OUTCOMES

PRE-INTERMEDIATE

STUDENT'S BOOK

HUGH DELLAR
ANDREW WALKLEY

Contents 3

Contents   5

1

IN THIS UNIT YOU LEARN HOW TO:

- ask and answer common questions about jobs
- talk about what you're doing at work at the moment
- talk about arrangements and appointments
- recognise and use collocations
- describe what different jobs involve

SPEAKING

1 **Work in pairs. Discuss the questions.**

- Look at the photo. What job do you think this person has?
- What do you think this person does during a normal day at work?
- What do you think is good about this job?
- What do you think is bad about it?
- Can you think of three questions to ask this person about their job?

2 **Work with a new partner. Discuss the questions.**

- Do you work? If yes, what do you do? Do you enjoy it? Why? / Why not?
- If not, what do you want do in the future?

JOBS

WHAT DO YOU DO?

VOCABULARY Talking about jobs

1 Which of the jobs in the box can you see in the photos? Check you understand the other jobs.

actor	nurse	politician
engineer	photographer	sales manager
journalist	pilot	scientist
lawyer	police officer	soldier

PRONUNCIATION

2 ▶ 1 Listen to the words in Exercise 1. Notice how the stress is stronger on one syllable than on the others. Underline the stressed syllable in each word. Then listen again and repeat.

actor

3 Work in groups. Discuss these questions.

- Do you know anyone who does any of the jobs in Exercise 1?
- Which of the jobs would you like to do? Why?
- Are there any of these jobs you could never do? Why not?

4 Look at the sentence beginnings in bold in 1–6. Match each sentence with a pair of alternative endings (a–f).

1 **I work in** a local hospital.
2 **I work** late most nights.
3 **I work for** Henning and Schmidt. It's a big law firm.
4 **I'm working on** a project for my class.
5 **I'm doing** work experience in a school at the moment.
6 **I run** my own company.

a a new product. / a new film.
b a local paper. / myself.
c a primary school. / the marketing department.
d nights. / very long hours.
e some research. / a training course.
f a hotel. / my own studio.

5 Work in pairs.

Student A: imagine you have a job in Exercise 1. Say something about the job using language from Exercise 4.

Student B: guess the job.

Student A: if B is wrong, say another sentence about the job.

DEVELOPING CONVERSATIONS

6   Match the common questions about work (1–6) with the answers (a–f).

1   What do you do?

2   Where do you work?

3   How long have you worked there?

4   Do you enjoy it?

5   What are the hours like?

6   Do you get on with the people you work with?

a   Yeah, it's good. Sometimes it's a bit boring – like any job – but basically it's fine.

b   A couple of years. I joined soon after university.

c   I'm a police officer.

d   In the local police department in Lyon.

e   Yeah, they're nice. We often go out together after work.

f   Not great. I often work nights, so it's hard. It makes family life difficult.

7   Spend two minutes memorising the questions in Exercise 6. Then close your books. Work in pairs, and see if you can remember all six questions.

LISTENING

8   ▶2 Listen to two conversations about work. Which questions from Exercise 6 do they ask in each conversation?

9   ▶2 Listen again. Note down the answers to each question.

10 Work in groups. Discuss these questions.

   • Who do you think has the better job? Why?

   • Could you work with people in your family? Why? / Why not?

   • Do you know anyone who travels a lot because of their job? What do they do? Are they happy?

GRAMMAR

11 Work in pairs. Look at the rules 1–7. Decide which are about the present simple (PS) and which are about the present continuous (PC).

1   It describes temporary, unfinished actions.

2   It describes something that is generally true.

3   It's often used with time phrases like *at the moment*, *this month* and *this week*.

4   It's often used with adverbs like *always*, *usually*, *sometimes* and *never*.

5   The third person form ends in an *-s*.

6   Negatives are formed with *am / is / are + not + -ing*.

7   Questions use *do / does* + the infinitive form of the verb (without *to*).

 Check your ideas on page 166 and do Exercise 1.

12 Complete the sentences with the correct form of the verbs. Use the present simple in one sentence and the present continuous in the other.

1   **run**

   a   My parents _____ a small family hotel.

   b   I _____ the shop while my boss is on holiday.

2   **try**

   a   As a good businesswoman, I always _____ to give my customers what they want.

   b   He _____ to get a job in TV, but it's very competitive.

3   **wait**

   a   I _____ to hear if I get the job or not.

   b   I usually _____ about an hour after eating before doing any exercise.

4   **do**

   a   I'm very busy because I _____ a course every night after work at the moment.

   b   We _____ most of our business in the United States, so I travel a lot.

13 Work in groups. Discuss the questions. Use the present continuous and present simple.

1   What two or three things are you doing at the moment that are different to your normal habits?

   I'm not eating chocolate. I'm trying to lose weight.

2   What are you working on at the moment – at school or in your job? Is it interesting?

   We're studying Business Law. It's a bit boring.

   I'm helping to organise a conference. It's good.

3   Is any construction work happening where you live?

   They're building new houses at the end of my street.

 For further practice, see Exercise 2 on page 166.

CONVERSATION PRACTICE

14 Think about how to answer the questions in Exercise 6 for either your own job or for a job you really want to do in the future. Then have conversations with other students in the class.

 1 To watch the video and do the activities, see the DVD-ROM.

TIME MANAGEMENT

SPEAKING

1 Check you understand the words in bold in the sentences below. Decide if the sentences are true or false for you, and why.

1 I am often late for things.

2 I often need to **rush** to get to places or to finish things.

3 I usually make a **list** of things I need to do during the day.

4 I hardly ever do everything I plan to do in a day.

5 I always do things which are a **priority** first.

6 I often **delay** doing things I don't like doing.

7 I never write down any **appointments** or things I **arrange** in a diary.

8 I occasionally miss appointments because I forget I have them.

9 I sometimes **stay up late** to finish things.

10 If I'm finding something very difficult to do, I usually **take a break**.

2 Work in groups. Compare your answers to Exercise 1 and discuss these questions.

• Which are good things to do and which are bad? Why?

• Who manages their time best in your group?

• Do you think you can learn to manage your time and be more efficient? How?

LISTENING

3 ▶ 3 Listen to two conversations. The first is between Martin and Tula, the second is between Rachel and her mum. Take notes on the work these people need to do this week.

1 Martin   2 Tula   3 Rachel

4 Work in pairs and compare your ideas. Do you think each speaker manages their time well? Why? / Why not?

5 ▶3 Listen again and complete the sentences with three words in each space. Contractions like *don't* count as one word.

1 I'm trying to write something for marketing, but I'm _____ .

2 Hey, _____ , are you going to that training session on Friday?

3 It said all _____ have to attend.

4 It's probably a _____ then.

5 I'm going. Can you do _____ things for me?

6 The washing machine's on. _____ the clothes outside?

7 You need to _____ , my girl. You're nineteen, not a child!

8 Yeah, but you _____ your work. And anyway, you're my mum.

6 Work in pairs. Discuss the questions.

- Do you think either of the conversations could happen in your country? Why? / Why not?
- What do you think is good or bad about working in an office?
- What things stop you from doing work?
- How much housework do you do?
- How much time do you have to relax? What do you do?
- Do you think you have a good balance between work and relaxation? Why? / Why not?

GRAMMAR

Present simple and present continuous for the future

We can use both the present simple and the present continuous to talk about the future.

7 Decide if these sentences refer to the future or not. When do you think we use the present continuous to talk about the future, and when do we use the present simple?

1 *I'm just answering some emails.*

2 *I'm meeting a customer at twelve.*

3 *I'm trying to watch this.*

4 *I'm giving that presentation on Friday.*

5 *Are you going to that training session tomorrow?*

6 *I've got an appointment with the dentist at one.*

7 *I've got a test tomorrow.*

8 *I often need to rush to get to places or finish things.*

9 *I need to leave at eight.*

10 *I work all day and then do housework.*

Ⓖ Check your ideas on page 166 and do Exercise 1.

8 Make a list of things to do each day this week. Include the following.

- any appointments and arrangements you have
- things you need to do at work or college
- housework or other things you need to do
- plans you have to go anywhere

9 Work in groups and explain your plans. Find out the following.

- Who has a very busy week?
- Who has a very quiet week?
- Who has a lot of social events this week?
- Who is doing something really interesting?
- What's the main priority for each person this week?
- When can you all meet to do something?

Ⓖ For further practice, see Exercise 2 on page 167.

UNDERSTANDING VOCABULARY

Collocations

Collocations are two or more words that we often use together. For example, on these pages you learned the word *appointment*. In English, we *make* or *arrange an appointment* and sometimes we *miss an appointment* (we forget to go or we're late); we *have / have got an appointment with the dentist*. Sometimes you can't arrange to do something because you *have a previous appointment* (one you made before).

Don't learn just the word *appointment*. Try to learn some verbs, adjectives or phrases that usually go with the noun. It's a good idea to learn words together because:

- it can help you hear and read more quickly.
- it's easier to use the word correctly.
- you see more words more often – and remember more.

10 Complete each group of collocations with one word from the box.

| contract | interview | job | meeting |
| priority | project | staff | training |

1 apply for a ~ / lose my ~ / have a well-paid ~ / a part-time ~

2 employ part-time ~ / need more ~ / train the ~ / friendly and efficient ~

3 have a job ~ / the ~ went badly / a phone ~ / a hard ~

4 need more ~ / give ~ / attend staff ~ / get basic ~

5 arrange a ~ / go to a ~ / have a staff ~ / a positive ~

6 (not) be a ~ / make it a ~ / agree what the ~ is / my main ~

7 have (got) a temporary ~ / sign the ~ / my ~ ends / agree a new ~

8 manage a ~ / work on a new ~ / a big ~ / launch a new ~

11 Work in pairs. Say one more collocation for each of the nouns in Exercise 10.

12 Work in groups. Discuss the questions.

- Do you know anyone with a well-paid job?
- Do you know anywhere that needs more staff? Why?
- Do you think phone interviews are good? Why? / Why not?
- Do you know anyone who gives training? What in?
- Do you ever go to meetings? What about?
- Do you know anyone on a temporary contract?

Unit 1 Jobs **11**

ALL WORK, NO PAY

SPEAKING

1 Work in pairs. Make a list of all the different kinds of work people do for no money.

2 Compare your list with another pair. Then discuss these questions in your group.
- Why do you think people do these different kinds of work?
- Do you know anyone who does any unpaid work?
- Do you think people should earn money for any of these different kinds of work? Why? / Why not?

READING

3 Read the article on page 13 about three people who are working for no money. Answer these questions.
1 What kind of work is each person doing?
2 Why are they doing this work?
3 How do they feel about working for no money?
4 What are their plans for the future?

4 Work in pairs. Can you remember which of the three people mentioned each of the things below and why?

Sulochana mentioned a website. Her organisation is planning to start a website to tell people about their situation.

1 a website
2 going on strike
3 it's a competitive area
4 got bored
5 a fixed salary and a pension
6 has a really positive attitude
7 making coffee
8 building the nation
9 advising
10 a new German film
11 my contract ends
12 the company is exploiting me

5 Read the article again and check your ideas from Exercise 4.

6 Work in groups. Discuss these questions.
- Do you agree that companies that don't pay young workers are exploiting them? Why? / Why not?
- Is voluntary work common in your country? What kind is most common?
- Do you agree that housewives play an important role in building the nation? Why? / Why not?

VOCABULARY Activities at work

7 Complete the sentences with the present continuous form of the verbs in the boxes.

advise	do	negotiate	organise	teach

1 I _____ currently _____ the government on how to improve hospitals.
2 This week I _____ some training with some new people. I _____ them how to sell over the phone.
3 I _____ a big party for a car company. They're launching a new car soon.
4 We _____ a big deal with a Chinese media company.

attend	do	give	install	work on

5 I _____ currently _____ some research on why people forget things.
6 I _____ a new collection of dresses for Milan fashion week.
7 I _____ a new kitchen in an apartment in town.
8 I _____ a conference this week. I _____ a talk on time management.

8 Work in pairs. Try to think of:
1 two more things you can **teach** people **how to** do.
2 two more things people sometimes **organise**.
3 two more things people **do research on**.
4 two more things people sometimes **install**.
5 two more things people sometimes **give talks on**.

9 Choose three things from Exercises 7 and 8 that you sometimes do. Tell your partner about them.
A: *I attend conferences for work once or twice a year.*
B: *Really? Do you give talks?*
A: *No. I just listen, and try to learn.*

SOUNDS AND VOCABULARY REVIEW

10 ▶ 4 Listen and repeat the sounds with /t/ and /d/. Are any of them difficult to hear or say?

11 ▶ 5 Work in groups. Listen to eight sentences using the words below. Together, try to write them down. Then listen again and check.

appointment	training	staff	test
delay	department	depend	develop

12 Work in teams. You have three minutes to write collocations or phrases for the words in Exercise 11.

*a **training** course, a **training** session, need more **training***

THERE'S NO MONEY IN IT

CLAUDIA, MUNICH, GERMANY

I graduated in Munich two years ago with a degree in Media Studies. After that, I applied for lots of jobs in film and television. I know it's a competitive area, but I didn't get any interviews! Not one! Everyone wanted me to have work experience, but how can you get work experience if nobody gives you a job?

In the end, I took unpaid work with a public relations company. To begin with, I hated it. I only did boring jobs like making coffee for people and photocopying, but recently I've started doing more interesting things. At the moment, I'm organising the European distribution of a new German film.

I'm not happy about working for no money, and sometimes I think the company is exploiting me, so I'm looking for other work. I can't live without pay for another year!

JEROME, SIERRA LEONE

I worked as a doctor in a small town in Switzerland for almost thirty years and I retired five years ago. To begin with, I enjoyed it, but I soon got bored. Then I saw an advertisement for Voluntary Service Overseas (VSO) and applied. They offered me a job working in Sierra Leone and I moved here nine months ago. They paid for my flight and they pay my rent, but basically I'm working for nothing.

I'm not complaining, though. It's amazing! I'm having the best time of my life. Life can be very hard for people here, but everyone has a really positive attitude. Now, I'm doing some training with local doctors and advising them on how to improve services. My contract ends in three months, but I'm planning to stay here for another year, if I can.

SULOCHANA, KERALA, INDIA

I'm a housewife but I'm also working for an organisation that's fighting for women's rights. I don't get paid, but I don't mind because we're hoping to make our government pay housewives like me a fixed salary and a pension for the work we do in the home. Venezuela did something similar a few years ago.

Women play an important role in building the nation. Without mothers and wives at home, men need to do more work – and this takes more energy. But men don't understand this and that's why we're organising ourselves.

We're planning to start a website to tell more people about our situation and we're also thinking of stopping work and going on strike. Let's see how men survive on their own then!

2

SHOPS

IN THIS UNIT YOU LEARN HOW TO:

- talk about shopping and things you buy
- make and respond to compliments
- talk about problems you can have with shopping
- offer help
- compare places and products
- have conversations with shop assistants

1 **Work in pairs. Answer the questions.**

- Who do you think the people are?
- How are they feeling? What do you think they might say to each other in this situation?
- Can you see any of these things in the photo?

coat	hat	jewellery	shoes	suit	T-shirt
dress	jeans	shirt	skirt	top	trainers

2 **Change partners. Discuss these questions.**

- Do you like the different clothes and things in the photo? Why? / Why not?
- Do you like going shopping? How often do you go?
- Who do you go with? Or do you prefer to go on your own? Why?
- Which of the things in the box in Exercise 1 can you see in your classroom?

WHERE DID YOU GET IT?

VOCABULARY
Describing things you bought

1   **Complete the sentences with these pairs of words. Check you understand the words in bold.**

comfortable + lie	fit + uncomfortable	suit + dark
complicated + follow	light + carry	thick + keep
designed + unique	quality + lasted	wear + smart

1   They're really good _____ – real **leather**. I had **a pair** before and they _____ for years.

2   I bought this nice _____ coat to _____ me **warm** in the cold weather. It's **pure wool**.

3   I bought them because they **look really nice**, but they actually don't _____ . They're a bit small and _____ to walk in.

4   They said it's **easy to use**, but it's really _____ and the instructions are difficult to _____ .

5   We bought a new sofa. It's really _____ to sit on and it's **nice and big** so you can _____ on it too.

6   We can't _____ jeans or T-shirts at work so I had to buy some _____ **trousers** and a jacket.

7   What do you think? Yellow doesn't usually _____ me. I think I **look better** in _____ colours.

8   I got a new laptop for work. It's really **cool**. It's so _____ and easy to _____ round.

9   My friend makes **jewellery** and she _____ this ring. It's the only one she made so it's _____ !

2   **Work in groups. Discuss the questions. Use a dictionary if you need to.**

1   Which words in bold in Exercise 1 are **materials**? Can you think of one more?

2   Why might something not **fit** you any more? What would you do with it?

3   What things can **last** a long time?

4   What things **keep you warm**? What's the opposite?

5   What's the opposite of **dark colours**?

6   What's **jewellery** usually made from?

7   When do people usually wear **smart clothes**?

8   Why might something be **complicated** to use?

3   **Work in pairs. How many of the words in Exercise 1 can you use to describe things you have?**

I've got a great pair of black leather boots. I've had them for ages. They're really good quality.

I've got a few nice thick winter coats that keep me warm. My favourite one is long and dark blue.

LISTENING

4   ▶ 6 **Listen to some friends talking about things they bought recently. Take notes on the three things they bought, where they bought them and what they say about them.**

16

5 Work in pairs. Discuss the questions.

- Where can you buy second-hand things?
- Do you ever buy second-hand things?
- Do you think it's good to buy any of these things second-hand? Why? / Why not?

a bike	a car	a computer game
a book	a coat	kids' clothes
boots	a computer	

GRAMMAR

Past simple

We use the past simple to talk about events and habits in the past.

6 Look at these sentences from Exercise 1 and the conversation. Then complete the rules.

a *They **lasted** for years.*

b *I **bought** this nice thick coat.*

c *I **got** these earrings.*

d ***Did** you **have** a nice weekend?*

e *What **did** you **do**?*

f *I **didn't find** anything that **fitted** me.*

g *They **weren't** very expensive.*

1 To make the past simple with most verbs, add _____ to the infinitive (without *to*). (*last – lasted*).

2 Many common verbs are irregular, for example: _____ – *went*; _____ – *got*.

3 To make a question, use _____ + *you / he / they*, etc. + infinitive (without *to*).

4 To make a negative, use *I / you / we*, etc. + _____ + infinitive (without *to*).

5 To make negatives of the verb *to be* use *wasn't* or _____ .

 Check your ideas on page 167 and do Exercise 1.

PRONUNCIATION

7 ▶ 7 Listen to the past forms said slowly and then faster. Notice how the sounds of the words change when said faster. Listen again. Practise saying them.

8 Write two past simple questions you might ask after someone says these sentences.

1 I went out for dinner at the weekend.

2 It was my birthday last week.

3 We went on holiday to Brazil.

4 I changed jobs recently.

5 I went to watch Barcelona play last weekend.

9 Work in pairs. Student A says a sentence from Exercise 8 and Student B asks their questions. Student A answers. Then change roles.

10 Work in pairs. Tell your partner about one of the following. Your partner should ask questions to find out more. Then change roles.

- a great present you bought for someone
- an amazing holiday shopping experience
- your last birthday
- your last holiday

 For further practice, see Exercise 2 on page 168.

DEVELOPING CONVERSATIONS

Complimenting

We often compliment people and then ask a question – or make another comment.

K: *That's really neat. **Where did you get it?***

C: *In Jessops in town. I'm really pleased with it.*

C: *I love your jacket. **It looks really nice and warm.***

D: *Yeah, it is. It's great. It's pure wool.*

11 Put the words in the correct order to make questions or comments.

1 I love your ring. did / where / you / it / get / ?

2 That's a great bag. new / is / it / ?

3 Hey, cool phone! you / it / long / had / how / have / ?

4 I love your shirt. really / a / design / it's / nice / .

5 I like your boots. comfortable / look / really / they / .

6 That's a lovely jacket. really / you / it / suits / .

12 ▶ 8 Listen and check your answers.

CONVERSATION PRACTICE

13 Choose one of these tasks. Take turns to start.

a Work in groups. Compliment other students in your group on their clothes, or other things they have. Use language from Exercise 11. Continue each conversation for as long as you can.

b Work in pairs. Have a conversation about what you bought at the weekend. Start by asking *Did you do anything at the weekend?* You can invent the details. Continue the conversation for as long as you can.

A: *Did you do anything at the weekend?*

B: *Yeah, I went shopping.*

A: *Really? Did you buy anything nice?*

B: *Well, I got a jacket in that new second-hand shop.*

 2 To watch the video and do the activities, see the DVD-ROM.

I BOUGHT IT ONLINE

SPEAKING

1 Read the fact file. Then work in groups. Discuss the questions.

- Which facts do you think are interesting, surprising or unsurprising? Why?
- How often do you buy things online? What was the last thing you bought?
- What kinds of things do you buy?
- What time of day do you usually shop online?
- Do you have any favourite sites for shopping?
- Do you think online shopping is bad for local shops where you live? Why? / Why not?

FACT FILE

- Globally, we now buy 22% of everything we need online.
- Most online shopping happens between eight and nine in the evening.
- 55% of us use a laptop to do our online shopping, while 20% use a smartphone.
- 29% of us sometimes buy things online while we are at work.
- 25% of what we spend online goes on books, music and software.
- Women return more than 20% of the clothes they buy online, men return less than 10%.
- Men spend 20–30% more money than women online.
- Online sales are increasing all the time, but in the UK over 10,000 shops close every year.

VOCABULARY Shopping online

2 Check you understand the words and phrases in bold. Then work in pairs. Which sentences describe good shopping experiences (G) and which describe bad ones (B)? Explain your ideas.

1 The camera I wanted was **out of stock**.
2 It was **in a sale**. It was £50 – **reduced from** £99.
3 Their **delivery service** was very **reliable**.
4 The delivery man **dropped** it.
5 They had a really **wide selection**.
6 When I **took** it **out of the box**, I found it was **damaged**.
7 I **returned** it and **got my money back**.
8 It didn't **fit** me. It was a bit too small.
9 It was a **bargain**. I **bid** twenty pounds for it on eBay – and **won**.
10 It cost a lot, but it was my own **fault**. I didn't check **the delivery fee**.

3 Work in groups. Tell each other about two of the following.

- a time you bought something that was in a sale
- a time you dropped something important
- a time you returned something and got your money back
- a time you bought something that didn't really fit you
- a time you found a bargain

READING

4 Work in pairs.

Student A: read the two stories on this page.

Student B: read File 1 on page 186.

As you read, think about these questions.
1 What did each person buy?
2 Why did they buy these things?
3 What problems did they have?
4 What happened in the end?

CLICK TO BUY!

SANDRA

Last month I bought a pair of shoes online. I didn't really need them, but a friend of mine recommended a new site so I had a look. They had a really wide selection – and lots of things in my size. I have big feet, and it's sometimes hard to find things that fit me. When they delivered my order, though, the shoes were the wrong colour – blue not black – and they were a bit too small. I returned them and got my money back, but it was annoying.

ADAM

It was my 40th birthday last year. My wife took me to a concert. It was great. We saw a band we both loved when we were at university. When I got home, my wife went to bed, but I went online – and suddenly decided to buy a guitar on eBay. I guess the concert inspired me. I wanted to bid £100, but I bid £1,000 by accident. It was stupid, I know, but I was tired! Anyway, I won, but it cost me £750! My wife was really angry when it arrived, but I'm having lessons now and I'm slowly learning!

5 With your partner, ask and answer the questions in Exercise 4 about the texts you read. Which story do you like best? Why?

6 Now read the two stories your partner read. Then decide which of the four people:
1 ordered something the company didn't have.
2 was happy to have lots of things to choose from.
3 bought something without really thinking about it first.
4 spent time looking for a good deal.

PRONUNCIATION

7 ▶ 9 Listen to the past simple forms of twelve regular verbs. Notice the different ways of saying the -ed endings. For each verb, decide if the -ed ending is pronounced /t/, /d/ or /ɪd/.

8 ▶ 9 Listen again and repeat each verb.

9 Work in pairs. Discuss the questions.
- Can you remember the last website someone recommended to you? Is it good?
- Can you play any musical instruments? If yes, which ones? How well?
- What do you think is the best age to buy laptops or smartphones for children? Why?
- Do you have any experience of terrible service from companies?

10 Match the verbs with the words they went with in the stories.

1	recommend	a	my order
2	deliver	b	to bed
3	take	c	the box
4	go	d	me to a concert
5	look at	e	a new part
6	open	f	a new website
7	order	g	to tell me
8	forget	h	lots of different sites

11 Work in pairs. Talk about the stories using the words and phrases in Exercise 10 and the past simple.

*Sandra's friend **recommended a new website** for buying shoes.*

SPEAKING

12 Work in groups of three. You are going to tell a story about an online shopping experience. One student begins by saying one of the sentences below. Take turns to add a line to the story.
a It was my grandfather's 70th birthday.
b Late one night, I decided to go online and have a look at eBay.
c I didn't really need it, but it was lovely.

CAN I HELP YOU?

LISTENING

1 Work in groups. Think of:

1 three reasons you might take things back to a shop.

2 three ways you might help another customer in a shop.

3 three reasons why you might complain about a shop.

4 three questions you might ask a member of staff in a shop.

5 three things a shop assistant might ask you when you pay.

2 ▶ **10** Listen to five conversations. Match each conversation (1–5) to one of the situations below and answer the question.

a a customer taking something back to the shop
Why do they take it back?

b a customer helping another customer
How do they help?

c a customer complaining
What do they complain about?

d a customer asking a member of staff a question
What do they ask?

e a shop assistant asking a question
What do they ask?

3 Work in pairs. Decide what conversations these phrases came from. Explain your decisions.

1 the button was loose

2 it's a bit plain

3 About time!

4 You'll grow into it.

5 a manufacturing fault

6 the stationery department

7 I have a lot to get.

8 they're at a reduced price

9 have something in stock

10 I've got the receipt.

11 I'll wrap it for you.

12 It's typical!

4 ▶ **10** Listen again and check your answers to Exercise 3. Look at the audio script for Track 10 on page 193 if you need to.

5 Work in groups. Discuss these questions.

• What was the last thing you did to help someone?

• What was the last present you bought? Who for? What was the occasion? Did you wrap it? Did they like it?

• When was the last time you took something back to a shop? What happened?

• Did your parents ever make you wear something you didn't like when you were a child?

• Did you have any favourite clothes when you were younger? What were they?

DEVELOPING CONVERSATIONS

Offering to help and responding

Look at the pattern for offering to help from the conversations in Exercise 2.

A: *Do you want to go first?*   (offer)

B: *Are you sure?*   (check)

A: *Yes, of course. I have a lot to get.*   (reassure)

B: *Great. Thanks.*   (accept)

We also often use *will* to offer (e.g. *I'll wrap it for you*) and *You don't mind?* to check.

6 Put a–e in the correct order in the two conversations. The first line in conversation 1 is done for you.

Conversation 1

a Gosh. That's heavy.   *1*

b Of course. I'm happy to help.

c Are you sure?

d That's great. Thanks so much.

e Do you want me to carry it to your car?

Conversation 2

a No, of course not. I'm actually going there too.

b I'll show you, if you like.

c Oh right. Thanks.

d You don't mind?

e Where's the men's clothes department?

7 Work in pairs. Write conversations like the ones in Exercise 6, starting with these sentences. Then practise reading them out.

1 I have a lot of bags.

2 It's raining. We're going to get wet walking there.

3 There's only one seat.

4 I'm in a rush and there's a long queue.

5 I'm quite hungry.

GRAMMAR

Comparatives

We use *more* or *-er* or *not as* with adjectives and adverbs to make comparisons.

8 Look at these sentences from the listening and complete the rules below.

a *Do you have this in a **smaller** size?*

b *It's a bit plain. Do you have anything **a bit prettier**?*

c *Their service is **much more reliable**.*

d *It's **not as nice as** the one we saw before.*

1 We add _____ to the end of adjectives / adverbs of one syllable.

2 Two-syllable words ending in *-y* change to _____ .

3 We use _____ before two- or three-syllable adjectives / adverbs.

4 To say there's a big difference, use _____ + comparative.

5 You can make a negative comparison using _____ + adjective / adverb

 Check your ideas on page 168 and do Exercise 1.

9 Complete the sentences with the correct comparative form of the word.

1 They're a bit loose when I walk. Do you have them in a _____ size? (small)

2 It looks too complicated for my gran. Do you have one which is _____ to use? (easy)

3 It's a bit tight round my shoulders. Do you have a _____ size? (big)

4 I need something suitable for an interview. Have you got anything a bit _____ ? (smart)

5 It doesn't look very strong. Have you got one which is a bit _____ quality? Something which will last a bit _____ ? (good, long)

6 It's a bit plain and dark. Have you got something a bit _____ , a bit _____ ? (bright, colourful)

7 It'll probably be _____ for the baby, but it's a bit heavy and it'll be difficult to carry up and down stairs. Have you got something _____ , something a bit _____ that you can fold _____ ? (comfortable, practical, light, easily).

10 Work in groups. Discuss what you think the people are talking about in each sentence in Exercise 9.

11 Check you understand the phrases that a shop assistant uses in the box below. Then work in pairs.

Student A: you are the customer. Read out one of 1–7 in Exercise 9.

Student B: you are the shop assistant. Answer your partner's question and try to sell something.

Then change roles and repeat.

Certainly sir / madam.

I'm afraid not.

We're out of stock. / They're the only ones we have. / It's the last one.

This one might be more suitable.

It's a bit more expensive, but ...

It's not as cheap, but ...

It'll last a lifetime.

It's the top of the range.

It really suits you.

G For further practice, see Exercise 2 on page 168.

SPEAKING

12 Work in groups. Choose five of the following to discuss. Then think of two examples of each.

- a supermarket
- a clothes shop / website
- an electronics shop / website
- a market
- a pool / sports centre
- a place to eat / buy food
- a mobile phone
- a car
- a TV channel

13 Decide which of the two examples you prefer in each case and explain why. Discuss your choices.

SOUNDS AND VOCABULARY REVIEW

14 ▶ **11** Listen and repeat the sounds with /s/ and /ʃ/. Are any of them difficult to hear or say?

15 ▶ **12** Work in groups. Listen to eight sentences using the words below. Together, try to write them down. Then listen again and check.

increase	missed	rush	service
last	receipt	selection	shirt

16 Work in teams. You have three minutes to write collocations or phrases for the words in Exercise 15.

*I **missed** the class last week, I **missed** the train, I **missed** the bus*

VIDEO 1

A CHILD'S GARDEN OF GATORS

1 **Work in groups. Look at the photo. Discuss these questions.**

- What do you think is happening in the photo?
- How do you feel when you look at the photo? Why?
- Which sentence below do you most agree with? Explain your ideas.
  - If you allow children to take risks, they learn to take care of themselves.
  - If you risk nothing, then you risk everything!
  - Parents today need to protect their children more because there are more risks.

2 ▶️ 3 **Work in pairs. Watch the video without any sound. Answer these questions.**

1 Where do you think they are?

2 What are they doing?

3 What risks are they taking?

4 What happens at the end of the film?

3 ▶️ 3 **Now watch the video with sound. Decide if these sentences are true (T) or false (F).**

1 The father doesn't want his son to catch alligators more than three feet long.

2 The son is ten years old.

3 The son looks right when his father tells him to look left.

4 He doesn't catch the first alligator he sees.

5 They make a special noise to scare the mother alligator.

6 The father tells his son to run.

4 **Choose the correct form to complete the sentences from the video.**

1 Along the canal, the lesson in gator catching *just gets / is just getting* under way.

2 Right now, big alligators *look for / are looking for* smaller gators.

3 They *eat / are eating* each other.

4 I think *I see / I'm seeing* one.

5 *I watch / I'm watching* for the mother.

6 *She looks for / She's looking for* her baby.

5 **Work in pairs. Discuss these questions.**

- Why do you think the father is teaching his son to catch alligators?
- Do you think it's a good thing for the son to learn? Why? / Why not?
- What were the best things your parents taught you to do?
- Did you learn different kinds of things from your mother and your father?

UNDERSTANDING FAST SPEECH

6 ▶️ 4 **Read and listen to this extract from the video said at natural pace and then slowed down. To help you, groups of words are marked with / and pauses are marked //. Stressed sounds are in CAPITALS.**

RIGHT NOW // I don't WANT him / CATching / Any Alligators / MORE than three FEET

7 **Now you have a go! Practise saying the extract at natural pace.**

REVIEW 1

1 Complete the text by writing the correct form of the verbs in brackets.

I'm at college and I ¹_____ (train) to become an electrician. I ²_____ (really like) the course and I ³_____ (do) quite well. Last week we ⁴_____ (learn) how to install all the electrics in a house. It's quite complicated, but I ⁵_____ (pass) the test with 90%. Every weekend I ⁶_____ (work) in a café in town. I mainly ⁷_____ (make) coffees and teas, but I sometimes ⁸_____ (help) in the kitchen. It's OK to get some money, but I ⁹_____ (want) to find a job with an electrician to get some experience. Last week I ¹⁰_____ (have) an interview, but I ¹¹_____ (not get) the job. The college ¹²_____ (organise) a meeting with several electrical companies next month so maybe I'll find something then.

2 Put the words in the correct order to make questions.

1 do / what / do / you
2 have / you / weekend / did / a / nice
3 are / meeting / what / you / tomorrow / Maria / time
4 long / last / did / how / the / meeting
5 work / your / does / you / brother / with
6 do / want / you / me / it / to / wrap

3 Complete the second sentence so that it has a similar meaning to the first sentence, using the word given. Do not change the word given. You must use between two and four words, including the word given.

1 The instructions were really difficult to follow so I asked for help.

I asked for help because _____ the instructions very well. **UNDERSTAND**

2 The internet connection at work is faster than mine here.

The internet connection I have here is _____ it is at work. **FAST**

3 Were those boots expensive?

_____ a lot for those boots? **PAY**

4 I've got an appointment at the dentist's tomorrow.

I _____ the dentist's tomorrow. **GOING**

5 I always buy well-known brands because the clothes last longer.

I always buy well-known brands because the clothes _____ . **QUALITY**

6 Do you have anything that isn't as complicated as this?

Do you have anything that is _____ than this? **USE**

4 ▶ 13 Listen and write the six sentences you hear.

5 Match the verbs (1–8) with the nouns they collocate with (a–h).

1 arrange / go to   a my own company
2 train / need   b a project
3 apply for / lose   c a new part
4 order / install   d a contract
5 negotiate / sign   e a job
6 work on / manage   f a sofa
7 run / start   g an appointment
8 buy / lie on   h staff

6 Decide if these words are connected to jobs and work, or clothes and shopping.

a bargain	a journalist	stock	a top
experience	smart	a strike	trainers
jewellery	a soldier	thick	training

7 Choose the correct option.

1 They don't have a very wide *select / selection* there, but it's cheaper.
2 I often buy things from that website and they are always very *rely / reliable*.
3 Could you *recommend / recommendation* a good place to buy shoes?
4 They don't charge anything to *deliver / delivery* your order.
5 I need to get some new boots. These ones are really *comfortable / uncomfortable*.
6 I'm looking for a job with a TV company, but it's so *competitive / competition*.
7 I work as a sales *manager / management* for a big company.
8 I need to get a *law / lawyer* to look at the contract.

8 Complete the text with one word in each space. The first letters are given.

Last week I ¹br_____ my laptop. It was my own ²fau_____ because I was late and so I was in a ³ru_____ . I didn't close my bag properly so the laptop ⁴dr_____ out of it as I ran across the road, and a car went over the computer! It was so badly ⁵da_____ , I lost everything on it. It's a big problem because I'm ⁶at_____ a conference next month and I'm ⁷gi_____ a presentation, so I really need a computer. A friend ⁸re_____ a website and I was really lucky because they had lots of things on ⁹sa_____ . I bought a really nice laptop that was ¹⁰re_____ by $300. But then the company rang me yesterday to say there was a ¹¹de_____ sending it to me, because they had so many ¹²or_____ . I hope they deliver it before my conference!

3

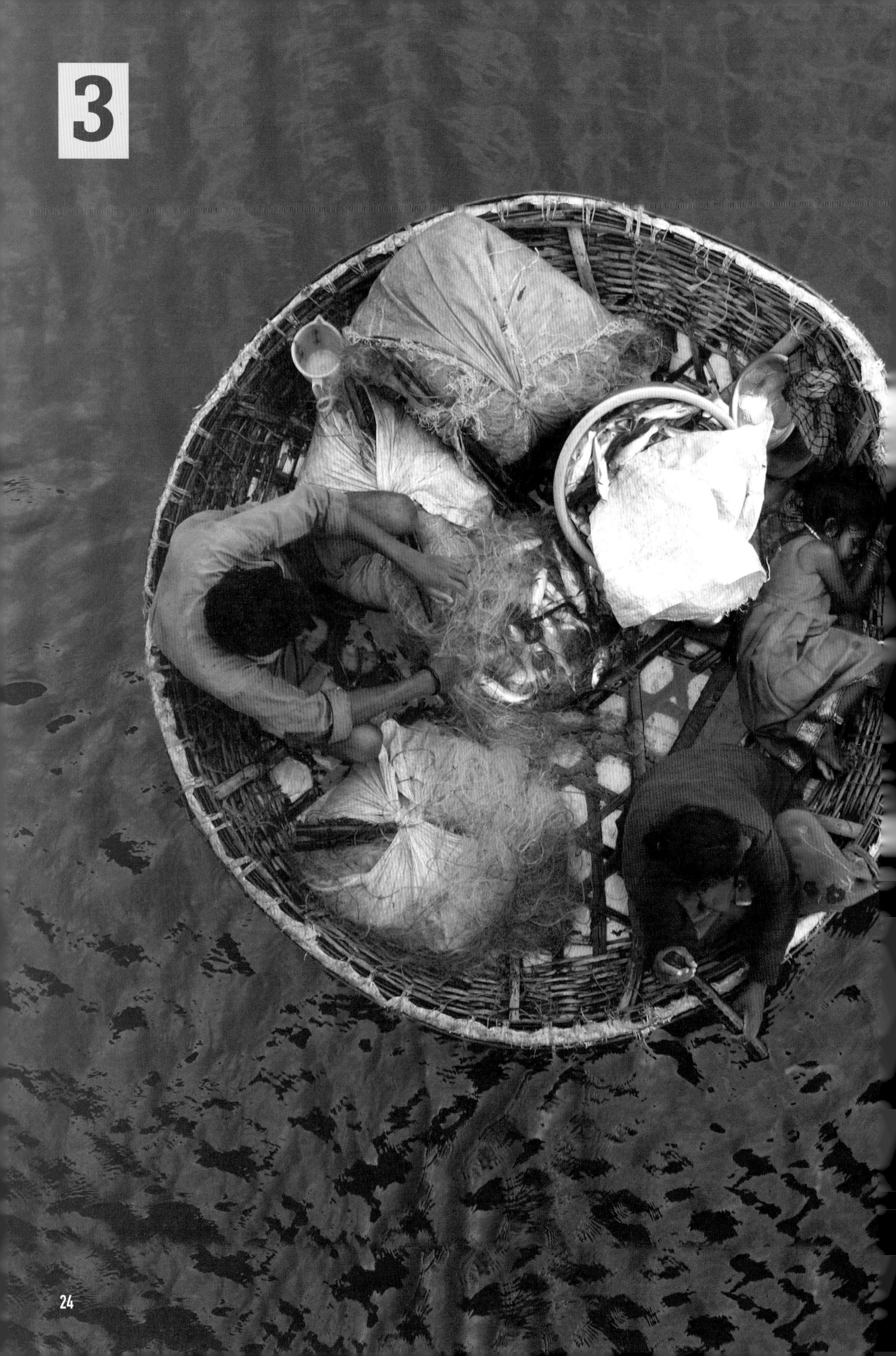

IN THIS UNIT YOU LEARN HOW TO:

- talk about buildings and places
- ask for and give directions
- tell stories better
- apologise for being late
- talk about different ways of travelling
- describe problems you can have on journeys

SPEAKING

1   Work in pairs. Look at the photo and discuss the questions.

- Where do you think this is? Why?
- Why do you think they are travelling in this way?
- What do you think is good about this way of travelling? Why?
- What do you think is bad? Why?

2   Work with a new partner. Discuss these questions.

- What different ways of travelling are there where you live?
- Which kind do you like most / least? Why?
- Can you think of any other ways of travelling that you want to try?
- Do you enjoy the journeys you make every day? Why? / Why not?

WE'RE LOST!

VOCABULARY Places in town

1 Label the picture with the words in the box.

a bridge	a monument	a sports ground
a church	a playground	a subway
a crossing	a police station	a town hall
a crossroads	a roundabout	traffic lights

2 Complete the sentences about places where people live with nouns from Exercise 1.

1 There's a nice _____ in the park near my house. I sometimes take the kids there.

2 In the centre of town, there's a big _____ to the people who died in the war.

3 My dad's a member of the local council. He works in the _____ .

4 When you come to the _____ , take the second exit.

5 They're building a new _____ over the river at the moment.

6 Is there a _____ near here? I need to report a crime.

7 I live really near a big _____ . It gets very noisy on match days.

8 There's a huge traffic jam in the centre of town because the _____ aren't working.

3 Work in pairs. Tell your partner about where you live, work or study. What things are there?

There's an old church near where I work.

There's a subway under the main road near my house.

LISTENING

4 ▶ **14** Listen to a couple on holiday asking for directions. Answer the questions.

1 Where are they trying to get to?

2 What problems do they have in each conversation?

3 How do they travel?

4 Do they get to where they want to go in the end?

5 ▶ **14** Choose the correct option. Then listen again and check your answers.

1 Do you know the *road / way* to the museum from here?

2 *It's / Is* better to get a bus.

3 It's directly *opposite of / opposite* the town hall.

4 Go down this road. *Take / Turn* the second road on the right.

5 What bus *he said / did he say* we need?

6 Is this the *correct / right* bus stop for the museum?

7 Is it *near to / near* here?

8 You *got off / went off* at the wrong stop.

9 Just keep *going / go*. It's maybe half a mile.

10 You can't *miss / lose* it.

6 Work in groups. Discuss these questions.

• Do you ever ask for, or give, directions? Can you remember the last time?

• Can you remember a time you had problems finding a place? What happened?

• Do you like going to museums? If yes, do you have a favourite? Why?

DEVELOPING CONVERSATIONS

Giving directions

Certain phrases are commonly used when people give directions. Keep a record of any new phrases you learn. Notice the prepositions used in each.

Go **down** this road.

Take the second road **on the right**.

You need to go **over the road**.

Go **past** a monument.

It's **on the left**.

7 Complete the directions with the prepositions in the box.

along	at	on	opposite
over	past	through	to

So first, cross [1]_____ this big road here. There's a crossing over there that you can use or you can go [2]_____ the subway, under the road. Then walk [3]_____ the edge of the park and [4]_____ an old church until you come [5]_____ some traffic lights. Turn left [6]_____ the lights and go straight on. It's [7]_____ your right – directly [8]_____ a big bookshop. You can't miss it.

8 Draw a map that shows the places in Exercise 7. Then draw a line to show the way.

9 Work in pairs. Compare your maps and discuss any differences.

10 Write a short email giving directions to your home from one of the following places:

• your school or workplace

• the nearest train station or bus stop

CONVERSATION PRACTICE

11 Work in pairs. You are going to roleplay conversations between a visitor to a town and a person who lives there.

Student A: look at File 2 on page 186.

Student B: look at File 6 on page 188.

Take turns asking for directions and marking the missing places on your map. Use these phrases.

Excuse me. Do you know the way to ...?

Excuse me. Is there a ... near here?

Excuse me. Is the ... near here?

5 To watch the video and do the activities, see the DVD-ROM.

I MISSED MY FLIGHT

VOCABULARY Travelling by plane

1   Match these phrases with the pictures (1–9).

   a   be late taking off

   b   call a taxi

   c   check in online

   d   check the departures board

   e   get stuck in heavy traffic on the way

   f   join the queue to board

   g   take ages to go through security

   h   land on time

   i   run to the boarding gate

READING

2   Read the introduction to a blog post. What can you guess about the writer?

LESSONS IN LIFE: TRAVELLING MAN

HOW NOT TO MISS FLIGHTS

Yesterday, I missed a flight. It was my *fifteenth* missed flight. Though, to be fair, it is several years since I last missed one. Anyway, this week's post is about how I missed all those flights and the lessons I (very slowly) learned.

3   Look at the lessons (a–f) the writer learned from his experiences. Work in pairs. Discuss how you think he missed his flight in each case.

   a   Airports are big places

   b   Check the travel news before you go

   c   Check your ticket

   d   Read, but don't choose a thriller

   e   See waiting as fun

   f   Set your alarm clock

4   Read the blog post. Match the lessons in Exercise 3 with the paragraphs.

1   I hated waiting. This was my big problem. It was even worse when they introduced online check-in, because you could get to the airport forty minutes before the flight and still catch it *if* nothing went wrong. Unfortunately, *when* I got stuck in heavy traffic, or the train was delayed or it took ages to go through security, I missed flights. But then a friend bought me a tablet and I realised that waiting was actually enjoyable. I could read, watch films, relax!

2   The first time I missed a flight, I actually left really early and planned to arrive almost two hours before my flight. However, when I got to the train station to go to the airport, I found that they were doing repairs on the line and there was a bus to replace the train – a very old, slow one. We eventually arrived at the airport three minutes after the check-in closed!

3   Once, I was catching a very early flight to go back home. I got to the boarding gate in plenty of time, but I was really tired, so I decided to have a little sleep while I was waiting. When I woke up, there were no passengers around me and the woman from the airline was walking away from the gate. There wasn't another flight for ten hours! I hate waiting!

4   One year, we were travelling to see family in Ivory Coast and we changed flights in Charles de Gaulle Airport, Paris. We had an hour to get the connection. We landed on time, but from the plane there was a bus; then we walked; we took a train; we walked and walked (more quickly); we queued for security again; we ran. We missed the connection.

5   I was going to see a friend once and I went to London Stansted airport. I checked the departures board, but I couldn't see my flight, which I thought was strange. I looked at my ticket again and it said *Gatwick* Airport – on the opposite side of the city!

6   Which brings me to my last and most recent lesson. I arrived early and sat down to read my book – a crime story by Jo Nesbø. As the story got more and more exciting, I completely forgot the time. I was reading the last few pages when I suddenly heard the last call for my flight. Unfortunately, airports are big places and when I got to the gate, it was closed. I sat down and finished my book.

26 *comments*

5 Work in groups. Based on what you read and on your own experiences, explain why you think the author:

1 started to enjoy waiting.

2 didn't take a taxi when the train was cancelled.

3 didn't wake when the flight was boarding.

4 didn't buy a ticket with more time to connect in Charles de Gaulle.

5 went to the wrong airport.

6 didn't wait at the boarding gate when he started reading his book.

GRAMMAR

Past simple and past continuous

When we tell stories, we show how actions relate to each other using the past continuous and the past simple.

6 Look at these sentences from the blog post. Answer the questions below.

a *When I **got** to the train station ..., **they were doing** repairs on the line.*

b *When **I woke up**, ... the **woman** from the airline **was walking away** from the gate.*

c ***I was reading** the last few pages when **I suddenly heard** the last call for my flight.*

1 Which verbs are in the past simple?

2 Which verbs are in the past continuous? How are they formed?

3 In each sentence, which action started first?

4 In each sentence, which action is completed?

Ⓖ Check your ideas on page 169 and do Exercise 1.

7 Complete the sentences with the past simple or past continuous form of the verbs.

1 They stopped him while he _____ through security and _____ all his bags, so he missed the flight. (go, search)

2 This baby _____ screaming when we were taking off and it _____ during the whole flight. It was a nightmare. (start, not stop)

3 A: It was so stupid. I _____ where I was going and I _____ into a lamppost. (not look, walk)

B: Oh no! _____ ? (anyone watch)

4 I was going through the arrivals hall at Madrid airport and these people were taking photos of me, which I thought was strange. Then I _____ round and I realised this famous actress, Penelope Cruz, _____ behind me! (turn, walk)

PRONUNCIATION

8 ▶ 15 Listen and write down the five past continuous phrases you hear. You will hear each twice: first fast and then slower.

9 Choose two of these situations. Spend a few minutes thinking about what you will say. Then work in groups and share your stories.

- a time you missed a flight / train / coach
- a time you had a problem or something funny happened on a flight
- a time you were late for something important
- a time you had / saw an accident
- a time you met / saw someone famous

Ⓖ For further practice, see Exercise 2 on page 169.

DEVELOPING CONVERSATIONS

Apologising for being late

When we are late, we often apologise and give a reason.

*Sorry I'm late. I **was chatting** to a friend and I completely forgot the time.*

*Sorry I'm late. I **was stuck** on the bus.*

You can accept the apology by using one of these phrases.

Oh well. Never mind. At least you're here now.

Don't worry. What was the problem?

It's OK. I haven't been here long.

10 Work in pairs. Take turns apologising for being late and accepting the apology.

COMPLETE CHAOS

VOCABULARY Transport

1 Match what the people say to the forms of transport in the box. Check you understand the words in bold.

bike	coach	plane	train	underground
car	motorbike	taxi	truck	van

1 A: How much did he **charge** you?

B: Eleven dollars plus a **tip**. Does that sound OK?

2 They usually stop at a **service station** on the **motorway** for half an hour to let all the **passengers** stretch their legs.

3 Our flight's **cancelled** because the air traffic controllers are **on strike**.

4 I bought this huge wardrobe at a market, and I had to **hire a vehicle** to get it home.

5 I cycle to work. There's a good **cycle lane** that goes from my house, so I don't need to go on the roads.

6 Sorry we're late. We were **driving** round looking for somewhere to **park**.

7 There's a really fast **rail service** between Rome and Milan.

8 It was going slowly because it was carrying **a huge load,** and there was **a long line of cars** stuck behind it.

9 Buy a **travel card** from the station. Then you can travel on all the **lines** in the city.

10 A: Do you need a **licence** to **ride** one?

B: Yes, you need to take a practical **test** of your riding skills, but it's quite easy.

2 Work in pairs. Take turns to choose five words or phrases from Exercise 1, and explain, act or draw them. Your partner should guess the words without looking at the book.

3 Think of six different forms of transport you have used. Then work in pairs and tell your partner where you went and how you travelled.

LISTENING

4 ▶ 16 Listen to the travel news. How many items of news are there? How many give good news?

5 ▶ 16 Listen again and complete the table.

Place	Problem	Cause	Advice
Airport	flights delayed / cancelled	air traffic controllers on strike	1_____ or 2_____
A516	3_____	truck crashed	4_____
M6 junctions 5–6	diversion causing slow traffic	5_____	take other routes
Northern Line	sections closed	repairs	6_____
East Ham station	7_____	flooding	–
Wembley concert	no parking	–	8_____

6 Complete the phrases from the listening with the missing prepositions. Look at the audio script for Track 16 on page 194 and check your answers.

1 There are terrible problems _____ a lot of places.

2 Passengers who are flying _____ the next few days should ring their airline.

3 Lanes _____ both directions are closed.

4 Elsewhere _____ the roads, the M6 motorway _____ junctions 5 and 6 is completely closed.

5 Also _____ the underground, East Ham station is closed.

6 The traffic lights are working again _____ the crossroads with the B761.

7 Go _____ foot or take public transport.

SPEAKING

7 Work in groups. Think of two possible causes for these situations.

1 a flight is cancelled

2 a rail service is delayed

3 an underground station is closed

4 one lane of a motorway is shut

5 there's a traffic jam in a city

8 Tell each other about two situations in Exercise 7 that you experienced. Explain what happened.

GRAMMAR

Quantifiers with countable and uncountable nouns

Countable nouns have both singular and plural forms. Uncountable nouns are things we don't count in English. They usually only have a singular form.

Some words we use to show quantity go with both countable and uncountable nouns. Others only go with one of these kinds of nouns.

9 Work in pairs. Look at the sentences from the travel news and decide if the statements 1–5 are true (T) or false (F).

a *Not **many** planes can fly over France.*

b *There's not **much** hope of a deal **any** time soon.*

c *This follows **some** heavy rain in the area overnight.*

d *There aren't **any** more problems on the A6.*

e *You can expect **some** delays there all day.*

f *There are terrible problems in **a lot of** places.*

g ***Plenty of** flights are delayed and quite **a few** (flights) cancelled.*

h *Expect **a bit of** trouble there.*

i *There's **no** parking in or around the ground.*

1 *Many* and *a few* only go with plural countable nouns.

2 *Much* and *some* only go with uncountable (singular) nouns.

3 *A bit of, any, a lot of, plenty of* and *no* only go with countable nouns.

4 *Much* and *many* are usually used in negative sentences.

5 *Any* is never used in positive sentences.

 **G** Check your ideas on page 169 and do Exercise 1.

10 Choose the correct option.

The situation on the roads isn't too bad in my city. Actually, at the moment, there's not ¹*much / many* traffic because it's a holiday this week. Oh, and there aren't ²*no / any* buses today either, because there's a strike. It's usually a bit busier. There are ³*some / any* cycle lanes here, but not ⁴*much / many*, so I don't cycle much, to be honest. I usually take public transport. There are always ⁵*plenty / a bit* of buses and it's easy to get to the city centre. I can take ⁶*many / any* bus from the stop near my house. They all go into the city.

One bad thing is that there's ⁷*no / any* underground here, which can be a ⁸*few / bit* of a problem sometimes. There are ⁹*a lot of / much* taxis, though. A ¹⁰*few / bit* of my friends take them, but I can't afford to! They're not cheap!

 **G** For further practice, see Exercise 2 on page 170.

11 Work in groups. Discuss the transport situation where you live using the language from this lesson. What's good? What problems are there? What's the best way to change things? Think about these things.

- the traffic
- the roads
- the parking
- the public transport (buses, trains, underground)
- taxis
- trains to the rest of the country
- planes to other countries

SOUNDS AND VOCABULARY REVIEW

12 ▶ **17** Listen and repeat the sounds with /k/ and /g/. Are any of them difficult to hear or say?

13 ▶ **18** Work in groups. Listen to eight sentences using these words. Together, try to write them down. Then listen again and check.

bags	crossroads	ground	strike
clock	gate	security	truck

14 Work in teams. You have three minutes to write collocations or phrases for the words in Exercise 13.

*pack my **bags**, put my **bags** in the car, heavy **bags***

4

EAT

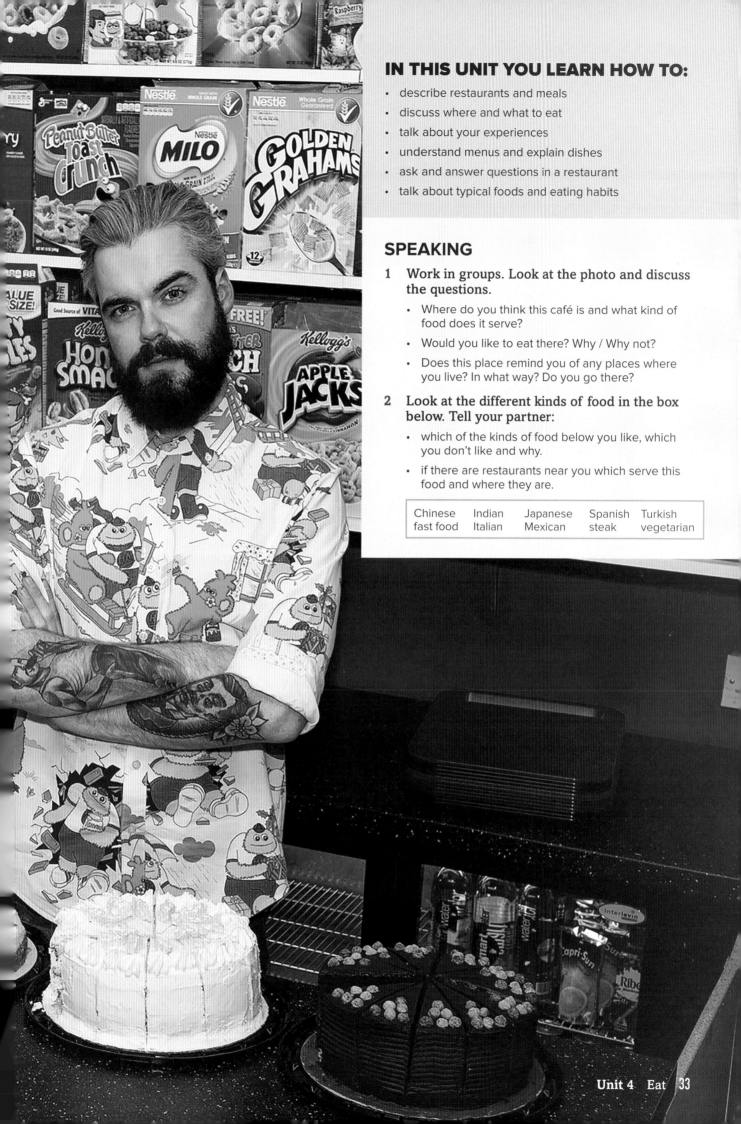

IN THIS UNIT YOU LEARN HOW TO:

- describe restaurants and meals
- discuss where and what to eat
- talk about your experiences
- understand menus and explain dishes
- ask and answer questions in a restaurant
- talk about typical foods and eating habits

SPEAKING

1   Work in groups. Look at the photo and discuss the questions.

- Where do you think this café is and what kind of food does it serve?
- Would you like to eat there? Why / Why not?
- Does this place remind you of any places where you live? In what way? Do you go there?

2   Look at the different kinds of food in the box below. Tell your partner:

- which of the kinds of food below you like, which you don't like and why.
- if there are restaurants near you which serve this food and where they are.

Chinese	Indian	Japanese	Spanish	Turkish
fast food	Italian	Mexican	steak	vegetarian

ARE YOU HUNGRY?

VOCABULARY Restaurants

1 **Complete the sentences with these pairs of words.**

busy + seat	dishes + choose	service + staff
choice + options	had + delicious	terrace + view
disgusting + rude	place + does	value + portions

1 There's a little Japanese _____ near my office, which _____ great sushi!

2 It often gets really _____ , so you sometimes have to wait for a while to get a _____ .

3 We often go to a small Spanish place near here. The _____ is great. The _____ are always really friendly.

4 They have a big selection of vegetarian _____ , so you'll have plenty to _____ from.

5 The first time I went there, it was really good _____ , but I went there again recently and it was quite expensive and the _____ were much smaller!

6 I went there once, and I had this dish which tasted _____ , but when I complained about it, the waiter was quite _____ .

7 They have a fixed menu, and there isn't much _____ . There are usually just two or three _____ for each course.

8 It's great. You can sit outside on the _____ there and get an incredible _____ over the city.

9 I really want to go there again. I _____ this amazing seafood dish when I went there. In fact it was all really _____ , but it's also really expensive.

2 **Think of two restaurants you've been to on holiday. Underline some of the language in Exercise 1 you can use to describe the places. Then work in groups and share your experiences.**

We went to a little Argentinian place in the north of Spain, which did amazing grilled meat. We sat outside on a terrace with a view over the sea. The food was delicious and the portions were really big. it was really good value.

LISTENING

3 ▶ 19 **Listen to two colleagues – Sara and Victor – discussing where to eat. Find out where they decide to go and why.**

4 ▶ 19 **Work in pairs. Decide if the sentences are true (T) or false (F). Listen again and check your answers.**

1 They both like Thai food.

2 The seafood place is in a department store.

3 Sara eats any kind of food.

4 They need to get a bus to go to Selale.

5 Sara doesn't like Turkish food.

6 They are definitely eating in Selale.

5 **Work in pairs. Discuss these questions.**

• Which of the three restaurants in Exercise 3 would you prefer to eat in? Why?

• How often do you eat out for breakfast, lunch or dinner? Where do you go? Who with?

GRAMMAR

Present perfect simple

The present perfect simple is formed using *have / has* + the past participle. We often use it to start conversations and find out about other people's experiences.

6 Look at the extracts from the conversations in Exercise 3 and decide if the statements below are true (T) or false (F).

S: *Well, there's a really nice Thai place just down the road.* **Have** *you ever* **been** *there?*

V: *Yeah, I go there a lot. I actually went there yesterday.*

V: *Well, why don't we go to Selale instead.* **Have** *you* **been** *there?*

S: *No.* **I've never heard** *of it. Where is it?*

V: *It's Turkish. It's really good.* **I've been** *there a few times.*

S: *Really?* **I haven't ever had** *Turkish food.*

V: *You're joking.*

1 The past participle is usually the same as the past simple form.

2 Always answer a present perfect question with a present perfect form such as *Yes, I have*.

3 Don't use the present perfect with a past time phrase such as *yesterday* or *a few years ago*.

4 Make the present perfect negative using *not* or *never* after *have / has*.

G Check your ideas on page 170 and do Exercise 1.

7 Complete each sentence with two ideas. Try to make them true and surprising!

- I've never eaten / drunk ...
- I've never been to ...
- I've never ...

8 Work in groups. Share your ideas from Exercise 7. Respond using some of these phrases.

You're joking! You should. You'll love it!

Really! Why not?

Me neither! I've never had the chance.

9 Complete the sentences using the present perfect or the past simple form of the verbs.

1 A: _____ anything unusual? (ever eat)

B: Yeah, I _____ bat soup once. (have)

2 A: _____ to an expensive restaurant? (ever go)

B: Yes, I _____ to a very famous Spanish place with work. Luckily, my boss _____ ! (go, pay)

3 A: _____ in a restaurant? (ever complain)

B: Yeah, a few times, actually. Last week I _____ in a café because the food _____ cooked properly. (complain, not be)

4 A: _____ a hair in your food? (ever find)

B: No, never, but I once _____ a piece of glass in a burger. I couldn't believe it! (find)

5 A: _____ any of Jamie Oliver's recipes? (try)

B: No, I _____ of him. (never hear)

6 A: _____ *Masterchef*? (watch)

B: I _____ it a few times, but I don't really like cookery programmes. (see)

PRONUNCIATION

10  ► 20 Listen to the six questions in Exercise 9. Notice how *have you ever* is pronounced /həvjʊːwevə(r)/.

11 Work in pairs. Take turns to ask your partner the questions in Exercise 9 and give true answers. Then write five more *Have you ever ...?* questions.

G For further practice, see Exercises 2 and 3 on page 171.

DEVELOPING CONVERSATIONS

Making and responding to suggestions

Look at how we make suggestions and respond to them.

A: *Where do you want to go?*

B: *There's a nice Indian place round the corner.* **How about that?**

A: **To be honest, I don't really feel like** *a curry today.*

B: **Well, why don't we** *go to Prego instead.*

A: *Oh, I went there once but I had a dish that tasted disgusting.*

12 Work in pairs. Write similar conversations using these ideas.

1 Gino's Pizzas / pizza yesterday / the Thai place next to it

2 Mexican place by the river / don't feel like / the seafood place near here

3 cafe round the corner / not much choice / a Chinese restaurant

4 Harvey's restaurant / last time service bad / order a takeaway

CONVERSATION PRACTICE

13 Spend a few minutes thinking of three places where you might go and eat with other students in your class. What's good / bad about them?

14 Have conversations similar to the one you heard in the listening. Use these questions to start. Reject at least one of your partner's ideas and explain why.

- Are you hungry?
- Do you want to get something to eat?
- Where are you thinking of going?
- Have you ever been there?

 6 To watch the video and do the activities, see the DVD-ROM.

WHAT ARE YOU HAVING?

SPEAKING

1 Work in groups. Discuss these questions.

- How often do you eat the following kinds of food? Explain why.

> beans   fruit   seafood   fish   meat   vegetables

- Which of these things have you eaten today?

- When you eat out, do you generally order the same thing – or do you like trying different things?

VOCABULARY Describing food

2 Add three words from the box to each column in the table below.

bitter	grilled	mild	roast	shell	soft
fruit	herb	raw	seafood	skin	stone

how eaten	taste and texture	part of food	kind of food
fried	hard	leg	meat
boiled	sweet	seed	vegetable

3 Match each description to one photo.

1 They're a kind of seafood. They're quite big and white, not very soft, with a mild taste – not very salty. They're usually fried or grilled in the shell. They have a big shell – almost the size of my hand.

2 It's a kind of fruit. It's green. It has a very thick skin, which you don't eat, and a very big stone in the middle. The inside is green and it's not really sweet or bitter. You usually eat it in a salad, or you sometimes make a kind of sauce with it.

4 Work in pairs. Take turns describing four different foods for your partner to guess.

LISTENING

5 Read the restaurant menu. Put a tick (✓) next to the dishes that look good to you, a cross (✗) next to any dishes that don't look good and a question mark (?) next to any dishes you don't understand.

6 Work in groups. Compare your ideas.

- Try to explain some of the dishes to the others.
- What would you order in this restaurant? Why?
- Is there anything you really wouldn't eat? Why?

THE GLOBE RESTAURANT

STARTERS

Grilled squid
Soup of the day
Six oysters
Mushrooms with garlic
Tomato and avocado salad

MAIN COURSES

Fried chicken with potatoes (roast, boiled or fried)
Aubergines stuffed with rice
Spaghetti with tomato and clams
Spicy scallops with noodles
Leg of lamb with vegetables
Lamb curry
Courgette and potato pie with Greek cheese

DESSERTS

Chocolate pudding with chocolate sauce
Fruit salad
Home-made strawberry and vanilla ice-cream
Carrot cake (with cream)
Plate of cheese (with biscuits)

Mango

Avocado

Scallops

Kiwi fruit

7 Work in pairs. Decide who you think asks each question (a–j) – a waiter (W) or a customer (C)?

a Could I just have a coffee, please?

b Would you like to see the dessert menu?

c Does it contain any meat?

d Shall we leave a tip?

e Could we get some water as well, please?

f Are you ready to order?

g Have you booked?

h Would you like a high chair for the little girl?

i Could we have the bill, please?

j Could you get us a cloth, please?

8 ▶ 21 Listen to six short conversations in The Globe restaurant. Put the questions (a–j) in Exercise 7 in the order you hear them.

9 ▶ 21 Work in pairs. Can you remember the answers to any of the ten questions? Discuss your ideas. Then listen again and check your answers.

DEVELOPING CONVERSATIONS

Offers, requests, suggestions

To make polite offers, we often use *Would you like ...?*

Would you like to see the menu?

To make polite requests, we often use *Could you / I / we ...?*

Could you get us a cloth, please?

Could I just have a coffee?

To make suggestions, we often use *Shall I / we ...?*

Shall we leave a tip?

10 Complete the questions with *would*, *could* or *shall*.

1 A: _____ we just have a jug of tap water, please?

   B: I'm afraid not, madam. You have to buy a bottle.

2 A: _____ we get the bill?

   B: Yeah, it's getting late and I'm tired.

3 A: _____ we have a half portion for the kids?

   B: Of course, sir.

4 A: _____ you like to see the drinks list, madam?

   B: No thanks. _____ we just have some water?

5 A: _____ we ring them and book a table?

   B: That's a good idea. They get quite busy.

6 A: _____ you move your chair a little so I can get past?

   B: I'll get up. There's not much room in here.

7 A: _____ you like me to order for everyone?

   B: Yes, if you don't mind. There's so much to choose from.

8 A: _____ we get a taxi or do you want to walk?

   B: Let's walk. It's a lovely night. It's so warm.

11 Work in pairs. Take turns asking the questions from Exercise 10. Give different answers.

SPEAKING

12 Work in groups. You are going to roleplay a conversation. One student is the waiter, and the others are a group of friends. Decide who will take which role. Look at The Globe restaurant menu and the guide below and think about what you will say.

Customers	Waiter
	Take drink order and check customers understand the menu.
Ask about different dishes.	
	Take the order and make an offer / suggestion.
Discuss what you're eating and make two requests to the waiter.	
	Respond to requests. Later, ask if they would like desserts.
Discuss desserts and / or ask for the bill.	
	Give the bill.
Discuss the bill and how you'll pay.	

13 Now roleplay the conversation.

Courgette

Squid

Aubergine

Oyster

START THE DAY

READING

1 Work in groups. Discuss these questions.

- What's the most important meal of the day for you – breakfast, lunch or dinner? Why?
- What time do you usually have each meal?
- Do you eat any snacks between meals? What?

2 Read the article about breakfast around the world and match each photo to a country. One country does not have a photo. Name the food and dishes you see.

3 Read the article again and match each sentence (1–6) to a country / countries.

1 People sometimes have a very sweet drink.
2 A local food has been linked to health.
3 Someone had a special food on a journey.
4 Some people only have two meals all day.
5 Habits have changed. (x 2)
6 People don't have the traditional breakfast at home. (x 2)

4 Look at the words in bold in the article. Complete the sentences below with the words from the article. Then work in pairs and discuss the questions.

1 What does your _____ breakfast _____ of?
2 How often do you _____ something quick to eat instead of taking time to have a proper meal?
3 Do you ever eat from food _____ in the street? Why? / Why not?
4 Have you ever had an upset _____ after eating food? What happened?
5 How _____ are you about your health and what you eat?
6 What do you think is the _____ for a long life?

GRAMMAR

too and not ... enough

We use *too* or *not ... enough* to show there is a problem. We use *too* when we **need less** of something, and *not ... enough* when we **need more** of something.

5 Look at the sentences from the article and then complete sentences 1–5 with one word in each space.

a *They're **not** adventurous **enough** to experiment with anything new at breakfast.*
b *Would you have them or are they **too** spicy, **too** fattening or just **too** different?*
c *... they don't have **enough** time to make breakfast.*
d *... fewer Irish eat the traditional Irish breakfast, or fry, because it has **too** much fat.*

1 I usually just heat something in the microwave. I'm _____ lazy to cook for myself.
2 My doctor says I'm eating too _____ sugar, so I should stop adding it to my tea.
3 Too _____ people these days eat fast food.
4 My daughter helps me cook, but she's not old enough _____ be left on her own in the kitchen.
5 They're closing down the restaurant on the corner, because it does _____ make _____ money.

G Check your ideas on page 171 and do Exercise 1.

6 Work in pairs. Use *too / not ... enough* to complain about the things in the box. Say what you would do to solve the problem.

| a coffee | a hotel | a meal | a room |
| a car | a jacket | a movie | a steak |

It's too hot to drink. Leave it to cool.

It's too weak for my liking. Leave it for a bit longer.

It's too bitter. Add some sugar.

G For further practice, see Exercise 2 on page 172.

SPEAKING

7 Work in groups. Do you agree or disagree with the statements? Explain why.

- People don't learn enough about cooking when they are at school.
- Kids eat too many sweet things these days.
- There aren't enough good places to eat near here.
- Food is sold too cheaply in the shops.
- The government isn't doing enough to improve people's health.
- Kids spend too much time on the internet.
- People's lifestyles are too busy these days.
- We get too much homework in this class.

SOUNDS AND VOCABULARY REVIEW

8 ▶ **22** Listen and repeat the sounds with /v/, /b/, /f/ and /p/. Are any of them difficult to hear or say?

9 ▶ **23** Work in groups. Listen to eight sentences using the words below. Together, try to write them down. Then listen again and check.

| view | bill | typical | fat |
| serve | book | portion | fixed |

10 Work in teams. You have three minutes to write collocations or phrases for the words in Exercise 9.

*a **view** over the city, get a good **view**, sit and look at the **view***

BREAKFAST AROUND THE WORLD

They say breakfast is the most important meal of the day. Maybe that's why many people may be **open** to trying foreign food at lunch or dinner, but they're not adventurous enough to **experiment** with anything new at breakfast. But what about you? Below, we look at **typical** breakfasts in five different countries. Would you have them or are they too spicy, too fattening or just too different?

SOUTH KOREA

The traditional breakfast is rice and soup. People then choose extra dishes to go with it such as grilled fish, vegetables and *kimchi*, which is pickled cabbage with chillies. *Kimchi* is so popular that the first Korean astronaut took some with him to the international space station! Of course, these days, many Koreans have such **busy** lifestyles they don't have enough time to make breakfast and just **grab** a quick coffee and some cereal or toast.

BULGARIA

Breakfast in Bulgaria **includes** tea or strong coffee, sesame bread and butter, cheese made from sheep's milk, honey, olives, boiled eggs and – most importantly – *kiselo mlyako*, a local yoghurt. Bulgaria has a lot of people aged over 100 and many believe that the **secret** behind this is their yoghurt, which most Bulgarians eat every day.

COSTA RICA

Many Costa Ricans start their day with the national dish, *gallo pinto*, which is a **mixture** of fried rice and black beans. It's lightly spiced and often **served** with fried plantain (a kind of banana used like a vegetable in a lot of Central American and Caribbean cooking), cream and fried eggs. There's usually some **strong** local coffee as well – or perhaps some agua dulce ('sweet water'), which is made from sugar cane juice.

EGYPT

Visit any town in Egypt in the morning and you'll find street **stalls** selling *foul medammes* – beans cooked with tomatoes and onions – and eaten with a boiled egg on top and lots of flat bread. Pickled vegetables are usually served as a side dish. For many poorer Egyptians, this is their only food until dinner. They say the dish is 'a rock in the **stomach**'.

IRELAND

As people become more **concerned** about their health, fewer Irish eat the traditional Irish breakfast, or *fry*, because it has too much fat. However, many still eat it if they stay in a hotel, or they cook it on a special day. It **consists** of bacon, black pudding (a kind of sausage made with **blood**), white pudding (another kind of sausage), fried eggs, fried mushrooms and toast – all served with strong Irish tea!

VIDEO 2

FORBIDDEN FRUIT

Cam Canh

1 **Work in pairs. Look at the photo. Discuss these questions.**

   • Do you know what this fruit is? Have you ever tried it?

   • Where do you think it might be most popular?

   • What problems might be connected to the fruit?

2 📹 **7** **Watch the video. Find three problems caused by the fact that this fruit is so popular.**

3 **Work in pairs. Can you remember:**

   1 the four different ways people described the smell of durian?

   2 why cheese was mentioned?

   3 the price of durian?

   4 where the smell of durians can spread to if people eat them in hotels?

   5 the ways of removing the smell of durians?

4 📹 **7** **Watch the video again to check your ideas.**

5 **Decide which sentences below are facts and which are opinions. Work in pairs. Compare your ideas and discuss how you reached your decisions.**

   1 The durian is a seasonal fruit.

   2 Durians are awful.

   3 Durians are banned from some hotels.

   4 They smell like a rubbish dump.

   5 Asian people think cheese smells disgusting.

   6 Durians don't bear fruit for at least fifteen years.

6 **Work in groups. Discuss these questions.**

   • What's your favourite fruit? Are there any fruits you really don't like? Why?

   • Would you try durian – if you haven't already? Why? / Why not?

   • Are there any smelly foods that you really like?

   • What other problems with guests do you think hotel staff sometimes face?

UNDERSTANDING FAST SPEECH

7 📹 **8** **Read and listen to this extract from the video said at natural pace and then slowed down. To help you, groups of words are marked with / and pauses are marked //. Stressed sounds are in CAPITALS.**

   Other CULtures / LOVE / FOODS / that SMELL STRONGly // CHEESE / a FAvourite / in the WEST // is ACtually ROtted MILK // a SMELL PEOple in Asia / find disGUSting

8 **Now you have a go! Practise saying the extract at natural pace.**

REVIEW 2

1 Complete the text with one word in each space. Contractions like *don't* count as one word.

I was surprised to find out my friend, Sergio, has
¹_____ travelled abroad before. It's funny, because
he's done a ²_____ of other unusual things. He
told me when he ³_____ driving me to the airport.
We were on the motorway and we ⁴_____ chatting
when I suddenly noticed that there weren't ⁵_____
signs to the airport. I asked him 'Are you sure this is
the ⁶_____ way?' and he said, 'I think so, but I
⁷_____ never been there before.' So we stopped at
a service station and ⁸_____ for directions, and of
course we were on the wrong road. Luckily, we still had
plenty ⁹_____ time before my flight took off and so I
¹⁰_____ miss it.

2 Make two questions from each group of words.

1 Did / Have / he / you / go / eaten / with / you / here /
before

2 What / Has / would / he / you / like / finished / for /
eating / dessert

3 Where / What / have / time / did / you / you / been /
get / here

4 How / How / much / long / has / did / she / lived / it /
cost / here /

5 Could / Who / I / were / have / you / talking / a /
coffee / please / to / earlier

3 Choose the correct option.

1 A: What are you having?

  B: Just *much / some* soup and bread. *I had / I've had*
  breakfast an hour ago and I'm not very hungry
  now.

2 A: *Shall / Could* you pass me the salt and pepper?

  B: Here's the pepper, but I'm afraid there's *any / no*
  salt left. We need to buy *any / some* more.

3 A: Have you ever *saw / seen* that programme *King
  Cook*?

  B: Yeah, *a few / plenty* times, but I *haven't liked /
  didn't like* it that much.

4 A: How *did / has* the accident happen?

  B: The other driver *was texting / texted* on his mobile
  phone, so he didn't see the stop sign.

  A: How stupid! You're lucky he didn't do *a bit of /
  much* damage to your car.

4 ▶ 24 Listen and write the six questions you
hear.

5 Write replies to the questions in Exercise 4 to
create short dialogues.

6 Match the verbs (1–8) with the nouns they
collocate with (a–h).

1 book		a	a big selection / a meal
2 join		b	the first exit / ages
3 go through		c	to work / a horse
4 taste		d	a flight / a seat
5 take		e	the queue / the army
6 ride		f	£10 / you for parking
7 charge		g	disgusting / like chicken
8 have		h	security / the traffic lights

7 Decide if these words are connected to flights,
driving or food.

cancelled	a licence	a roundabout	skin
check in	mild	seafood	a truck
land	roast	a service station	a vehicle

8 Complete the sentences. Use the word in
brackets to form a word that fits in the space.

1 On the way to the meeting, I got _____ in traffic,
so I arrived late. (stick)

2 The plane was delayed so we were waiting in the
_____ lounge for three hours. (depart)

3 We were at the end of the queue at the _____
gate. (board)

4 The staff were all very helpful and _____ , even
though people were angry. (friend)

5 We went to a _____ place near here last night. It
was great. (Japan)

6 Do you know it? It's _____ opposite the entrance
to the park. (direct)

7 There wasn't a big _____ of dishes but all the
food was delicious. (choose)

8 I had _____ fish for my main course. (grill)

9 Complete the email with one word in each
space. The first letters are given.

Hi there Simon,

Just a quick email about arrangements for Saturday.
The match starts at five, so shall we get to the stadium
around four? There are sometimes big ¹qu_____
to get in so it's good to arrive early. Don't drive there –
it's almost impossible to ²pa_____ . The easiest
way to go is to take the ³und_____ . Donostia
is the nearest station to the football ⁴gr_____ .
It's on the red ⁵li_____ . When you come out
of the station, you'll see a big department store
on the ⁶ma_____ road. Go past the store and
⁷ke_____ going along that road until you come to a
square with a big ⁸mo_____ in the middle of it. You
can't ⁹mi_____ it. Let's meet there at four. It's five
minutes' walk from there.

After the match, shall we go for something to eat?
There's a really nice Mexican place near there. The
food's ¹⁰de_____ , the ¹¹po_____ are big and
it's great ¹²va_____ . It's the perfect place to go
after a game.

Hugh

5

RELAX

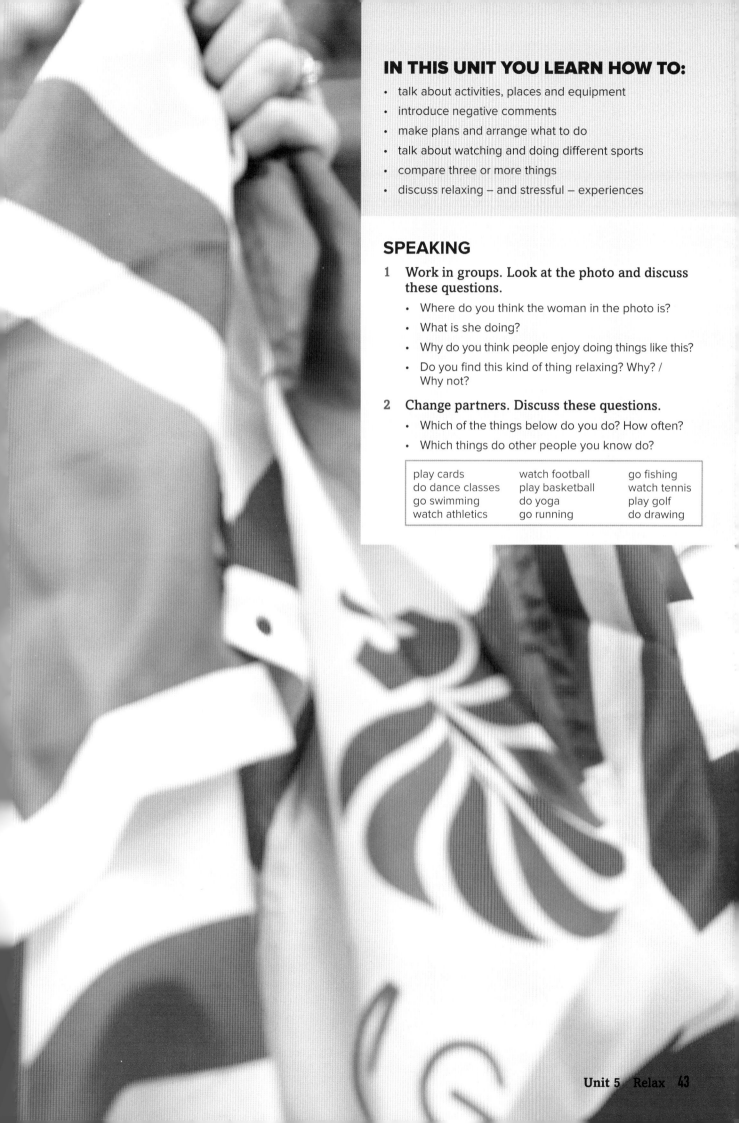

IN THIS UNIT YOU LEARN HOW TO:

- talk about activities, places and equipment
- introduce negative comments
- make plans and arrange what to do
- talk about watching and doing different sports
- compare three or more things
- discuss relaxing – and stressful – experiences

SPEAKING

1 **Work in groups. Look at the photo and discuss these questions.**

- Where do you think the woman in the photo is?
- What is she doing?
- Why do you think people enjoy doing things like this?
- Do you find this kind of thing relaxing? Why? / Why not?

2 **Change partners. Discuss these questions.**

- Which of the things below do you do? How often?
- Which things do other people you know do?

play cards	watch football	go fishing
do dance classes	play basketball	watch tennis
go swimming	do yoga	play golf
watch athletics	go running	do drawing

WHAT ARE YOUR PLANS?

VOCABULARY Places and equipment

1 Match each sport (1–6) with a pair of words (a–f).

1	swimming	a	rod / gear
2	running	b	court / racket
3	golf	c	pitch / boots
4	tennis	d	pool / trunks
5	football	e	track / shoes
6	fishing	f	course / clubs

2 **Work in pairs. Have six short conversations about the activities in Exercise 1. Use the questions below and words from Exercise 1.**

Do you want to ... with me on Saturday?

Is there a ... near here?

Is there anywhere I can buy ... near here?

Do you have any ...? / a spare ...?

Can you hire ... there?

A: *Do you want to play golf with me on Saturday?*

B: *Yeah, maybe. Is there a course near here?*

A: *There's one about 30km away.*

3 **Work in groups. Discuss the questions.**

- Can you think of five more places or pieces of equipment connected to the activities on page 43?
- What sport facilities are available near you?
- What sports equipment do you have in your home?

LISTENING

4 ▶ 25 **Listen to a conversation between Corinne and her friend, Maribel, who is visiting her. Tick (✓) the plans and arrangements for the weekend that they talk about.**

- relaxing and doing nothing special
- looking round the shops
- taking a flight
- watching a sports event
- doing some exercise
- going to a dance class
- going on a trip to the country
- going to a swimming pool

5 ▶ 25 **Listen again and complete the sentences with two or three words in each space. Contractions like *I'm* count as one word.**

1 What are you going to do while _____ ?

2 I'm just going to _____ .

3 Yes – and Saturday morning, _____ .

4 I'm sorry, but _____ are coming.

5 There's actually an athletics track just _____ .

6 To be honest, though, _____ a park or somewhere like that.

7 Do you have any plans for us _____ ?

8 We're thinking of going _____ in the mountains near here.

9 Oh right. Do you have any _____ ? I don't have anything with me.

10 If we want to _____ of the day, we need to leave early.

6 Work in groups. Discuss the questions.

- Does the trip Corinne planned for Sunday sound good to you? Why? / Why not?
- What time do you usually get up at the weekend? Why?
- Do you prefer swimming in a pool, a river or the sea? Why?
- Are there any particular activities you like doing outside or in the countryside?
- Where's the nicest place you've ever been walking, running or swimming?

DEVELOPING CONVERSATIONS

Introducing negative comments

We often add a short phrase before making comments that are negative in some way.

To be honest, I'd prefer a park.

I must admit, I'm a bit soft.

I have to say, I hate sport.

7 Work in pairs. Tell your partner about negative characteristics you have using *to be honest / I must admit / I have to say*. You may want to use some of the words in the box. Explain your ideas.

a bad loser	conservative	lazy	messy
bad with money	forgetful	loud	unfit

8 Tell your partner five negative opinions. Think about free-time activities and interests, famous people, places, food, music, films, etc.

To be honest, I don't think German food is very nice.

I must admit, I hate golf.

I have to say, I can't stand Jason Statham.

GRAMMAR

Plans and arrangements

To talk about future plans and arrangements we make with other people, we can use *going to* + infinitive (without *to*), the present continuous, *be thinking of* + *-ing* and *might* + infinitive (without *to*).

9 Match each sentence below to one of these meanings.

a a definite arrangement or plan for the future

b a possible plan not fully decided

1 I'm just going to take it easy.

2 I might go shopping in the morning.

3 Some important clients are coming.

4 I'm not going to be up before eleven.

5 I'm going to go for a walk after dinner.

6 Some friends might come round on Saturday.

7 I'm thinking of leaving quite early.

G Check your ideas on page 172 and do Exercise 1.

10 Put the words in a and b into the correct order to make questions.

1 We're having a picnic on Sunday if you're interested.

a else / who / going / is / ?

b going / are / where / it / to / you / have / ?

2 I might go to watch Leeds United play on Saturday.

a are / who / playing / they / ?

b of / when / tickets / thinking / are / you / getting / the / ?

3 My friend Jane's coming to visit.

a long / how / she / stay / going / is / to / ?

b you / are / while / of / what / doing / she's / thinking / here / ?

11 Work in pairs. Have conversations using the ideas in Exercise 10.

12 Make sentences that are true for you using the ideas below. Change or add words if you need to. The first one is done for you.

*I **might go out and meet some friends** tomorrow night. I'm not sure yet.*

*I'm just going to stay in and **relax** tomorrow night.*

1 I'm going to stay in and study tomorrow night.

2 I'm going to the cinema at the weekend.

3 My grandparents are coming for dinner tonight.

4 I'm meeting a friend for a drink tomorrow.

5 I'm playing basketball on Thursday.

6 A friend of mine is having a party on Friday night.

13 Work in pairs. Tell your partner your sentences from Exercise 12. Your partner should ask questions to find out more.

G For further practice, see Exercise 2 on page 172.

CONVERSATION PRACTICE

14 Work in pairs. Imagine a friend is coming to visit you for the weekend. Make a list of fun or interesting things to do in your town / area.

15 Now have a conversation similar to the one you heard in the listening. Take turns being A and B. Use the guide below to help you.

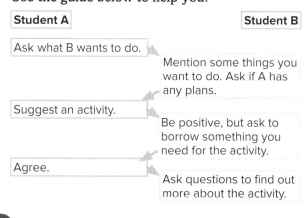

Student A	Student B
Ask what B wants to do.	
	Mention some things you want to do. Ask if A has any plans.
Suggest an activity.	
	Be positive, but ask to borrow something you need for the activity.
Agree.	
	Ask questions to find out more about the activity.

▶ 9 To watch the video and do the activities, see the DVD-ROM.

THE BEST GAME IN THE WORLD

VOCABULARY Sports and games

1 Complete 1–8 with the correct form of the verbs in the box.

beat	kick	support	time
draw	score	throw	win

1 I once _____ a medal in a running race at school.

2 I _____ 185 the last time I went bowling. That's my best ever.

3 A: How fast can you swim 100 metres, then?

   B: I don't usually _____ myself, but I guess it's around two minutes. I usually do about 30 lengths in 20 minutes.

4 We _____ our last match 1–1. We were winning until the 89th minute!

5 My brother always _____ me when we play cards. I'm sure he cheats!

6 I was playing football in the street and I _____ the ball through my neighbour's window by mistake.

7 Don't _____ it to me! I'm terrible at catching.

8 A: Who do you _____ ?

   B: Slavia Prague. I've got a season ticket, so I go to all their home games.

2 Work in pairs. Take turns to choose five words or phrases from Exercise 1, and explain, act or draw them. Your partner should guess the words without looking at the book.

   B: *This means you like a football team, and you always want them to win.*

   A: *Support?*

   B: *Right.*

3 Work in groups. Discuss these questions.

- Are you good at sport or at any other games?
- Have you ever won anything?
- Do you know how fast you can swim / run / cycle?
- Do you support any teams? Why?
- If you support a team, how're they doing at the moment?

LISTENING

4 Work in pairs. Think of three reasons to explain why football is so popular around the world, and three reasons why some people don't like it.

5 ▶ 26 Listen to a short talk about football's popularity. What two reasons does the speaker give for why people might not like the sport? What four reasons does he give to explain its popularity?

6 Work in groups. If you are a football fan, explain why and argue against the reasons for not liking it. If you're not a fan, explain why not and argue against the reasons for liking it.

GRAMMAR

Superlatives
We use superlatives when comparing more than two things.

7 Look at the sentences from the talk. Then work in pairs and discuss the questions below.

   a *Football is **the most popular** sport in the world.*

   b *Football is **the simplest** game to play.*

   c *The basic rules are among **the easiest** to grasp of any sport.*

   1 When do we use *most* to form superlatives?

   2 When do we use *-est* to form superlatives?

   3 Why do we use *-iest* (not just *-est*) in sentence c?

G Check your ideas on page 172 and do Exercise 1.

8 Complete the sentences so they are true for you. Use the superlative forms of the adjectives in brackets.

   1 _____ is _____ person I know. (tall)

   2 _____ person I know is probably _____ . (fit)

   3 _____ is _____ person I know. (clever)

   4 _____ person in my family is _____ . (relaxed)

   5 _____ is _____ building in my town. (ugly)

   6 _____ thing I've ever done is _____ . (exciting)

PRONUNCIATION

9 ▶ 27 Listen and notice how we usually pronounce *-est* as /ɪst/. Practise saying the sentences.

10 Work in groups. Compare your sentences from Exercise 8. Give extra details. For example:

   A: *My brother-in-law, Javier, is the tallest person I know. He's almost two metres.*

   B: *Really? OK. Well, I have a friend, Dimitry, who's two metres five. He's a giant!*

G For further practice, see Exercise 2 on page 173.

READING

11 Work in pairs. Look at the photos and discuss the questions.

- Do you recognise any of the sports in the photos?
- Where do you think each sport is most popular?
- What do you think are the basic rules of each sport?
- What do you think is good / bad about each sport?

12 Read about three different sports. Match each sport to one photo.

THERE'S MORE TO SPORT THAN FOOTBALL

Although it's doesn't attract big crowds or money, *pato* is the national sport of Argentina. It was invented in the 17th century and originally involved two teams on horses trying to **prevent** each other from carrying a duck (*pato* in Spanish) to their farmhouse. The sport was **banned** for a while because of violence – not only to the duck, but also to other players. Some were killed in fights or because horses kicked them. The modern game (sometimes also known as 'horseball') is a lot safer. Teams of four riders fight for the 'duck' (now a ball with handles) and throw and catch it to try and score in their **opponent's** net.

Since 1948, *keirin* has become one of Japan's biggest sports with over 20 million spectators a year attending events. People now **bet** over $15 billion dollars on the **outcome** of the races. Keirin is like horse racing, but with cyclists. Nine competitors ride round a track, following a cyclist who sets the **pace** at about 50km/h. He then leaves the track so the riders can race each other for the last part of the race, reaching speeds of 70km/h. There are often crashes as there is so little space to race in. Riders have to train 15 hours a day in special schools to be able to race, and can win millions of dollars.

Bossaball is quite a new game with a small but growing number of fans. It was invented in 2004 by a Belgian, Filip Eyckmans, and first became popular in Spain. It's played on a special inflatable pitch and is a mixture of volleyball, football, gymnastics and dance. Players bounce up and down and **aim** to pass, kick and head the ball over the net. The rules are quite complicated, but you basically lose a point when the ball touches the floor. The **referee** is also a DJ who plays Brazilian music as the teams play.

13 Work in pairs. Decide which of the three sports:

1 is the most popular.
2 is the oldest.
3 is the newest.
4 was once the most dangerous.
5 is the most dangerous now.

14 Match the words in bold in the article with these meanings.

1 try
2 stop
3 the result
4 the speed something happens at
5 the person who you try to beat when you play
6 the person who stops anyone cheating
7 made illegal by the government
8 try to win money by guessing the winner

SPEAKING

15 Work in groups. First, discuss the questions by talking about the sports in the texts. Then talk about other sports / games you know. Explain your ideas.

- Which sport / game do you think is the most fun to do?
- Which do you think is the best to watch?
- Which do you think needs the most skill to do?
- Which do you think needs the most fitness?
- Which do you think needs the most strength?

TAKE THE STRESS OUT OF LIFE

SPEAKING

1   Work in groups. Look at the activities below. Discuss if they are relaxing or stressful for you. Explain why. Use some of the patterns in the box.

cooking or baking	making or repairing things
drawing or colouring	shopping
going to or having a party	using computers
having a massage	working or studying

It depends what for. I mean, I love shopping for clothes.

It depends how much time I have. Sometimes I'm just too busy.

It depends how easy it is. I'm OK with simple things.

LISTENING

2   You are going to listen to a conversation about two popular hobbies. First, work in pairs and do the following.

- Check you understand the words in the box below.

- Discuss which words you think might go with each of these topics.

   - colouring books for adults

   - the maker movement (people making things for themselves, by hand, instead of buying them)

depression	furniture	pattern
personal	publish	retail therapy

3 ▶ **28** Now listen to the conversation and check your ideas. What is the connection between the two hobbies?

4 ▶ **28** Work in pairs. Discuss how to end the sentences. Listen again and check your ideas.

1 **Make-up**, shopping and boys is the reason the presenter _____ .

2 One of the biggest areas of **growth** in publishing is _____ .

3 The French publishers got a **dramatic** increase in sales by adding _____ .

4 The **task** of colouring is similar for children and adults because _____ .

5 In the adult books, some of the designs are _____ .

6 Karen thinks colouring has **made a difference** because she's more relaxed and _____ .

7 The sociologist, Professor Townsend, believes many people don't like the fact that life has become _____ .

8 Shopping involves difficult decisions, **debt** and worrying about what others have, but making things involves _____ .

5 Work in pairs. Decide what the words in bold in Exercise 4 mean.

6 Work in groups. Discuss these questions.
- Do you like the idea of colouring books? Why? / Why not?
- Do you ever make things? If not, why not? If yes, what? How did you learn?
- Do you think stress and / or depression is a problem in your country? In what ways do people deal with these problems? Are they good or bad ways?
- Do you ever sleep badly? What advice would you give to someone who can't sleep?
- Do you agree with Professor Townsend's views on shopping and making? Why? / Why not?

UNDERSTANDING VOCABULARY

Word families

Word families are words connected in form and meaning. For example, in the listening you heard colouring books are *one of the biggest* **growth** *areas in publishing* and *there's* **growing** *interest in making things. Growth* (n) and *growing* (adj) are connected to *grow* (v). Different forms in a word family often appear in the same text, and knowing one word in a family helps you to understand the meaning of other word forms. Try to also notice the different collocates that go with each word form.

7 Look at the audio script for Track 28 on page 197. Find as many forms based on the words in the box as you can. Decide if they are nouns, adjectives, adverbs or verbs.

child	person	occupy	sell
drama	publish	relax	stress

8 Complete each sentence with one of the words from the word family.

1 *expensive* (adj), *expense* (n), *inexpensive* (adj)
   a The company I work for pays for all my **travel** _____ when I go abroad.
   b Tickets to see matches are quite _____ , so they always have big crowds.

2 *add* (v), *added* (adj), *addition* (n), *additional* (adj)
   a I think you need to _____ **some salt** or something to it, to make it taste better.
   b **In** _____ **to** having simple rules, it needs very little equipment.

3 *support* (v), *support* (n), *supporter* (n)
   a The government doesn't have **much** _____ **for** its transport plans.
   b The police arrested several people at the ground after fighting between **rival** _____ .

4 *heat* (v), *heat* (n), *heating* (n), *heated* (adj)
   a It's really cold in here. Can you **turn the** _____ **on**?
   b In August we usually go to the mountains **to escape the summer** _____ .

5 *manage* (v), *management* (n), *manager* (n), *manageable* (adj)
   a I don't _____ **to do everything** I need to do, as I have too much work and too little time.
   b I just don't like his **style of** _____ .

6 *secure* (adj), *secure* (v), *security* (n), *insecure* (adj)
   a They do their best **to** _____ **the airports** and flights against terrorist attacks.
   b When the president visited, the _____ **was very tight**.

9 Can you explain or translate each of the collocations in bold in Exercise 8?

10 Discuss these questions.
- What are your biggest **expenses**? What's the most **expensive** ticket you've ever bought?
- Who are **rival supporters** in your country? Is there ever any trouble between them? Are there any policies you **strongly support** at the moment?
- Do you like **the heat**? Do you need **heating** in your home? For how long in the year?
- Would you be a good **manager**? Why? / Why not?

SOUNDS AND VOCABULARY REVIEW

11 ▶ **29** Listen and repeat the sounds with /l/ and /r/. Are any of them difficult to hear or say?

12 ▶ **30** Work in groups. Listen to eight sentences using these words. Together, try to write them down. Then listen and check.

play	race	threw	sale
pool	relax	track	simple

13 Work in teams. You have three minutes to write collocations or phrases for the words in Exercise 12.

play a game, *play* cards, *play* the piano

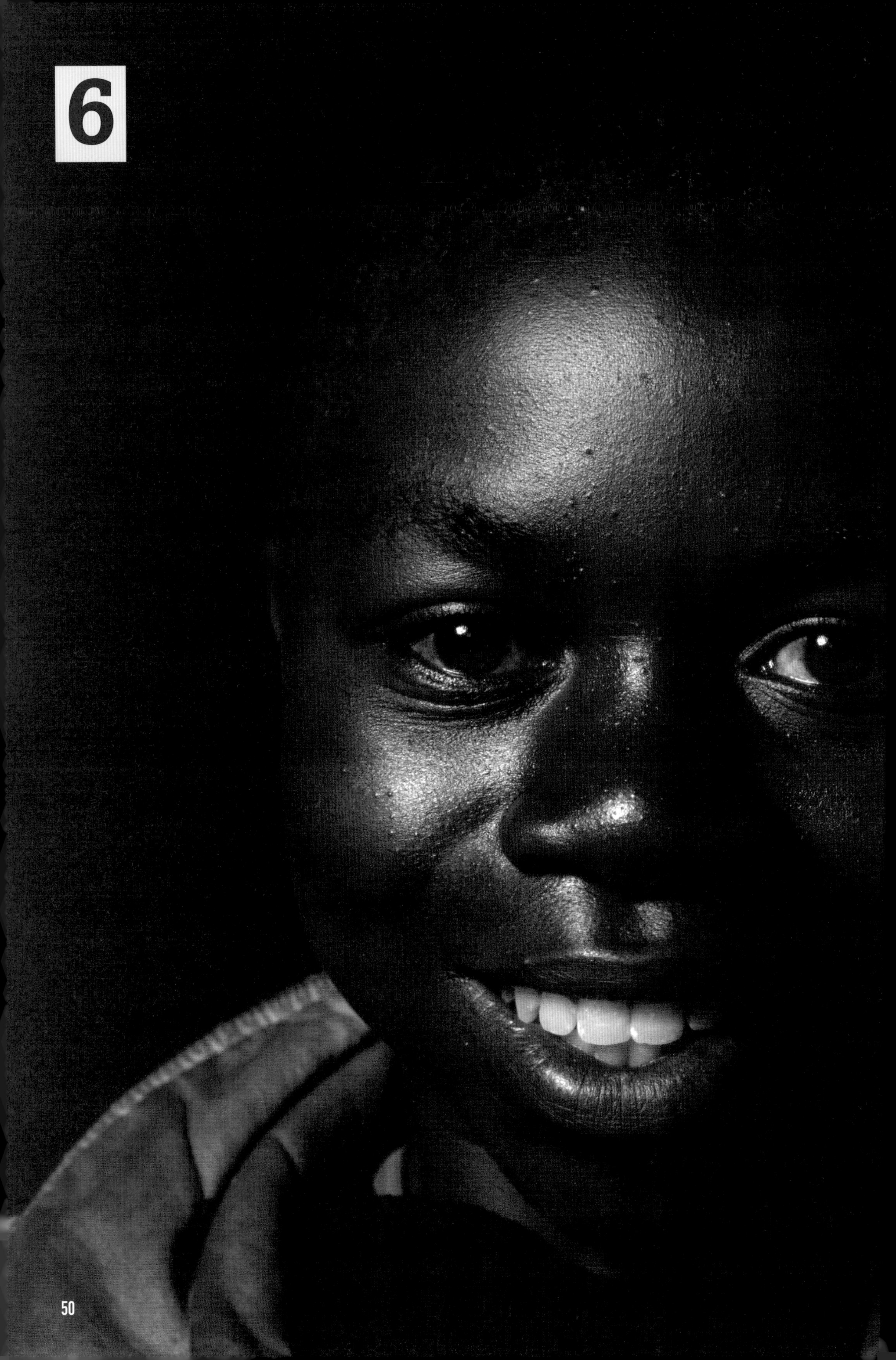
6

IN THIS UNIT YOU LEARN HOW TO:

- describe people you know
- explain who people are – and which people you mean
- ask and answer common questions
- discuss similarities and differences
- describe character and abilities
- discuss uses of social media and online habits

SPEAKING

1   Imagine you are the photographer. Think about these questions.

- Why did you take the photo of the boy?
- Who are the people in the small photo?
- Who is the boy and how does he know the people in the small photo?
- What has happened since the black-and-white photo was taken?

2   Work in pairs. Take turns to tell your stories.

3   Change partners. Tell your partner about:

- how often you take photos and what of.
- a favourite photo that you have. Explain who or what is in it, and why you like it.

FAMILY AND FRIENDS

WHO'S THE GUY IN THE MIDDLE?

LISTENING

1 ▶ 31 Listen to a conversation between two friends, Laura and Maya. They talk about the people in the photo. Who are the people?

2 ▶ 31 Complete the questions from the conversation with the words in the box. Then listen again and check.

Do	How long	Is	Who
How	How old	What	Why

1 A: _____ have you been here?
   B: About half an hour.

2 A: _____ else is coming?
   B: My little sister.

3 A: _____ do you know her?
   B: I met her on a business trip.

4 A: _____ she just visiting?
   B: No, she's working here.

5 A: _____ does he do?
   B: He's a teacher.

6 A: _____ did he go there?
   B: His girlfriend is from there.

7 A: _____ is he?
   B: 34.

8 A: _____ you get on well?
   B: No, not really.

3 Work in pairs. B's responses in Exercise 2 are incorrect. Try to remember what Laura and Maya actually said. Look at the audio script for Track 31 on page 197 and check your ideas.

VOCABULARY Family and friends

4 Decide if the words in the box refer only to females, or to both males and females.

1 aunt	6 flatmate	11 neighbour
2 classmate	7 girlfriend	12 mum
3 colleague	8 gran	13 mother-in-law
4 cousin	9 little sister	14 partner
5 ex-wife	10 niece	15 sister-in-law

5 What are the male equivalents of the female words in Exercise 4?

6 Check you understand the phrases in bold. Which people from Exercises 4 and 5 are the sentences talking about?

1 My brother and his wife have recently **had a baby** girl.

2 We **got to know each other** because we **work closely** together.

3 We **shared an apartment** in Gas Street when I first **moved** here.

4 She got the house when we **got divorced**.

5 They moved next door last year and we **immediately got on**.

6 I **don't really get on with him**. He doesn't think I'm good enough for his daughter.

7 He's over 70, but he only **recently retired**. So my dad **runs the company** on his own now.

8 In age, there's **a big gap** between us, but we're **very close** because I often picked her up from school and looked after her until Mum or Dad got home.

7 Choose six of the phrases in bold from Exercise 6 to talk about friends and family. For example:

*My cousin **had a baby** boy last year.*

*My uncle **works closely** with my dad, because they run a bar together.*

*I'm **very close** to my sister-in-law, because she was my best friend when she met my brother.*

GRAMMAR

Question formation

Most questions are formed using the pattern:

auxiliary verb	pronoun / noun	verb form
Do	you / your brothers	get on?

8 Look at these questions from the conversation. Answer the questions below.

a *How long **have you been** here?*

b *What **does he do**?*

c ***Is she** just **visiting**?*

d *Why **did he go** there?*

1 Which question(s) are in:
   - the present simple?
   - the present continuous?
   - the present perfect?
   - the past simple?

2 What are the auxiliary verbs and pronouns in each question?

G Check your ideas on page 173 and do Exercise 1.

9 Put the words in the correct order to make questions. The first one is done for you.

1 live / do / where / you / ?   *Where do you live?*
2 know / you / anyone / in / the / do / class / ?
3 known / have / how long / them / you / ?
4 you / are / English / studying / why / ?
5 this school / have / studied / you / in / before / ?
6 enjoying / you / the / are / class / ?
8 you / have / did / nice weekend / a / ?
9 you / did / do / what / ?

PRONUNCIATION

10 ▶ 32 Listen to the questions from Exercise 9 – first said slowly, then faster. Notice the stressed sounds in the faster speech.

11 Work in groups. Ask and answer the questions.

G For further practice, see Exercises 2 and 3 on page 174.

DEVELOPING CONVERSATIONS

Explaining who people are

When we ask or answer questions about people, we often add a phrase to explain who exactly we are talking about. The phrase starts with a preposition or an *-ing* form.

Who's the other girl **in the picture?**

Who's the guy **with the blue suit?**

The girl **with the red hair** *is my sister.*

We use an *-ing* form to say what they're doing.

Anna was the woman **sitting next to me** *in class yesterday.*

12 Complete the sentences with one word in each space.

1 A: Who's the the boy _____ the black-and-white photo?

   B: That's me when I was six.

2 A: Who's the guy _____ the hat?

   B: He's a friend _____ university.

3 A: Who was the woman sitting _____ to you in class today?

   B: That was my cousin, Wardah.

4 A: How was the film?

   B: The film was OK, but the man _____ behind me kept talking to his partner and the guy in _____ of me had a really annoying laugh!

5 A: Who's the woman _____ the baby?

   B: That was a colleague _____ the place I worked in Italy. I've forgotten her name now.

13 Work in pairs. Talk about the photo below. Ask and answer questions about who the different people are and make comments about them.

CONVERSATION PRACTICE

14 Think of three people you know. Choose one friend, one family member, and one other person from school, work or other activities. Either draw simple pictures of the three people or, if you have photos of them on a mobile phone, use those.

15 Have conversations like the one you heard in the listening. Show your pictures to your partner. Your partner should start by asking: *Who's that?* and continue the conversation by asking at least four more questions about each of the people.

🎥 10 To watch the video and do the activities, see the DVD-ROM.

DA GINO'S FOCACCERIA 232—90

A FAMILY BUSINESS

SPEAKING

1 Work in pairs. Discuss these questions.

- Do you know anyone who runs a family business? What's the business? Which members of the family are involved in the business? How?
- What do you think is good / bad about family-run businesses?
- Would you like to work with people in your family? Why? / Why not?
- Do / Did you want to do what your parents do / did as a job? Why? / Why not?

LISTENING

2 ▶ 33 Listen to a woman, Angela, talking about her family business. Answer the questions.

1 What is her business?
2 How successful is it?
3 Who is involved in the business? In what ways do they help with the business?
4 Who does she want to take over the business?

3 ▶ 33 Listen again and complete the sentences with three words in each space. Contractions like *don't* count as one word.

1 I was a model _____ younger and I did work for several wedding magazines.
2 My husband was very supportive _____ to start my company.
3 I think he thought it would always be small – something like a hobby – but it _____ .
4 I hope my daughter, Sophie, will _____ business eventually.
5 _____ are both very determined – she doesn't stop until she succeeds at something!
6 And then, she also shares her father's _____ .
7 He loves fashion and design, but I don't think he has _____ .

4 ▶ 34 Listen to two of Angela's children, Sophie and Jerome, talking about the business. In what ways do they agree / disagree with what their mother said?

5 Decide if you agree or disagree with these statements about Angela's family. Then work in groups and discuss your ideas.

- This kind of poor communication is common in families.
- I don't understand Sophie's attitude to taking over the business.
- The mother should support Jerome more. He can learn to be harder in business.
- Daughters normally have their mother's character and sons have their father's character.
- Being the middle brother or sister is the most difficult place in the family.
- The baby of the family always has an easy time – especially when there's a big age gap.

GRAMMAR

Similarities and contrasts

We can use *both*, *neither*, *all* and *none* to show similarities, e.g. how two or more people / things share the same characteristics.

6 Look at the sentences from the listening. Answer the questions below.

a *We have three kids now and they're **all** part of the business too.*

b *She and I are **both** very determined.*

c *They're **both** very good at negotiating prices, whereas I think maybe my son, Jerome, is a bit too soft.*

d *I actually don't want to run the business – **none of us** do!*

e ***Neither of them** take no for an answer.*

1 How many people do the words in bold refer to?

2 Which words show people are the same in *not* doing / being something?

3 When do you need *of* after *all*, *both*, *none* or *neither*?

4 What word has a similar meaning to *but*?

G Check your ideas on page 174 and do Exercise 1.

7 Work in pairs. Ask questions to find out what you have in common with your partner. How many similarities can you find in five minutes?

8 Join another pair of students and explain your similarities and differences. Use *both (of us) / neither of us* and *whereas*.

9 Now explain to the class what different things the students in your group have in common. Use *all* and *none* (of us).

G For further practice, see Exercise 2 on page 175.

VOCABULARY Character and habits

10 Match the sentences about general characteristics (1–9) with the explanations (a–i).

1 She and I are both very **determined**.
2 My granddad's still very **fit**.
3 Neither of us are very **practical**.
4 Neither of us are very **organised**.
5 We're all very **friendly and open** in our family.
6 My dad's quite **strict**, whereas my mum's a bit **soft**.
7 None of us are very **patient**.
8 My sisters are both very **bright.**
9 My brother's very **calm and confident**.

a We're not very good at building or repairing things.
b We're always happy to welcome people into our home.
c We don't give up. We keep going till we succeed.
d We often forget appointments and we're both quite messy.
e We get frustrated quickly and start shouting.
f He goes running every day for about an hour.
g He's just very positive and sure of himself, whereas I worry about things more.
h I always ask her for things because she usually agrees.
i They always get top grades. I sometimes feel a bit stupid in comparison.

11 Use each adjective in bold in Exercise 10 to talk about you and your family.

*To be honest, I'm not very **determined**. I give up quite easily.*

*We're all quite **fit** in my family. We all love sport.*

PRONUNCIATION

12 ▶ **35** There are lots of pairs of words in English like *friendly and open*. The 'and' is often pronounced /ən/ and the three words are said as one. Listen and practise saying the word pairs you hear.

13 Work in pairs. How many pairs of words from Exercise 12 can you remember? Look at audio script 35 on page 198 and check.

SPEAKING

14 Work in pairs. Which of your friends and family would be good at these tasks in a business? Use your own ideas and language from this lesson to explain why.

controlling costs and finance	managing staff
developing new products	negotiating prices
doing sales	networking
giving presentations	organising transport
keeping the office tidy	sorting out arguments
making decisions	writing contracts

MY SOCIAL NETWORK

READING

1 Work in groups. Read the short text below. Then discuss these questions.

   1 What exactly do you think the girl did wrong?

   2 Why do you think she did it?

   3 Does this story remind you of any other similar stories?

   4 How do you keep in touch with your close friends and family?

   5 Do you have online friends that you've never met in real life? Who?

> Everyone enjoys meeting new people and making friends – and the internet's made ¹this much easier. However, online friends don't always behave in the way we expect our real life friends to. For instance, I recently read about a teenage girl who posted inappropriate photos of a school friend on the web. The photos soon went viral. Over 100 people shared ²them almost immediately – and ³thousands more saw and commented on them. Following a complaint from ⁴her friend's parents, the head teacher spoke to the girl. 'How did ⁵this happen?' ⁶he asked. The girl then explained she had more than a thousand online friends, so things spread very quickly. When asked how many of ⁷these people were real friends, ⁸the girl immediately replied 'Six!'.

2 Work in pairs. What do the words in bold in the text refer to?

3 Read the quiz on page 57. Choose one answer for each question. Think of the reasons for your choices.

4 Complete the definitions below with words from the quiz.

   1 If you _____ an online picture, you add the names of the people in it.

   2 If someone does something without your _____ , they do it before you say it's OK.

   3 If you _____ fun of someone, you laugh at them and make jokes about them.

   4 If you _____ someone, you remove them from your list of online friends.

   5 If you post _____ status updates, it's not clear how you feel or what has happened.

   6 If you _____ someone, you stop them from seeing your status updates, photos, etc.

5 Work in groups of three. Discuss your answers to the quiz, and explain your choices. Who are you more similar to in your group?

UNDERSTANDING VOCABULARY

Words with the same verb and noun forms

Nouns and verbs in the same word family sometimes have different forms. For example: *grow* (verb) – *growth* (noun), *secure* (verb) – *security* (noun), etc. However, often a word can be used as both a verb *and* a noun, e.g. *phone*.

6 Six of the words in the box can be used as both verbs and nouns. Which two words can't?

accept	email	post	stream
comment	ignore	quote	update

7 Complete each sentence with the correct form of one of the words in the box in Exercise 6.

   1 She _____ all these awful photos of her ex-boyfriend online last week.

   2 I wanted to _____ on that post, but I just didn't have time.

   3 I know. I saw her status _____ on Facebook earlier.

   4 Can you _____ me the details later?

   5 To _____ my dad: your best friends are made by time.

   6 We managed to find a live _____ and so we watched the game online.

8 Work in pairs. Think of three more words that can be used as both verbs and nouns. Write examples showing how to use both the verb and the noun for all three words.

SOUNDS AND VOCABULARY REVIEW

9 ▶ 36 Listen and repeat the sounds with /w/ and /g/. Are any of them difficult to hear or say?

10 ▶ 37 Work in groups. Listen to eight sentences using these words. Together, try to write them down. Then listen again and check.

weekend	negotiate	vague	wedding
quote	quiz	work	gap

11 Work in teams. You have three minutes to write collocations / phrases for the words in Exercise 10.

*Have a great **weekend**.*

*I might go shopping at the **weekend**.*

*I went there last **weekend**.*

WHAT KIND OF AN ONLINE FRIEND ARE YOU?

1 A friend posts and tags a picture of you online without your permission. Do you:

a 'like' the post?

b add a comment to show you're not happy about the photo?

c send a message asking your friend to remove the photo?

2 A friend often posts pictures of cute animals doing funny things. Do you:

a share the pictures with all your online friends?

b sometimes look at them and smile to yourself?

c hide any further posts from this person?

3 A few of your friends post lots of 'selfies' – photos they took of themselves. Do you:

a comment on how great your friends look in the photos?

b make fun of your friends – in a nice way – by writing the opposite of what you really think?

c 'unfriend' them?

4 A friend often posts vague status updates – things like *So angry right now!* Do you:

a try to find out why your friend feels like this?

b not comment yourself, but watch other people's comments to find out what's happening?

c show you're annoyed by posting things like *Nobody cares?*

5 Your brother posts photos of almost every meal he ever eats. Do you:

a sometimes comment and write things like *Wow! Looks delicious?*

b not comment or spend any time looking at the photos, but then start feeling hungry yourself?

c make fun of him by posting pictures of disgusting things and writing that they're your dinner?

6 Your sister often takes online quizzes – and wants you to do the same. Do you:

a take them all, but only post your score when you do well?

b generally ignore them, but sometimes quickly take one or two?

c write – and share – your own quiz called *How much time can YOU waste on quizzes?*

7 One of your cousins often posts inspiring quotes like *Follow your dreams*. Do you:

a share them with all your friends because you love positive ideas?

b comment occasionally on ones you like, but mostly just not look at them?

c hide the posts if you can – and if you can't, unfriend your cousin?

8 Your grandmother loves playing online games – and wants you to join her. Do you:

a accept and play whenever you get the chance?

b politely explain that you'd really like to, but don't have time?

c post a message telling friends to never ask you to play any online games – ever?

9 A friend of a friend sends a friend request – and says they like your photo. Do you:

a accept because it's always good to make new contacts?

b ignore the request and pretend it didn't happen?

c delete the request and block the person?

10 An old friend starts posting a lot about his ex-girlfriend. Do you:

a phone him or arrange to meet face to face to discuss his problems?

b try to write positive comments when you have time?

c feel uncomfortable and unsure of what to say?

VIDEO 3

WOMAD

1 Work in pairs. Look at the photo. Say:
   - what's happening in the photo.
   - what kind of performances happen at a place like this.
   - what's good and bad about these kinds of events.

2 ◀ 11 Watch the first part of the video (0.00–1.22) about the WOMAD festival. Find out:
   1 who takes part in the festival.
   2 what WOMAD stands for.
   3 who co-founded the festival.
   4 why he founded it.

3 Work in groups. Discuss these questions
   - Would you like to go to a festival like WOMAD? Why? / Why not?
   - Who are the most famous foreign musicians in your country?
   - What kind of music do they play? Do you like what they do?
   - Are any musicians from your country famous abroad? Where?

4 ◀ 11 Watch the second part of the video (1.23–4.24), about a band called Spaccanapoli. Are the sentences true (T) or false (F)?
   1 Eight people play in the band.
   2 They've played at WOMAD several times.
   3 Marcello taught himself to play the tambourine.
   4 Their music mixes different styles.
   5 They don't normally sing in the streets.
   6 The song he sings at the end is a love song.

5 Complete the second phrase with the correct form of the word in bold. The first one is done for you.
   1 **combine** different styles
      a _combination_ of dance and drama
   2 **perform** on the main stage
      give a great _____
   3 find him **inspiring**
      get _____ from the world around me
   4 get on with my **neighbours**
      live in a nice _____
   5 **personally**, I don't like it
      express my _____ view
   6 **celebrate** my birthday
      it's a _____ of our culture
   7 continue the **tradition**
      wear _____ clothes

6 Work in pairs. Take turns to talk about one of the following topics. Your partner should ask questions to find out more.
   - a festival I know about
   - music I like

UNDERSTANDING FAST SPEECH

7 ◀ 12 Read and listen to this extract from the video said at natural pace and then slowed down. To help you, groups of words are marked with / and pauses are marked //. Stressed sounds are in CAPITALS.

   and THERE were these // REAlly sTUNning // VOICes / DOing // much BEtter than I ever could / so THAT was // really insPIring for me

8 Now you have a go! Practise saying the extract at natural pace.

REVIEW 3

GRAMMAR

1 Complete the text with one word in each space.

Tina,

Just a quick one to tell you what ¹_____ happening on Saturday. We've decided that ²_____ easiest way to get to the festival is to drive. Kwab can take the others, and my brother's ³_____ with us now and has a car. He's ⁴_____ to pick us up at ten. One thing to mention – he ⁵_____ bring his two kids too, if he can't find a babysitter. I hope you don't mind. Neither of ⁶_____ are any trouble and I think they're ⁷_____ quite excited by the idea of going to a real rock music festival. We're ⁸_____ taking any food with us. We ⁹_____ just going to buy something from one of the food stalls there. ¹⁰_____ you looked at the programme yet? Who ¹¹_____ you want to see? I'm ¹²_____ of going to see Los Enemigos first. What about you?

Luisa

2 Make two questions from each group of words.

1 Why / How / long / did / have / you / you / move / known / here / each / other

2 How / When / old / are / is / they / thinking / your / gran / of / leaving

3 Who / What / are / happened / you / going / last / night / with

4 What / What / team / is / the / do / quickest / you / way / to / support / get / there

3 Complete the second sentence so that it has a similar meaning to the first sentence, using the word given. Do not change the word given. You must use between two and four words, including the word given.

1 Is this your first ever yoga lesson?
   _____ yoga before? **YOU**

2 We might go swimming in the lake later.
   We _____ swimming in the lake later. **OF**

3 We are both really competitive.
   _____ likes to lose. **US**

4 I've never seen anything so funny.
   It was _____ I've ever seen. **THING**

5 No-one in my family likes football.
   We _____ in my family. **HATE**

6 He beat the world record for swimming 50m.
   He _____ in the world. **SWIMMER**

4 ▶ 38 Listen and write the six sentences you hear.

5 Write a sentence before and after the sentences in Exercise 4 to create short dialogues.

VOCABULARY

6 Match the verbs (1–8) with the nouns they collocate with (a–h).

1	hire	a	an update / a comment
2	score	b	the ball out / it hard
3	kick	c	a baby boy / a spare racket
4	have	d	my own company / a hotel
5	control	e	20 points / twice
6	post	f	films / music
7	run	g	some skis / some clubs
8	stream	h	costs / the crowd

7 Decide if these words and phrases are connected to sport or friends and family.

age gap	draw	opponent	retired
bet	forgetful	pitch	soft
classmate	niece	race	track

8 Complete the sentences. Use the word in brackets to form a word that fits in the space.

1 There has been a huge _____ in the number of people cycling in recent years. (grow)

2 Stopping smoking has made a huge _____ . I can run a lot faster now. (different)

3 You can't play tennis in this _____ . Let's play later, when it's cooler. (hot)

4 The football club has tried to improve _____ at matches, but there are still some problems. (secure)

5 There was some trouble at the match between the rival _____ . (support)

6 My sister's room is quite messy, but in other ways she's very _____ . (organise)

7 My mum taught for years and she's given me lots of _____ advice since I started as a teacher. (practice)

8 I'd like to get a job in _____ , when I finish university. (publish)

9 The _____ of the books haven't been very good, unfortunately. (sell)

10 We probably need to do some _____ marketing to sell more. (addition)

9 Complete the text with one word in each space. The first letters are given.

My best friend is probably my flatmate, Dietmar. We first met playing at a tennis ¹cl_____ . We didn't really ²g_____ o_____ immediately, maybe because he ³su_____ Bayern Munich, ⁴wh_____ I'm a fan of Schalke, but mainly because he usually ⁵be_____ me at tennis. I have to ⁶ad_____ , I am a very bad ⁷lo_____ . He doesn't get upset, he's usually quite ⁸c_____ when he loses. Gradually, I got to ⁹k_____ him better and realised he's just a really great guy – very friendly and ¹⁰o_____ . I guess that's one reason he's such a good salesman, because people are always happy to talk to him and he's really good at ¹¹ne_____ . On top of that, he's really ¹²de_____ , so when there's a chance of a sale he doesn't give up.

7

IN THIS UNIT YOU LEARN HOW TO:

- explain where you are from
- describe your town and area
- ask useful questions when staying with people
- ask for permission to do things
- show guests round your house or apartment

SPEAKING

1 **Work in pairs. Look at the photo and discuss the questions.**

- Where do you think this is? Why?
- What kind of building might this be?
- Why do you think the map of the world is here?
- Where's your home on the map?
- How many countries or areas on the map can you name?

2 **Work with a new partner. Discuss the questions.**

- Which places in your own country have you visited or lived in?
- Do you have a favourite town, city or area in your country? Why?
- Do you have any family or friends in other parts of the country?

YOUR PLACE

WHEREABOUTS EXACTLY?

LISTENING

1   You are going to hear conversations with people from Italy, Texas and Oman. First, work in groups. Discuss what you know about each place. Think about:

- any famous towns, cities or regions – and what they're like.
- any famous people or companies from each place.
- the climate in each place.

2   ▶ 39 Listen to the three conversations. Find out:

1   where exactly the second speaker in each conversation is from.

2   what each place is like.

3   Work in pairs. Decide which conversations these phrases came from. Explain your decisions.

a   My geography isn't very good.

b   It's a small city in the north-east.

c   The climate's lovely.

d   Lots of people from different countries live there.

e   It's easy to get round.

f   It spreads along the coast.

g   Did you catch anything?

h   You can walk along the banks.

i   What a small world!

4   ▶ 39 Listen again and check your answers to Exercise 3. Look at the audio script for Track 39 on page 198 if you need to.

5   Work in pairs. Discuss these questions.

- Which place sounds like the best place to live in? Why?
- Which place sounds like the best place for a holiday? Why?
- Are any famous companies based where you live?
- Have you ever met anyone who made you think it's a small world? Who? Why?

DEVELOPING CONVERSATIONS

Explaining where places are

When people ask where exactly we're from, we often first say the name of the place and then explain where it is. This can mean saying which part of the country it's in, or where it is in relation to more famous places the other person might know.

E: *So where are you from Chuck?*

F: *Texas.*

E: *Whereabouts?*

F: *I doubt you'll know it. It's a little town called Harlingen. It's right in the south – by the Mexican border.*

6 Look at the map of Scotland. Match the sentences (1–8) to the places (a–h) on the map.

1 It's a port on the north-east coast.
2 It's a tiny village in the centre of the country.
3 It's a small market town in the north-east.
4 It's a big city in the west of the country.
5 It's a small industrial town about halfway between Edinburgh and Glasgow.
6 It's an island off the west coast.
7 It's an area in the south-west that borders England.
8 It's quite a small town right up on the north coast.

7 Work in pairs. Cover the sentences in Exercise 6. Take turns starting a conversation, and answer using the map of Scotland and the language from Exercise 6.

A: *Where are you from?*
B: *Scotland.*
A: *Really? What part?*
B: *Inverness. Do you know it?*
A: *No, where is it?*
B: *Oh, it's a port on the north-east coast.*

8 Write five sentences to describe places you know – in your country or somewhere else in the world. Then work in groups. Take turns to describe a place. Can the rest of the group guess the place?

A: *It's an important port. It's on the north-west coast of Russia. It's near the border with Finland.*
B: *Murmansk?*
A: *You got it.*

VOCABULARY Describing places

9 Work in pairs. Discuss which is the odd one out in each group. Explain your decisions.

1 dry / climate / warm / cold / buildings
2 industrial / a forest / steel / factories / a car plant
3 green / parks / trees / dirty / countryside
4 churches / traffic / transport / pollution / the underground
5 village / exciting / cinemas / bars / 24-hour culture
6 agriculture / fields / squares / farms / rural
7 coast / desert / fishing / port / ocean / beach
8 museum / old / historic / city wall / modern
9 crime / lovely / dangerous / murder / steal
10 river / bridge / financial / boat / bank

10 Work in pairs. Try to think of a place that fits each description below. Discuss what you know about each place. Have you ever been to any of the places?

• a place on the coast with a warm climate, where old people often retire
• an industrial city with a big steel factory or car plant
• a town or city with a good transport system
• a city that's quite dirty, but that's surrounded by nice countryside
• a very exciting city with a 24-hour culture
• a rural area with a lot of farms and agriculture
• a town by the sea with a fishing industry
• a historic city that has a wall round part of it
• a place which is quite dangerous with a lot of crime
• a town with a river going through it

CONVERSATION PRACTICE

11 Think about how to answer the questions below. You can give answers that are true for you – or invent answers.

Where are you from?   Where's that?
Whereabouts (do you live)?   Where's that?
What's it like?

12 Have conversations with other students to find out where they are from and what it's like.

🎥 **13** To watch the video and do the activities, see the DVD-ROM.

A BIG MOVE

VOCABULARY Where I live

1   **Work in pairs. Discuss the questions.**

- What is good or bad about living in each of the different places below?
- Do you know anyone who lives, or has lived in, places like this? When? Why? Do / Did they like it?

  1   university halls of residence
  2   the top floor of a block of flats
  3   an army base
  4   an old people's home
  5   a shared house
  6   a studio flat

2   **Match each place in Exercise 1 with a pair of phrases below.**

  a   take the lift / have a great view
  b   do military service / at war with another country
  c   noisy students / have my own sink
  d   not much space / absolutely tiny
  e   staff treat people with respect / have a good reputation
  f   split the bills / take turns to clean the bathroom

DONG MEI

I'm from Harbin, in the north-east of China, but I moved to Wales last year to do a Master's degree. It's the first time I've lived away from home, so I miss my family, but most of the time I love it. I'm living in the university halls of residence. I have my own room with a sink to wash in, but I have to share the bathroom. That's not great. Sometimes you have to wait or people leave it dirty. I also share the kitchen, but that's OK because it's a good place to meet the other students and talk. I've taught some of my flatmates to cook some Chinese dishes! Some of them didn't know to cook eggs, so it's really helped to make friends.

I think I'm more confident now, maybe because I have to do things for myself and I find I can do them well. Well, I can do them OK. And I love the freedom to do what I want. I can come home late and I don't have to answer questions about where I've been.

READING

3   **Work in groups of four: two As and two Bs.**

Student As: read the two stories on these pages.

Student Bs: read File 13 on page 190.

With the person who read the *same* texts, answer the questions.

  1   Whereabouts is each person living?
  2   What kind of place is each person living in?
  3   Why did they move there?
  4   What's good / bad about each person's situation?

4   **Now work in pairs: one Student A and one Student B. Ask and answer the questions in Exercise 3 about the texts you read.**

5   **Read the two stories your partner read. Then decide which of the four people:**

  1   isn't earning very much.
  2   has lost someone close to them.
  3   doesn't have a high position in a company.
  4   has relatives who helped find their new home.
  5   notices other people's bad habits.
  6   sometimes feels down because they're on their own.
  7   wants to make a positive difference.
  8   has had a change in character.

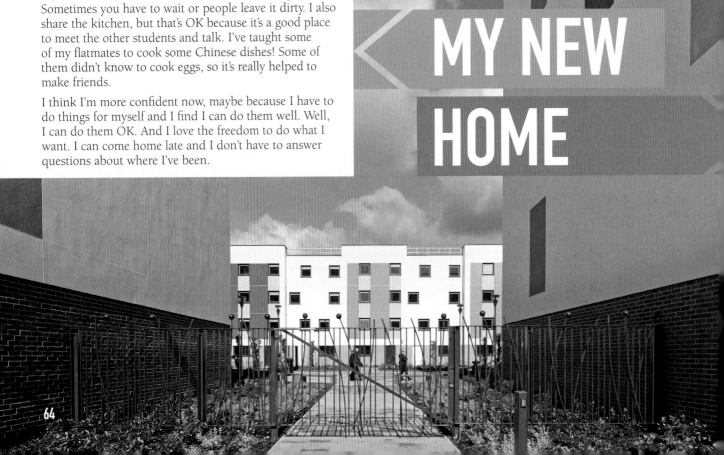

MY NEW HOME

6 Do you agree or disagree with these statements? Work in groups and discuss your ideas.

- The hardest thing to learn when you first leave home is how to manage your money.
- Living apart from your husband or wife is a good test of a relationship.
- Military service is a good idea.
- It's better to stay and help your country develop than to leave it.
- Children should look after their parents – instead of putting them in homes.

GRAMMAR

have to, don't have to, can and *can't*

7 Look at the sentences from the stories. Then complete the rules in the Grammar box.

   a *I **have to** share the bathroom. Sometimes I **have to** wait.*

   b *I **can** come home late and I **don't have to** answer questions about where I've been.*

   c *Sometimes junior staff don't want to go, but they **can't** say no.*

1 To talk about rules – or things that are necessary to do, use _____ + verb.

2 To talk about things that are not necessary, use _____ + verb.

3 To show something is possible and you are free to do it if you want, use _____ + verb.

4 To show something is not possible and you have no choice, use _____ + verb.

G Check your ideas on page 175 and do Exercise 1.

8 Complete the sentences with the correct form of *have to, don't have to* or *can*.

1 My flat's quite close. We _____ walk there in ten minutes.

2 Do you _____ pay extra for the bills or are they included?

3 My parents are quite liberal. For example, friends _____ stay at my house if they want to.

4 She's really lucky! She _____ do any housework at all!

5 My parents are quite strict. I _____ help with all the cooking and cleaning.

6 I don't get on with my sister. I _____ talk to her without having an argument!

PRONUNCIATION

9 ▶ 40 Listen to the sentences from Exercise 8. Notice that in normal speech *have to* is usually pronounced /hæftə/ and *can* is pronounced /kən/. Then listen again and practise saying the sentences.

10 Make a list of good and bad things about where you live. Use *have to, don't have to, can* and *can't*.

11 Work in groups. Compare your ideas. Who lives in the best place? Why? Does anyone know a person outside the group who lives in a better place?

G For further practice, see Exercises 2 and 3 on page 175.

KENTA

I work for a big Japanese car company. It's a secure job and the money's good, but because I'm a junior member of staff, I have to work in different places overseas every couple of years. Sometimes junior staff don't want to go, but they can't say no, because refusing can affect their future career. However, I always think it's a great opportunity and I learn about other cultures. Anyway, I'm currently based in Togliatti in Russia, about 500 miles south-east of Moscow. It's very different to my home town, Fukuoka. It's colder, of course, and the food is very different too, but I have a nice apartment on the top floor of a big block.

The hardest thing for me this time is that my wife and two children are still in Japan. I can visit three times a year, and we keep in touch online, but I get very lonely sometimes and I miss my kids terribly. On the positive side, though, I'm getting more experience and learning a lot, and that's very useful to get a senior job in the company.

LET ME SHOW YOU ROUND

LISTENING

1 Work in groups. Discuss which of the following you expect to do in the first half an hour after arriving at someone's house to stay. What might the people say in each case?

- kiss each other
- be introduced to everyone in the house
- talk about your journey
- take your shoes off
- have a wash or shower
- have something to drink or eat
- see all the rooms in the house
- give a present to the host

2 ▶ 41 Listen to a conversation between Maksim from Uzbekistan and the family he is visiting. Which four things in Exercise 1 happen?

3 Work in groups. Discuss these questions.

- Would you like to receive Maksim's presents?
- Have you had any presents from people who have visited you? Do you still have the present?
- When was the last time you stayed in someone's house? How long did you stay? Where did you sleep? Were there any rules for the house?

DEVELOPING CONVERSATIONS

Asking for permission

In the listening you heard Maksim ask for permission like this: *Is it OK if I ...?* and *Do you mind if I ...?* Look at the positive and negative ways to respond to these requests.

A: *Is it OK if I take my shoes off?*

B: **Sure. Go ahead.** (+)

B: *Well,* **actually, I'd rather you didn't.** (-)

A: *Do you mind if I smoke?*

B: **No, of course not. Go ahead.** (+)

B: *Well,* **actually, I'd rather you didn't** inside. (-)

4 Match the questions 1–6 to the responses a–f.

1 Do you mind if I open the window?
2 Do you mind if I use your computer?
3 Do you mind if I borrow your phone for a minute?
4 Is it OK if I leave class early today?
5 Is it OK if I close the window?
6 Is it OK if I leave these papers here?

a No, of course not. It is quite hot, isn't it?
b I'd rather you didn't. I'm trying to tidy up.
c No, of course not. One minute. I'll just log off.
d Yes, of course. It is quite cold, isn't it?
e Yes, of course. Just make sure you do your homework.
f Actually, I'd rather you didn't. I don't have much credit.

5 ▶ 42 Listen and check your answers. Notice how the words link together in *Do you mind if I* and *Is it OK if I ...?* Then work in pairs. Practise asking and responding to the questions in Exercise 4.

6 ▶ 43 Listen to the second part of the conversation between Maksim, Oliver and Isabel. Take notes on:

- the rooms Isabel mentions.
- any comments connected to each room.

7 ▶ 43 Work in pairs. For each sentence, decide where the speakers are and what / who they are talking about. Use your notes to help you. Then listen again and check.

1 He won't bite you. I promise. He's very friendly.
2 I'll do it for you if you like.
3 You'll probably have to watch repeats of *The Big Bang Theory*.
4 We won't go in there. It's a mess!
5 I'll get you some towels in a moment.
6 He'll remind me of home.
7 I think you'll be warm enough.

GRAMMAR

will / won't

We use *will / won't* + infinitive (without *to*) to talk about future actions or give opinions about the future. We often use *will / won't* as an immediate response to situations or things people say.

8 Look at the examples of *will / won't* in Exercise 7. Find the following.

a two examples of offers
b three examples of opinions
c one example of a decision
d one example of a promise

G Check your ideas on page 175 and do Exercise 1.

9 Work in pairs. Use *will / won't* to respond to these sentences. You can make a promise, an offer, a decision or you can give / ask for an opinion about the future.

1 These bags are really heavy.
2 Is it OK if I make myself something to eat?
3 Do you mind if I go out later?
4 Have you finished that book I lent you?
5 I'm sorry. I'm looking for the station.
6 Say goodbye to your brother for me.
7 What clothes do you think I need to take?
8 Are you ready to order?

10 With the same partner, have three-line conversations using your ideas and the sentences in Exercise 9.

A: *These bags are really heavy.*

B: *I'll carry one for you, if you want.*

A: *Well, if you don't mind. Thank you. It's very kind of you.*

 For further practice, see Exercise 2 on page 176.

VOCABULARY Staying with people

11 Complete the sentences with these verbs.

borrow	hang	leave	lock	take off
clear	help	lend	show	use

1 Do you want me to _____ my shoes before I come in?

2 Can I _____ an umbrella? They said it might rain later.

3 That was delicious! Shall I help you _____ the table?

4 You can just _____ your bag and things in the corner there.

5 You can _____ your coat on the back of the door there.

6 Could you _____ me a phone charger?

7 Make sure you _____ the door if you come home late.

8 Let me _____ you round the house.

9 Do you mind if I _____ your bathroom?

10 _____ yourself to anything to eat or drink.

SPEAKING

12 Work in pairs. You are going to roleplay a conversation between a guest and the host, who shows the guest round their house.

Student A: read File 3 on page 187.

Student B: read File 10 on page 190.

Now roleplay the conversation.

SOUNDS AND VOCABULARY REVIEW

13 ▶ **44** Listen and repeat the sounds with /æ/, /ɑː/ and /aɪ/. Are any of them difficult to hear or say?

14 ▶ **45** Work in groups. Listen to eight sentences using the words below. Together, try to write them down. Then listen again and check.

bank	farm	island	market
climate	financial	map	mind

15 Work in teams. You have three minutes to write collocations or phrases for the words in Exercise 14.

*walk along the river **bank**,*

*sit on the **bank**,*

*see people fishing on the **banks***

8

EDUCATION

IN THIS UNIT YOU LEARN HOW TO:

- describe your academic experiences
- respond with surprise to negative sentences
- talk about future situations
- talk about the education system in your country
- discuss cheating in education – and in other areas of life

SPEAKING

1   Work in groups. Look at the photo and discuss the questions.

- What do you think the people are learning?
- Where do you think it is?
- Why do you think they are learning this? Do you think it's a good idea?
- What adult education programmes are there where you live?
- Have you studied or learned a skill outside of school or university? What?

2   Work with a new partner. Look at the subjects in the box and explain which subjects:

- you liked at school.
- you are good at / not very good at.
- you are still interested in.

art and design	economics	history	maths
computing	geography	languages	science

GET THE GRADES

VOCABULARY Stages of education

1 Complete the sentences with the words in the box.

a year off	left school	primary school
do a Master's	my finals	second year
graduated	nursery	university

1 My three-year-old starts _____ next month, so I can go back to work.

2 When I was at _____ , I wanted to become a doctor, but when I went to secondary school I got bad grades in science.

3 My brother's in his _____ at secondary school.

4 I _____ when I was sixteen because I wasn't interested in studying.

5 I'm taking _____ . I'm working and saving money for my university fees.

6 I'm studying English at _____ because I want to become a teacher.

7 I've got _____ next term. Hopefully, I'll pass.

8 When I _____ , I wanted to get a job in the media, but it was impossible to find one.

9 If I want to get a good job, I'll have to _____ .

PRONUNCIATION

2 ▶ 46 Listen to these words. Match each one to a stress pattern below.

design	graduate	nursery	university
economics	history	primary	
geography	interested	secondary	

1 oO   2 Ooo   3 ooOo   4 oOoo   5 ooOoo

3 Work in groups. Discuss these questions.

- How old do you think the people are in each sentence in Exercise 1?

- Which of the stages of education in Exercise 1 have you been through? Was each one a good time of your life? Why? / Why not?

- Did you have any hopes or plans at each stage? What were they? Did they come true?

- Do you know anyone who is at primary school / secondary school / university at the moment? Do they enjoy it? What are their plans for the future?

LISTENING

4 ▶ 47 Listen to three conversations about school / university. Answer the questions for each conversation.

1 Is the second speaker studying at the moment?

2 How do they feel about their studies? Why?

3 What subjects do they mention? Why?

4 Do they mention any plans for the future?

5 ▶ 47 Work in pairs. Try to complete the questions below. Then listen again and check your answers.

Conversation 1

1 _____ school, Ollie?

2 What _____ favourite subjects?

3 How long _____ left?

4 What are you going to do _____ ?

Conversation 2

5 What course _____ , Pep?

6 What year _____ ?

7 Have you _____ yet?

Conversation 3

8 Did you go _____ , Dhanya?

9 What _____ study?

10 And did _____ it?

6 Can you remember the answers to the questions above? Work in pairs and compare your ideas, then look at audio script 47 on page 200 to check.

7 Work in groups. Discuss these questions.

- Who should decide each of the things below – parents or their children? Why?

  - which school / university to go to

  - which subjects to do at school

  - whether to go to university or not

  - which degree to do

- What are the advantages and disadvantages of NOT going to university?

DEVELOPING CONVERSATIONS

No?

When someone says a negative sentence that surprises us, we often respond by asking *No?* We then expect the other person to explain what they mean. You can also say *Really?*

A: *Dad doesn't want me to, though.*

B: *No?*

A: *No, he just wants me to stay in the system and go straight to university.*

8 Work in pairs. Take turns starting conversations with the sentences below. Follow the pattern in the box above.

1 I don't want to go university.

2 I'm not really enjoying the course.

3 I didn't really like sports when I was at school.

4 I haven't done my homework.

5 I didn't study for the test.

6 I don't want my son to study Fashion!

GRAMMAR

First conditionals

First conditionals are sentences of two parts – one to talk about possible future situations or actions and the other to talk about results of those actions.

9   Look at the sentences from the conversations. Decide if the statements below (1–4) are true (T) or false (F).

a   *Well, **if** it all **goes** well, **I'll have** two more years.*

b   ***If** I **get** the grades I want, **I'll** probably **do** a Master's.*

c   *You **won't pass if** you **don't start** working harder!*

d   *What **will** you **do if** you **don't get** into university?*

1   The *if*-part of the sentence refers to a future situation / action.

2   The *if*-part uses *will* / *won't* because it's about the future.

3   When we use *will* / *won't*, it shows we are certain of the result, but we can use *probably* or other words to show we are less certain.

4   The conditional sentence always starts with *if*.

Ⓖ Check your ideas on page 176 and do Exercise 1.

10   Complete the sentences with the correct form of the verbs.

1   My parents are going to pay for the course, and if I _____ more money, I _____ part-time. (need, work)

2   My parents have promised me that if I _____ all my exams, they _____ me a car! (pass, buy)

3   If I _____ the score I need in the IELTS exam, I _____ it in a couple of months. (not / get, retake)

4   If I _____ the grades I want, I _____ my first-choice university! (not / get, not / get into)

5   They _____ your application if you _____ the deadline. (not / consider, miss)

6   A: What _____ you _____ if you don't get a place on the course? (do)

    B: I'm not sure. I guess that if that _____ , I _____ probably just _____ looking for a job. (happen, start)

11   Work in pairs. Take turns to complete each sentence. Who can think of the most correct endings?

1   If everything goes well in the next few months, …

2   I'll call you if …

3   If I can save enough money, …

4   I might look for a different job if …

5   If I fail my finals, …

6   I won't become fluent in English if …

7   If I have enough time this weekend, …

8   Our education system won't improve if …

Ⓖ For further practice, see Exercise 2 on page 177.

CONVERSATION PRACTICE

12   Look at the questions in Exercise 5 and think of answers you might give. The answers can be true or you can invent them.

13   Now have conversations with other students in the class. Ask each other three or four questions. Then change partners and have another conversation.

🎥 14 To watch the video and do the activities, see the DVD-ROM.

A GOOD SYSTEM

SPEAKING

1 Work in groups. Look at the photo. Discuss the questions.

- What do you think is happening in this class?
- What do you think is good and bad about the class?
- Did your classroom look like this? Why? / Why not?

VOCABULARY Education systems

2 Work in pairs. Check you understand the words in bold. Then answer the questions.

1 What's an example of **a good grade** at school / university?

2 Do you normally **pay fees** at **a state school**?

3 Why might parents choose to **send their children to a private school**?

4 Give two examples of **bad behaviour** in school and two of **good behaviour** in class.

5 If **a subject is compulsory,** do you have to do it? What's the opposite?

6 What **qualification** do you get at university?

7 Who **sets a test** at school? Who **studies for a test**?

8 What happens if you **fail your final exam**?

9 Give two examples of **resources** a school might have.

10 How do you **get into a top university**?

11 Why might students have to **copy from a textbook**?

12 Say two things a teacher does if they have a **traditional approach to teaching**. What do the students do?

LISTENING

3 ▶ 48 Listen to an interview with Rebecca, a fourteen-year-old girl with a Spanish mother and an English father. The family moved from England to Madrid when she was eleven. Which sentence best describes her opinion?

a She prefers Spanish school.

b She prefers English school.

c She has mixed feelings about the different systems.

4 Work in pairs. Decide if these sentences are true (T) or false (F). Listen again and check your ideas.

1 Rebecca and her brother both made friends straight away.

2 She needed help with Spanish.

3 She did the last year of primary school in both England and Spain.

4 English students get more homework.

5 There are fewer years of secondary school in Spain.

6 In primary school, she had several different teachers in Spain, but not in England.

7 The approach of the Spanish teachers was different.

8 Her friends in England seem to like school more.

9 In both England and Spain, students sometimes have to repeat a year.

5 ▶ 49 Now listen to Rebecca's father. Which of the following does he talk about?

| approach | fees | qualifications | tests |
| behaviour | holidays | resources | textbooks |

6 ▶ 49 Work in pairs. Discuss what Rebecca's father said about the topics in Exercise 5. Then listen and read the audio script for Track 49 on page 201 and check your answers.

SPEAKING

7 Work in groups. Discuss if each statement is true for the education system in your country and if you think it's a good thing. Give examples to support your ideas.

- Fees are low, even for the top universities.
- You can choose the school or subjects depending on if you want to work or go to university.
- A lot of people send their children to private schools.
- Individual teachers decide how to deal with bad behaviour.
- Students do a lot of group work in classes.
- The government provides a lot of technological resources such as computers and interactive whiteboards.
- People usually have to buy their own textbooks.
- The summer holidays are five weeks long.
- A lot of students leave school without any qualifications.
- Over 50% of people go to university.
- At university, the grade depends more on essays and projects than exams.

GRAMMAR

had to and could

In Unit 7 we looked at how we use *have to* and *can* to talk about rules and what's possible. *Had to* and *could* are the past forms. The negative forms are *didn't have to* and *couldn't*.

8 Complete these sentences from the listening with *could, couldn't, had to* or *didn't have to*.

1 I _____ understand very much. It was horrible.

2 _____ you _____ do extra Spanish classes?

3 We _____ do much in primary in England – a bit of reading or something.

4 Sometimes we just _____ copy from the book.

5 My wife and I _____ organise our holidays to be at home with the kids most of the time.

Ⓖ Check your ideas on page 177 and do Exercise 1.

9 Complete the sentences with a past or present form of *have to* or *can*. You may also need to use a negative or question form.

1 I _____ come to class last week. _____ we _____ do any homework?

2 I _____ go out tonight because I _____ finish an essay for class.

3 At primary school, we _____ do a spelling test once a week.

4 We have about 20 hours of classes a week, but we _____ go to all of them. Some are optional.

5 In the past, everyone _____ study maths, English language, and French, but they were the only compulsory subjects. You _____ choose the others. Now you don't really have any choice.

6 When I was at school, there were strict rules about dress. You _____ wear a tie, a black jacket and black trousers, a blue jersey and grey socks. You _____ wear any different colours or jewellery.

7 I _____ get up very early when I was a student because classes didn't start till ten, but with this job I _____ be there by eight.

10 Choose two pairs of situations below. Write sentences comparing the two situations, using *had to* and *could* for the past, and *have to* and *can* for the present.

*When I was at primary school, I **could go** home for lunch, but at secondary school I **had to stay** at school.*

- primary and secondary school
- secondary school and university
- school / university and work
- living with my parents and living on my own
- being single and being married
- life before having your first child – and life after

11 Work in pairs. Tell each other your sentences. Ask each other questions to find out more information.

Ⓖ For further practice, see Exercise 2 on page 177.

HE CHEATED!

SPEAKING

1 Work in pairs. Discuss these questions.

- Do you think cheating is a problem in schools / universities in your country? Why? / Why not?
- Can you think of different ways students sometimes cheat in tests?
- Can you think of different ways students sometimes cheat in homework?
- In your experience, what usually happens if teachers find out students have cheated?

READING

2 Read the introduction to an article about cheating in education. Decide if the sentences are true (T) or false (F). Underline the parts of the introduction that support your answers.

1 Cheating is more common now than it was in the past.

2 The biggest problem is at Harvard University.

3 In the survey, about the same number of students said they cheated as said they didn't.

4 It's generally believed that weak students cheat more than strong students.

5 Some students pay people to do their homework for them.

6 Students are using technology to help them cheat.

3 Work in groups. Look at the headings (a–e) for the five main paragraphs in the article. Explain what you think each paragraph will say. Can you think of any other reasons why students might cheat?

a Cheating is easier than hard work

b Adults cheat too!

c Schools value test scores more than real learning

d Cheats don't get caught

e Kids are under extreme pressure to succeed

4 Now read the rest of the article. Match each heading in Exercise 3 to a paragraph (1–5). What do you think the main reason for cheating is? Why?

5 Complete the definitions below with words from the article.

1 If you _____ kids to get good scores, you make them study hard even if they don't want to.

2 If you lose _____ , you stop enjoying and wanting to do something that you enjoyed in the past.

3 If you don't have much _____ , you get angry when you have to wait for things.

4 If you make an _____ to do something, you try hard to do something that's difficult.

5 If you're _____ to do something bad or dangerous, something makes you want to do it.

CHEATING THEIR WAY TO THE TOP

Cheating in schools and universities has become very widespread. For instance, a couple of years ago, Harvard University – often thought to be the best in the world – had to ask over fifty students to leave after they cheated in their final exams. Sadly, this is just part of a much bigger problem.

6 If you're one _____ ahead of someone, you're better prepared than they are.

7 If you _____ someone who's cheating, you stop them and say they're doing something wrong.

8 If a company makes big _____ , they make a lot of money.

6 Work in groups. Discuss how you think cheating can be prevented. What can parents, teachers, schools and universities do?

VOCABULARY Cheating

7 Complete the sentences about cheating with the pairs of words.

claimed + check	lied + resign
ordered + pretended	declare + earned
got stuck + complete	taking + improve

1 She _____ she had some qualifications that she doesn't really have. She'll be in trouble if they _____ !

2 I _____ on the same level so I looked on the internet and found a cheat to _____ it.

3 I cheated. I _____ all the food online and then just _____ it was my own work.

4 They arrested him last night. They say he didn't _____ all the money he _____ last year.

5 They banned him after they caught him _____ drugs to _____ his performance.

6 She _____ about her expenses and when they found out, she had to _____ .

8 Match each sentence in Exercise 7 to one of the areas of life below. There are two you do not need.

cooking	relationships
game shows	sport
job interviews / CVs	tax and personal finances
politics	video / online games

9 Work in groups. Discuss these questions.

- In what other ways do people cheat in the areas of life in Exercise 8? Do you think it is acceptable to cheat in any of these situations? Why? / Why not?

- What do you think are suitable punishments for each different kind of cheating?

SOUNDS AND VOCABULARY REVIEW

10 ▶ 50 Listen and repeat the sounds with /ʃ/, /tʃ/ and /dʒ/. Are any of them difficult to hear or say?

11 ▶ 51 Work in groups. Listen to eight sentences using the words below. Together, try to write them down. Listen again and check.

application	challenge	education	section
approach	check	project	subject

12 Work in teams. You have three minutes to write collocations / phrases for the words in Exercise 11.

reject my **application**, *consider my* **application**, *fill in an* **application** *form*

In a recent survey, the majority of the students questioned said they sometimes cheated – and contrary to expectations, it's not only weaker students who cheat, but also the strongest and best. Many students don't just copy from the internet, they also buy essays from online firms that write to order. Of course, while the desire to get an advantage by cheating is nothing new, modern technology is constantly coming up with clever ways of breaking the rules. There are websites with whole sections selling hi-tech 'exam equipment'!

Why is this happening now? What's causing the huge growth in cheating? Well, there are five main reasons.

1 Parents and schools often push kids to get the best test scores. Kids then start to feel scared that if they don't do well, they won't get good jobs – and bad economic situations also make people feel less secure. On top of all that, kids are growing up in a world where great emphasis is placed on money and winning!

2 Schools in many different contexts need to show that their students are doing well if they want more money from the government. A school with poor test scores starts to fail: it gets less money and has fewer resources, so smart students go elsewhere, and teachers may well lose motivation. As a result, more and more importance is placed on doing well in tests. Students soon realise this – and some then decide to cheat.

3 Technology can make people impatient. Kids grow up expecting to get what they want when they want it. As a result, kids have less patience and less desire to work hard. Cheating seems to offer a way to get what you want without waiting or effort. Of course people are tempted!

4 All too often, cheats win! Partly this is because kids today are better at cheating and are sometimes one step ahead of teachers; partly it's because it's simply too much trouble to check and challenge every person that cheats. Kids see some of their classmates cheating – and succeeding – and decide to try it themselves.

5 Kids see stories in the news about famous sports stars who have used drugs to improve their performance, business people who have lied to make bigger profits, people who have got jobs using CVs that were not completely true, and politicians who have lied about their expenses. Is it any surprise that some kids decide to copy them?

So what can we do to prevent cheating? Well, that's what I will explore in part two.

VIDEO 4

FAINTING GOATS!

1 Work in pairs. Look at the photo and discuss the questions.

- Where do you think these people are?
- What do you think their lives are like? Think about how they spend their days, what they eat, etc.
- What do you think they might miss most if they go to the United States on holiday?

2 📹 15 Watch the first part of the video (0.00–0.40) about two Maasai runners visiting another country. Find out:

1 where they are.

2 what they're missing and why.

3 what they decide to do about it.

3 Check you understand the words in bold below, from the second part of the video. Then work in pairs. Discuss how you think each word is connected to the Maasai men in the video.

1 Both my grandfathers are **dead**.

2 My leg **muscles** really hurt. I ran too far yesterday!

3 Student numbers **expanded** by 20% last year.

4 They've found the **gene** that causes the disease.

5 I wanted to, but in the end I **got scared** and decided not to do.

6 Be careful you don't **fall over**. The floor is really wet.

7 We were camping in Kenya and one night we heard a **hyena** making a really strange noise.

8 **Cross** the road and then walk to the bridge.

4 📹 15 Watch the second part of the video (0.41–3.48) and check your ideas. Then work in pairs. Try to remember how the people used the words in bold in Exercise 3. Compare your ideas.

*When they first met the goats, the goats **played dead**.*

5 📹 15 Choose the correct option. Then listen again and check your answers.

1 The goats are between six and seven *months / years* old.

2 The goats behave this way because *they have eaten the wrong food / of their genes*.

3 The men *joke about taking / are planning to take* a goat back to Africa with them.

4 You *can / can't* get the same medical problem the goats have if you eat cooked goat meat.

5 In the end, they decide *to / not to* buy a goat to eat.

6 Work in groups. Discuss these questions.

- What kinds of things do you miss most when you are away from home?
- Have you ever seen anyone faint? When? Where? What happened?
- What kinds of things are you most scared of?
- What do you usually do when you're scared?
- Do you know of any other animals that have strange habits?

UNDERSTANDING FAST SPEECH

7 📹 16 Read and listen to this extract from the video said at a natural pace and then slowed down. To help you, groups of words are marked with / and pauses are marked //. Stressed sounds are in CAPITALS.

… and when they GET SCAred // their MUScles / TIGHten UP // and they CAN'T WALK / and when they TRY to WALK / they FALL Over

8 Now you have a go! Practise saying the extract at a natural pace.

REVIEW 4

1 Complete the text with one word in each space.

A: Hi there. How are you?

B: OK.

A: Is it ¹_____ if I sit here?

B: Of ²_____ . I ³_____ move my things.

A: I haven't seen you in class for a while.

B: No. I ⁴_____ to do a course at work for the last two weeks so I ⁵_____n't come.

A: Well, ⁶_____ you want to get the notes from the classes you missed, you ⁷_____ copy mine.

B: That would be great. Do you ⁸_____ if I take them with me after the class and I ⁹_____ copy them at work tomorrow.

A: Actually, I'd ¹⁰_____ you didn't. We ¹¹_____ to do a test next class and I want to study.

B: Oh, really?

A: Yes, but there's a copy shop next door. We ¹²_____ go there after the class.

2 Choose the correct option.

1 We're in the middle of the countryside so we *have to / don't have to* drive everywhere.

2 I *can't / couldn't* help you tonight, but I could come tomorrow.

3 When I was at school, we *didn't have to / had to* do much homework.

4 They *can't / don't have to* grow much in that region because it's so dry.

5 If the steel plant *will close / closes*, there won't be many other places to work.

6 A: Do you mind if I open a window?

   B *Of course / Of course not*. Go ahead.

7 A: Oh dear – I'm falling asleep.

   B: Let's stop for a bit and I *make / I'll make* some coffee.

8 A: What if you *don't / won't* pass?

   B: I *will / might* probably take the test again.

3 Write two endings for each question.

1 Do you have to ...?

2 Why did you have to ...?

3 Why can't you ...?

4 What will you do if ...?

4 ▶ 52 Listen and write the six sentences you hear.

5 Write a sentence before and after the sentences in Exercise 4 to create short dialogues.

6 Match the verbs (1–8) with the nouns they collocate with (a–h).

1 steal		a	me €10 / her bike
2 lend		b	you round / him how
3 lock		c	turns / drugs
4 show		d	my bag / all my money
5 take		e	my exam / the whole year
6 set		f	the front door / my bike
7 fail		g	good grades / into university
8 get		h	the class a test / my alarm

7 Decide if these words and phrases are connected to education, places or cheating.

an approach	claim	graduate	resign
an army base	compulsory	lie	a square
a car plant	a desert	pretend	a textbook

8 Complete the sentences. Use the word in brackets to form a word that fits in the space.

1 My favourite subject at school was _____ . (computer)

2 Maybe I enjoyed it more because it was an _____ subject. (option)

3 Fortunately, there's not much bad _____ at his school. (behave)

4 It's a very _____ school. They all have to wear uniforms. (tradition)

5 No-one checked her _____ when they gave her the job, and apparently she invented them! (qualify)

6 Part of teachers pay now depends on their students' _____ in exams. (perform)

7 He has this amazing flat with a view of the _____ old town and city walls. (history)

8 I wouldn't say it's _____ round there. You just need to be careful. (danger)

9 It was a very _____ city, but a lot of the factories have closed now. (industry)

10 She works in La Défense, which is the _____ district of Paris (finance)

9 Complete the text with one word in each space. The first letters are given.

I am from a ¹ti_____ place called Gnowangerup (population: 624). It is a very rural part of Western Australia – it's just miles and miles of ²fi_____, and my parents run a sheep ³fa_____ there. The ⁴pr_____ school I went to when I was six only had ten kids! Now I'm thirteen, I go to a ⁵se_____ school in Albany, two hours from my home, so I live in student halls of ⁶re_____ . It's a ⁷st_____ school so we don't pay any ⁸f_____ , which is good. The staff are quite strict, but they ⁹tr_____ us really well and it's so good to be with kids my own age. It's not exactly a 24-hour ¹⁰cu_____ here, but there's still more to do than in Gnowangerup. Albany is a port on the south ¹¹co_____ , so we often go to the beach and surf. We've also been out on the ¹²oc_____ and seen sharks and whales.

9

IN THIS UNIT YOU LEARN HOW TO:

- describe common illnesses and their symptoms
- give advice and understand medical advice
- ask and answer common questions about illness
- give instructions
- understand instructions on medicines

SPEAKING

1 **Work in groups. Look at the photo and discuss:**
- where you think the people are.
- what time of year you think it is.
- what's happening – and why.
- whether you think this is a good idea or not.

2 **Work with a new partner. Discuss these questions.**
- Do you feel physically / mentally different at different times of the year?
- What time of year do you usually feel happiest? Why?
- What time of year do you usually feel healthiest? Why?
- Which illnesses / health problems are connected to different times of the year?
- What solutions can you think of for these problems?

MIND
AND BODY

UNDER THE WEATHER

VOCABULARY
Illnesses and health problems

1   Match the health problems in the box to the pictures (a–i) they relate to.

an allergy	hay fever	a sore throat
asthma	a headache	a temperature
the flu	a nosebleed	an upset stomach

a an inhaler

b a cat

c flowers

d a thermometer

e some aspirin

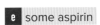

f honey & lemon

g oysters

h a bed

i tissues

2   Work in pairs. Compare your answers and explain your choices.

3   Work in groups. Discuss the questions.
  - Which of the health problems in Exercise 1 do you think is the most / least serious? Why?
  - Do you know anyone who suffers from hay fever, asthma or an allergy? How does it affect them?
  - Can you remember the last time you had any of the other health problems in the box?

4   Check you understand the words and phrases in bold. Then match the symptoms to a health problem in Exercise 1.

  1   It happens every spring. It's horrible. **My eyes get red and sore** and I **sneeze** all the time.

  2   I think it's because of something I ate. **I was sick** three times last night – and I still feel awful today.

  3   If I eat any kind of chocolate, I **get a horrible red rash** all over my body.

  4   I **get out of breath** very easily and I **cough** a lot at night.

  5   I've had it all morning. I **can't concentrate on** anything. I took some aspirin earlier, but they **didn't work**.

  6   I feel awful. I've got a temperature, my **whole body aches**, I've got a horrible cough and I've **lost my appetite**.

  7   It hurts when I **swallow** – and I'm **losing my voice** as well.

  8   I sometimes just suddenly get them. I don't know why. On bad days, they can **last** for up to 20 minutes!

  9   It was 38 degrees the last time I checked. I feel hot and cold and I'm **sweating** a lot as well.

5   Work in pairs.

Student A: close your book.

Student B: explain, act or draw five of the words / phrases in bold from Exercise 4.

Student A: guess the word or phrase.

Then change roles.

B: *This means you don't want to eat, you don't feel hungry.*

A: *I've lost my appetite.*

B: *Right.*

80

LISTENING

6 ▶ 53 Listen to two conversations where people talk about how they are feeling. Answer the questions for each conversation.

1 What problems do they have?

2 What extra information do you hear about the problems?

3 What advice are they given?

4 Do they take the advice?

7 ▶ 53 Listen again and complete the sentences with three words in each space. Contractions like *don't* count as one word.

Conversation 1

1 Oh no! _____ . Are you sure it's not just a cold?

2 I just feel really _____ all the time.

3 No-one will thank you if you _____ it.

4 Well, you take it easy and _____ .

Conversation 2

5 I always get like this at this _____ .

6 I really want to rub them, but that just _____ .

7 That's not _____ , actually.

8 You never know. It might _____ .

GRAMMAR

Giving advice

We use three main structures to give advice – to say what we think is the best thing to do. They all mean basically the same thing.

8 Complete the sentences from the conversations with one word in each space. The first letters are given.

1 Maybe you s_____ go home and get some rest.

2 W_____ d_____ y_____ get some sunglasses to protect your eyes a bit?

3 Maybe you o_____ t_____ try it.

G Check your ideas on page 177 and do Exercise 1.

9 Complete the sentences with one word in each space.

1 That leg looks really bad! I think you _____ see a doctor about that.

2 Maybe you _____ to just go to bed early tonight and get some rest.

3 You really _____ make an appointment. _____ don't you call the doctor now and see if you can go in tomorrow?

4 I don't think you _____ go out if you're not feeling very well.

5 It's a big decision. Why _____ you think about it for a few days?

6 What _____ we do about the cat? If you have an allergy to him, maybe we _____ think about finding him another home.

7 That cough doesn't sound good. Maybe you ought _____ take something for it.

8 A: It's not right, the way he talks to you. You _____ to complain about it.

B: I know I _____ , but I'm worried everything will just take longer if I do.

A: Well, if you feel like that, why don't _____ just change your doctor?

10 Work in pairs. Decide what advice to give in each of the situations below.

1 I'm really unfit.

2 I'm really tired. I'm not sleeping well at the moment.

3 I feel quite depressed for some reason.

4 My knee really hurts.

5 I'm really worried about my exams.

6 My parents don't give me enough money.

G For further practice, see Exercise 2 on page 177.

DEVELOPING CONVERSATIONS

Common questions about illness

When someone isn't very well, we often ask them common fixed questions. Usually the answers people give are also quite fixed.

11 Match each question (1–3) with two possible answers (a–f).

1 Are you OK?

2 Have you been to the doctor's about it?

3 Are you taking anything for it?

a Yes. The doctor gave me some tablets the other day.

b No, not really. I've got a terrible headache.

c No, not yet, but I've got an appointment this afternoon.

d No, not really. I'm just drinking lots of water. That's all.

e Yes, I went yesterday. He just told me to go home and take it easy.

f No, not really. I've got a bit of a cold.

12 Work in pairs. Think of two more possible answers to each question.

CONVERSATION PRACTICE

13 You are going to roleplay two conversations similar to those you heard in the listening. First, imagine you have a health problem. Decide how serious it is, what the symptoms are, if you've been to the doctor's or taken anything for it, etc.

14 Work in pairs. One student should start the conversation by asking: *Are you OK?* Use as much language from this lesson as you can. Then change roles and repeat.

📹 17 To watch the video and do the activities, see the DVD-ROM.

THE POWER OF THE MIND

READING

1 Work in groups. Read the introduction to the article on page 83. Then discuss these questions

- In your country, is healthcare paid through tax or do people have private health insurance?
- Is the cost of healthcare a problem in your country? Why? / Why not?
- Why do you think the cost of healthcare is increasing in some countries?
- How can the power of the mind help good health?
- Have you heard of any of the following? Say what you know about them.

hypnotherapy	meditation	nocebos	placebos

2 Read the rest of the article. Find out how the following can affect health.

emotional reactions	hypnotherapy	nocebos
exercise in old age	meditation	placebos

3 Read each sentence and decide whether it is an argument the writer makes.

1 Asthma sufferers don't need drugs.
2 With a placebo, there can be changes in the body.
3 All side effects of drugs are caused by the nocebo effect.
4 Some people can change their body temperature by thinking about it.
5 How well you deal with pain depends completely on your character.
6 Using hypnotherapy instead of drugs can mean operations are more successful.
7 You are as old as you feel.
8 As you get older, you are more likely to get injured playing sport.

4 Complete the second phrase with the correct form of the word in bold. All the missing words are in the article.

1 several **different** solutions   see a big _____
2 provide **treatment** for free   _____ cancer
3 study **science**   become a _____
4 **experience** difficulties   no previous _____
5 control my **emotions**   give _____ support
6 **operate** on his leg   the _____ went well
7 make a good **recovery**   _____ from the flu
8 get **injured** playing football   a bad knee _____

5 Work in groups. Discuss the following.

- Give other examples of some of the six suggestions in the article. Think about your own experience, knowledge, people you know or stories in the news.
- Say how each of the six suggestions could reduce the cost of healthcare.

UNDERSTANDING VOCABULARY

Phrases with *mind* and *matter*

In the article, you saw the quote: '*Age is a question of **mind over matter**. If **you don't mind, it doesn't matter!**'* Some words like *mind* and *matter* are mainly used as part of fixed phrases. You need to learn the phrases rather than just the single words.

6 Complete the sentences with *mind* or *matter*.

1 You say *It's just a question of mind over* _____ to explain that you can do something very difficult or horrible by concentrating and using your thoughts.
2 You ask *What's the* _____ ? if you think someone looks worried or ill and you want to know the reason.
3 You say *I don't* _____ when you are happy with all the choices and want someone else to decide.
4 You say *It doesn't* _____ when what you said or did is not important and you don't want to continue to talk about it.
5 You say *Never* _____ when you are telling someone not to worry or be sad.
6 You say *To make* _____s *worse* when you're telling a story about a problem and want to say something caused extra problems.
7 You ask *You don't* _____ ? *or Would you* _____ ? to check that someone is sure they are happy to do something.
8 You say *I've got a lot on my* _____ to say you have problems you are worrying about.
9 You say *That's a* _____ *of opinion* when you disagree with what someone said.

PRONUNCIATION

7 ▶ **54** Listen and notice which sounds are stressed. Then listen again and repeat.

8 Complete these short dialogues with phrases from Exercise 6.

1 A: So I was already late and then _____ , the bus broke down.
   B: Well, _____ . At least you're here now.
2 A: How could you make such a silly mistake?
   B: Sorry. _____ at the moment.
3 A: What do you want to eat tonight?
   B: _____ .
4 A: They don't spend enough on healthcare.
   B: Well, _____ . I pay enough in taxes already!
5 A: _____ ?
   B: Oh, nothing really. I just have a bit of a headache.
   A: Shall I go to the shop and get some aspirin?
   B: _____ ?
   A: No, of course not.

MIND OVER MATTER

In many countries, the cost of healthcare is increasing, but people don't want to pay extra taxes to pay for it. Perhaps because of this, interest is growing in how the power of the mind can help us stay fit, prevent illness and even treat ourselves when we are ill. Here are six ways that mind power could make a difference.

PLACEBOS

If you give asthma sufferers 'medicine' and tell them it will help their condition, many of them will report that they feel better after taking it, even when that 'medicine' wasn't actually real – it was a placebo. Sometimes doctors can measure physical changes after patients take a placebo. For example, their blood pressure may fall. So it seems the placebo effect is not just a trick of the mind.

NOCEBOS

The nocebo effect is a kind of opposite of the placebo effect. You get an illness because you believe you will. When doctors give a patient a drug to treat a serious illness, they tell them about problems (or side effects) that the drug might cause, like a headache or a rash. Experiments show that a percentage of people get these side effects even when the drug they receive is just a sugar pill.

MEDITATION

Scientists have studied monks who have learned to control their bodies by meditating. In one experiment, a monk sat in a cold room with a wet sheet over his shoulders. Most people would get very very cold, but the monk concentrated and increased his body temperature to 40°C. He actually dried the sheet!

THE PAIN'S NOT SO BAD

Scientists have shown that when some people experience pain, for example in a marathon or at the dentist's, they deal with it better for two reasons. Firstly, they prepare themselves beforehand – they imagine the pain. Secondly, when they feel the pain, their reaction is less emotional: they think 'Oh I notice there's a pain in my tooth', rather than 'Ahhh! That hurts so badly! Help me!' The psychologist Dr Martin Paulus has also shown that people can learn how to do this with training.

HYPNOTHERAPY

In 2014, the singer Alama Kante had a successful operation on her throat in France. She was hypnotised before it, so she did not need any drugs and she could sing during the operation. This way her voice was not damaged and she recovered more quickly. Hypnotherapy has also been successful in other areas, such as helping people give up smoking.

DON'T GIVE UP

There is a quote that 'age is a question of mind over matter. If you don't mind, it doesn't matter!' In the past, many people stopped playing sport, not because of injury, but because they *thought* they were too old. However, science is discovering that our bodies can work well into old age, if we don't stop practising. Like Fauja Singh: he ran his first marathon when he was 89 and continued to run after he was 100!

DON'T WORRY. YOU'LL BE FINE.

VOCABULARY Parts of the body

1 Label the photos with the words in the box.

arm	eye	hair	lip
back	face	hand	mouth
chest	foot	knee	shoulder
ear	finger	leg	stomach

2 Complete each group of collocations with a part of the body from Exercise 1.

1 have a bad ~ / a pain in my lower ~ / have his ~ to me

2 my ~ are wet / have big ~ / wipe your ~

3 cut my ~ shaving / bite my ~ / ~-read

4 long straight ~ / brush your ~ / have my ~ cut

5 a pretty ~ / pull a ~ / have a big smile on your ~

6 work on an empty ~ / have an upset ~ / take something to settle my ~

3 Work in pairs.

Student A: imagine you are a doctor. Say instructions 1–5 below to your partner.

Student B: close your book. Listen and do what your partner tells you.

Change roles for instructions 6–10.

1 Stand up and then bend your knees.

2 Put your feet together.

3 Bend forwards and touch the floor with your hands.

4 Sit down and lift your leg straight.

5 Open your mouth and say 'ahh'.

6 Take a deep breath so I can listen to your chest.

7 Turn your head so I can look in your ear.

8 Relax your face, shoulders and arms.

9 Raise your arm above your head.

10 Follow my finger with your eyes, don't move your head.

LISTENING

4 ▶ 55 Listen to three conversations. Decide where the speakers are in each one.

a at the dentist's   d in someone's house

b in a hospital   e in a chemist's

c in a restaurant

5 ▶ 55 Listen again and answer these questions.

1 What problem does the woman have in conversation 1?

2 What did she do to cure the problem?

3 Which problem does the customer have in conversation 2: diarrhoea, indigestion or vomiting?

4 What instructions is she given?

5 What two problems does the man have in conversation 3?

6 How did each one happen?

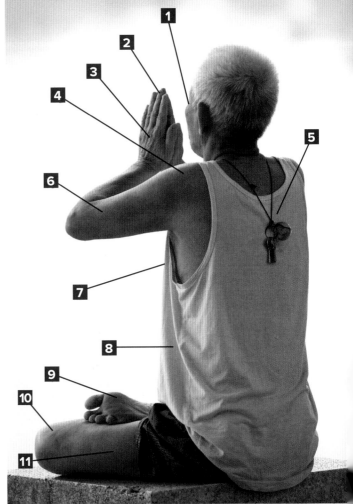

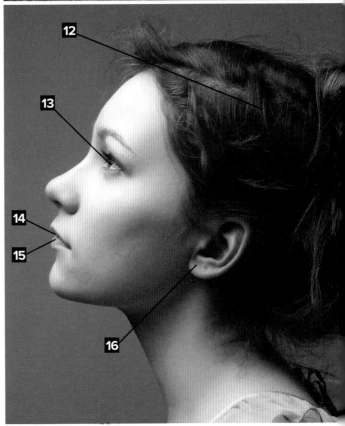

6 Work in groups. Discuss these questions.

- What's your cure for hiccups? For indigestion?
- Have you ever had any stupid accidents? Has anyone you know? If yes, what happened?
- Do you think the hospitals in your country are good? Why? / Why not?
- Have you ever been to hospital? Why? What was the service like?

GRAMMAR

7 Read the information and the sentences in the Grammar box. Then decide if the statements below are true (T) or false (F).

Imperatives

To make imperatives, we use the infinitive form of the verb (without *to*).

Swallow the water slowly.

*If they don't solve the problem, **talk** to your doctor.*

To make negative imperatives, we use *don't*.

***Don't take** more than four tablets in a day.*

1 To make imperatives, we don't use a subject before the verb.
2 We only use imperatives to give instructions.
3 We often use conditional *if*-clauses with imperatives.
4 Imperatives always sound rude.

 Check your ideas on page 178 and do Exercise 1.

8 Choose the correct form.

1 *Take / Don't take* any more today! That's the third one you've had.
2 *Eat / Don't eat* something first and then take them.
3 *Put / Don't put* the bottle in the fridge. It'll go bad if you leave it out.
4 *Stop / Don't stop* taking them. You have to finish the prescription.
5 *Try / Don't try* to drink it or eat it.
6 *Wash / Don't wash* your hands after using it.
7 *Put / Don't put* it there in the sun. Put it in the cupboard.
8 *Let / Don't let* me drive if you're feeling sleepy.

9 Match the sentences in Exercise 8 to the warnings given with medication below.

a Store in a cool dry place.
b Keep refrigerated.
c May cause tiredness.
d Complete the full course.
e Don't take on an empty stomach.
f Don't exceed three doses in 24 hours.
g For external use only.
h Avoid contact with your eyes.

10 Work in pairs. Take turns adding an imperative ending to the conditional sentence starters below. Continue until one person can't think of another ending. Then play again using the next sentence starter.

A: *If you need any help, call me.*
B: *If you need any help, ask.*
A: *If you need any help, look on the internet.*
B: *If you need any help, ... – I can't think! You win.*

1 If you need any help, ...
2 If you've got a cold, ...
3 If you're feeling stressed, ...
4 If you see the teacher, ...
5 If the alarm rings, ...
6 If you can't sleep, ...

 For further practice, see Exercise 2 on page 178.

SPEAKING

11 You are going to tell someone about a scar you have. If you don't have one, use your imagination and invent one! Use the questions below to plan what you are going to say.

- How did you get the scar?
- When did it happen? How old were you?
- Where were you? What were you doing?
- Was anyone else with you?
- What did the other people do? Did anyone help you?
- Did you have to go to hospital or have stitches?
- Did you have to wait a long time to see a doctor?
- How long did it take for the cut to heal / for you to recover?

12 Work in groups. Share your stories.

SOUNDS AND VOCABULARY REVIEW

13 ▶ 56 Listen and repeat the sounds with /e/, /iː/ and /eɪ/. Are any of them difficult to hear or say?

14 ▶ 57 Work in groups. Listen to eight sentences using the words below. Together, try to write them down. Then listen again and check.

ache	bleed	feet	raise
bend	breath	pain	sweat

15 Work in teams. You have three minutes to write collocations or phrases for the words in Exercise 14.

*my muscles **ache**,*

*have a head**ache**,*

*have awful tooth**ache***

10

PLACES TO
STAY

IN THIS UNIT YOU LEARN HOW TO:

- describe places you stayed in
- book somewhere to stay
- apologise for bad news
- explain and deal with problems in hotels
- talk about imagined situations
- talk about past habits

SPEAKING

1 **Work in groups. Look at the photo of a planned new resort and discuss the questions.**

- Do you think it's a good place for a resort? Why? / Why not?
- Would you go there? Why? / Why not?
- What are the big resorts in your country? What can you do there?
- Have you been to any resorts? Where? Where did you stay? What did you do there?

2 **Work in pairs. Discuss the questions.**

- What do you look for when you choose somewhere to stay? Think about these things.

| entertainment | facilities | food | location | price |

- Which of these things are most important / least important to you? Why?

BOOKING A ROOM

VOCABULARY Places to stay

1   Complete the sentences with the collocations in the box.

babysitting service	provided meals
basic furniture	put up the tent
free wi-fi	real fire
heated pool	reduced rate
including breakfast	share a room
low season	shower block

   1   It only cost €200 to rent for the week because it was still the _____ .

   2   It was £50 a night for a double room _____ .

   3   It normally costs $25 a night with electricity, but there was a _____ for groups.

   4   They had a _____ , so we left the kids and went out on our own a couple of nights.

   5   It was difficult to _____ because the ground was so hard.

   6   There was a kitchen the guests could use, but they also _____ .

   7   It had a _____ in the living room, which was nice.

   8   We didn't have to _____ with lots of other people. They had some smaller family rooms.

   9   There was a _____ which was shared by the whole block.

   10 You had to walk a long way to get to the toilet and _____ , but at least there was plenty of hot water.

   11 It had quite _____ , but the kitchen was OK and it was all very clean.

   12 They charged a lot for internet access in the room, but there was _____ in the reception area.

2   Match each sentence in Exercise 1 to one of these places.

an apartment	a campsite	a hostel	a hotel

3   Work in groups. Can you think of:

   1   two other things you can **share** in a hostel?

   2   two other kinds of **room** in a hotel?

   3   two other **services** a hotel or hostel **provides**?

   4   two other things that can be **included in the price**?

   5   two reasons you get a **reduced rate**?

   6   the opposite of **putting up a tent**?

   7   when the **low** and **high season** is in your country?

4   Work in pairs. Think of a hotel, apartment, hostel or camping site you stayed at. Tell your partner about it. Would you recommend it? Why? / Why not?

LISTENING

5   ▶ 58 Listen to a phone conversation. David is phoning a hotel for a friend who wants to visit Dublin with his wife and small child. Look at the questions David wants to ask. Then listen and note down the information.

> *Triple rooms?*
> *How much for everyone?*
> *With breakfast?*
> *Dates: Prefer 12th – 17th August*
> *Car hire cheaper from hotel?*
> *Parking available?*
> *Deposit?*

6   ▶ 58 Work in pairs and compare your notes. Then listen again and check.

7   Look at the audio script for Track 58 on page 202. Underline five words or phrases that you think are useful to learn. Compare what you chose with a partner.

DEVELOPING CONVERSATIONS

Apologising

We often say *I'm afraid* to apologise for giving bad news.

I'm afraid we're fully booked that weekend.

To reply to questions, we use *I'm afraid not / I'm afraid so.* We often also add a comment.

D: *And breakfast is included too?*

R: ***I'm afraid not.*** *It's 125 with breakfast.*

D: *So if, for whatever reason, they didn't come, they'd lose that money?*

R: ***I'm afraid so.*** *The complete payment is made on arrival.*

8   Work in pairs. Take turns asking these questions. Your partner should reply with *I'm afraid so* or *I'm afraid not* and add a comment.

   1   Is there free wi-fi?

   2   Do I need to pay a fee if I cancel?

   3   Is the swimming pool heated?

   4   Can we make a fire on the campsite?

   5   Did it reject my credit card again?

   6   Are there any tickets left for tonight's performance?

   7   Is it going to rain again tomorrow?

   8   Can't you do something about it?

9 Work in groups. You have three minutes to write as many things as you can that a hotel employee might say to guests using *I'm afraid*. Which group can think of the most sentences? Which group has the funniest ones?

I'm afraid we're full.

I'm afraid the air conditioning is broken.

10 ▶ 59 Listen to the receptionist taking another customer's credit card details. Complete the form below.

Name on the card:

Card number:

Security number:

Expiry date:

Contact number:

PRONUNCIATION

11 ▶ 60 Listen to the alphabet and put the letters next to the correct vowel sound.

/ɪː/	b	/eɪ/	a
/e/	f	/aɪ/	i
/əʊ/	o	/uː/	q
/ɑː/	r		

12 Invent some card details like the ones in Exercise 10 and write them on a piece of paper. Then work in pairs. Take turns asking for and giving these details. Note down your partner's details and compare them with what your partner wrote.

CONVERSATION PRACTICE

13 You are going to have two conversations similar to the ones you heard in Exercise 5.

Student A: read the role card in File 4 on page 187.

Student B: read the role card in File 12 on page 190.

Think about what information you need and write down the questions you want to ask.

14 Take turns being the receptionist and the customer ringing for information. Roleplay the conversations. The receptionist should apologise for at least two things using *I'm afraid*. Start like this:

A: *Hello, I'm ringing on behalf of some friends. They want some information about the hostel.*

B: *Sure. What would you like to know?*

■◀ 18 To watch the video and do the activities, see the DVD-ROM.

WE'LL DEAL WITH IT RIGHT AWAY

SPEAKING

1 Work in groups. Discuss the questions.

- What problems might people have in a hotel? How many problems can you think of?
- Have you ever asked a hotel receptionist for anything? What happened?

VOCABULARY Solving hotel problems

2 Match the sentences (1–10) with the follow-up questions (a–j). Check you understand the words in bold in the sentences.

1 There's a lot of **noise outside** our room.
2 My room is **boiling**.
3 That's more expensive than I expected.
4 Are you sure you don't have a **record of my booking**?
5 I've forgotten my **toothbrush** and **toothpaste**.
6 I only have a **morning free for sightseeing**.
7 I have an **upset stomach**.
8 I have an **early flight**.
9 I have to leave before you start **serving breakfast**.
10 I **can't get** the air conditioning **to work**.

a Do you have any?
b Could you give me **a wake-up call** and **book a taxi**?
c Could I get something to take with me?
d Could you tell me what **the bill includes**?
e Could we **change rooms**?
f Could you **check again** please?
g Do you have anything that will help, or is there **a chemist** nearby?
h Is there any way I can **turn down the heating**?
i Could you **send someone up** to **have a look at it**?
j Where would you **recommend going**?

3 Spend a few minutes memorising the questions in Exercise 2. Then work in pairs and test each other.

Student A: say a sentence (1–10) from Exercise 2.

Student B: close your book. Say the follow-up question.

4 Work with a new partner. Choose four problems from Exercise 2 and roleplay the conversations. Take turns to be the guest and the receptionist.

G: *Excuse me. There's a lot of noise outside our room. Could we change rooms?*

R: *You can, but I'm afraid the only rooms available are more expensive.*

LISTENING

5 Work in pairs. Look at the photos. Discuss how they might be connected to problems with a hotel guest. What do you think the guest asks for?

6 ▶ 61 Listen to a conversation between a guest and a hotel receptionist. Check your ideas from Exercise 5. Can the receptionist give the guest what they ask for?

7 ▶ 61 Put the sentences in the order you heard them in the conversation. Then listen again and check your ideas.

   a I'm afraid that's just not possible.

   b We really didn't have much time to prepare them.

   c I doubt I can find one.

   d I'm calling on behalf of Lady Zaza.

   e You've got hundreds of rooms in this place.

   f I'm sure that if she was, she'd tell you exactly the same thing.

   g There was no way we could stay in that last place.

   h I'll make sure they're taken out.

8 **Which of the adjectives below do you think describe Lady Zaza? Work in pairs and compare your ideas. Explain your choices.**

ambitious	demanding	lazy	selfish	tidy

9 **Work in groups. Discuss these questions.**

   • Can you think of any other adjectives to describe Lady Zaza? Do you know anyone else with these characteristics?

   • Have you ever heard of anyone else making similar demands? What did they ask for?

   • Why do you think people make demands like this?

   • Why do you think people agree to these demands? Would you?

GRAMMAR

Second conditionals

Second conditionals are sentences of two parts. The *if* part uses past tenses to talk about imagined situations, or things that are unlikely or impossible; the *would* part gives the imagined results or further actions.

10 **Look at the sentences from the conversation. Answer the questions below each one.**

   a *She'**d be** very ill **if she ate** one by mistake.*

   1 Is she ill? Is it likely that she will eat a chocolate with nuts? Why not?

   b *I **would move** them **if I could**.*

   2 Does he want to move the people from the room below? Can he move them?

Ⓖ Check your ideas on page 178 and do Exercise 1.

11 **Complete the sentences with the correct form of the verbs in brackets.**

   1 I don't think I _____ so calm if I _____ deal with someone like Lady Zaza. I'd probably say something rude to them. (be, have to)

   2 To be honest, I don't really like camping. I _____ it if I _____ the money to stay in hotels, but that's too expensive with a family. (never do, have)

   3 The hotel was awful! Honestly, I _____ there again even if you _____ me! (not stay, pay)

   4 A: The hotel was very noisy because of all the bars on the street.

      B: Really? I _____ a review on the web if I _____ you. It's good to warn other people. (post, be)

   5 A: Which _____ ? Moscow or St Petersburg? We don't really have time to visit both. (you recommend)

      B: Difficult! They're both great, but if I _____ choose, I _____ to St Petersburg, just because the traffic isn't as bad. (have to, probably go)

   6 A: If you _____ only visit one place in your country, where would it be? (can)

      B: Probably New York. There's so much to see and do there.

12 **Complete each sentence 1–5 in two different ways using your own ideas. Then work in groups and share your ideas.**

   1 If I had more money, I'd _____ .

   2 I wouldn't _____ even if you paid me!

   3 If I had to choose between _____ and _____ , I'd _____ .

   4 If I could only _____ , I'd _____ .

   5 If I wasn't _____ , I'd _____ .

13 **Work in pairs. Look at these situations. Discuss how would you react and what you would do. Explain why.**

   1 You're a receptionist and a customer is refusing to pay for the drinks he has taken from the minibar in his room. He says he didn't take any and is getting quite angry.

   2 You're in a hotel and you can't get to sleep because of noise next door.

   3 You're camping. It's raining and water is coming in through your tent.

   4 You're sharing a kitchen in a hostel and you see someone leave their dirty dishes.

   5 You've rented an apartment and the air conditioning is broken. It's boiling and the owner of the apartment isn't answering their phone.

   6 You're a cleaner, and you find $100 left on the bed when you are cleaning the room after a guest has left.

Ⓖ For further practice see Exercise 2 on page 179.

BEST HOLIDAY EVER!

SPEAKING

1 Look at the different kinds of holidays for primary school children. Rank them from 1 (best holiday for kids) to 6 (worst holiday).

- going to Disneyland with the family
- going to stay with relatives in the countryside
- going with other kids to a summer camp
- going camping with parents
- renting a place near the beach with the whole family
- two weeks with parents in a hotel in a foreign city

2 Work in groups. Explain your choices. Discuss what's good / bad about each kind of holiday.

READING

3 Read the series of messages from a social media site on page 93. Find out:

1 why Mark started the thread about holidays.
2 two ways Zinaida's holidays were different to kids' holidays today.
3 which three people often stayed near water.
4 who had a close encounter with danger.
5 who has nice memories of cooking.
6 who sometimes stayed in a theme park.
7 who suffered a loss.
8 who spent two weeks with each set of relatives every year.
9 who last went somewhere over 20 years ago – and why they're going back.

4 Match the verbs 1–8 with the words (a–h) they were used with on the social media page. Can you remember who used these words – and why?

1	mess around	a	on the fence
2	sit	b	for long walks
3	rent	c	breakfast on the terrace
4	climb	d	a cottage
5	have	e	by the river
6	get	f	chickens
7	scare	g	a tree
8	go	h	bored

GRAMMAR

> ### used to
>
> We often use (*never*) *used to* + infinitive (without *to*) instead of the past simple to describe past habits or states – especially to talk about things that have changed since.
>
> *Used to* does not have a present form. For habits in the present, use the present simple + *sometimes, never, two or three times a week*, etc.

5 Look at these sentences from the social media page and answer the questions below.

a *My parents **used to own** an apartment on the beach.*
b *We **went** swimming all the time.*
c *We **once made** cornflake cakes.*
d *My son **usually spends** his summers like this.*
e *It **was** so strict.*
f *They **used to take** us on day trips.*

1 Which sentences describe past habits?
2 Which sentences describe past states?
3 Which sentence describes a single event in the past?
4 Which sentence describes a present habit?

 Check your ideas on page 179 and do Exercise 1.

6 Decide which of these sentences you can rewrite using (*never*) *used to* and rewrite them.

1 I didn't like camping, but I love it now.
2 I did judo when I was younger, but then I stopped.
3 We usually camp, but we rented a flat this year.
4 He's quite fit and healthy now, but he smoked quite heavily when he was younger.
5 I had really long hair when I was at college, but I had it cut short a few years ago.
6 It's become very popular. It wasn't crowded before.

PRONUNCIATION

7 ▶ 62 Listen and check your answers to Exercise 6. Notice that *used to* is pronounced /juːstə/.

8 Work in groups. Tell each other about:

- something you never used to like, but do now.
- a place, activity or thing that used to be popular.
- three things you used to love doing and three things you used to hate doing when you were a kid.
- three things that have changed in your life.

G For further practice, see Exercise 2 on page 179.

SOUNDS AND VOCABULARY REVIEW

9 ▶ 63 Listen and repeat the sounds with /ʌ/, /ɒ/, /ʊ/ and /uː/. Are any of them difficult to hear or say?

10 ▶ 64 Work in groups. Listen to eight sentences using the words below. Together, try to write them down. Then listen again and check.

booking	holiday	money	room
deposit	look	pool	toothbrush

11 Work in teams. You have three minutes to write collocations / phrases for the words in Exercise 10.

 Mark Reed Am returning to the place I spent my childhood holidays this week. First time in more than two decades. Started me thinking. Where did you all spend your holidays when you were kids?
5 hours ago   Like

 Zinaida Vozgova I used to spend holidays with my grandparents out of town – that meant lots of fresh air, messing around by the river, fresh fruit and vegetables … and no TV or technology, which isn't typical for our kids now …
5 hours ago   Like

 Biggi Wimmer Went to Italy every year. Near Trieste. My parents used to own an apartment on the beach. We went swimming all the time. Can't remember what my parents did! By the way, **Mark**. Where did YOU use to go as a kid? And how come you're going back?
4 hours ago   Like

 Julia Tcvetkova Used to spend a fortnight in a tiny village out in the countryside in Siberia. Sounds dull, but I never used to get bored. Remember sitting on the fence before sunset, watching the cows being brought back to the village. And running around the fields after my dog … before the neighbours took him away for scaring their chickens!
4 hours ago   Like

 Mark Reed Eastbourne on the south coast of England, **Biggi**. Used to be my favourite place in the world. Not sure I'll feel the same anymore!
3 hours ago   Like

 Christina Rebuffet-Broadus We either went to Disneyworld in Florida or the Smoky Mountains in Tennessee in the summer! At Disney, we stayed in the Polynesian Village. In the Smokies, we used to rent a cottage in the mountains. We woke up one morning to find a black bear climbing a tree near the terrace we used to have breakfast on!
1 hour ago   Like

 Mark Reed **Julia**: so sad to hear about your dog! **Christina**: Wow! Crazy! Oh, and **Biggi** – work trip. Meeting new clients.
55 minutes ago   Like

 Biggi Wimmer Got you **Mark**. Hi **Julia**. Mad story. Where are you from?
48 minutes ago   Like

 Zinaida Vozgova There was another option – summer camp, which I did a couple of times. I really hated it! It was so strict. Nowadays, though, everything's changed – camps have become more creative and child-friendly, with lots of activities and English classes and so on. My son usually spends his summers like this.
41 minutes ago   Like

 Julia Tcvetkova Siberia-Lithuania-St. Petersburg-Cape Town-London.
37 minutes ago   Like

 Biggi Wimmer Wow! Complicated life. :-)
26 minutes ago   Like

 Julia Tcvetkova But interesting!
10 minutes ago   Like

 Sandy Millin My brother and I always spent a fortnight with each set of grandparents – one in Gloucester, the other near Liverpool. They used to take us on day trips to places all over the south- and north-west – to places like Bristol and the castles of North Wales. We also spent time playing board and card games and going for long walks in the local area, among many other things. Food was also a big part of it: for example, I remember making homemade pizzas with one grandma and I think we once made cornflake cakes with the other. Really fond memories. Cool question **Mark**. Thanks for asking and reminding me.
3 minutes ago   Like

VIDEO 5

THE FUTURE OF A VILLAGE

1 Work in groups. Look at the photo of Essaouira, Morocco and discuss:

- what you think the main industry in Essaouira is.
- what difficulties a place like this might have and why.
- how the people there might solve these problems.

2 ▭ 19 Watch the video and take notes on Essaouira, its economy and how it's changing.

3 ▭ 19 Work in pairs. From your notes, try to complete the summary and the definitions below. Then listen again to check.

Local fishermen don't have regular work now because there are fewer [1]_____ , some work has moved [2]_____ and they can't [3]_____ with big ships. The town is trying to increase [4]_____ to replace employment in the fishing industry. Essaouira used to be well-known in the [5]_____ , and lots of rock stars and other people visited it because of the historic old town, which is on [6]_____'s World Heritage List. Since 1996 there has been a [7]_____ in the number of tourists. This has caused concern among local people about water, land use and [8]_____ .

Glossary

Trawlers are [9]_____ .

The *Medina* is [10]_____ .

4 Work in groups. Discuss these questions.

- Would you like to stay in Essaouira for a holiday? Why? / Why not?
- How has the economy changed in your country?
- What industries used to be stronger? Why did they decline? What's replaced them?
- Do you know any places where tourism has increased a lot? Has that been a good thing? Why? / Why not?

UNDERSTANDING FAST SPEECH

5 ▭ 20 Read and listen to this extract from the video said at natural pace and then slowed down. To help you, groups of words are marked with / and pauses are marked //. Stressed sounds are in CAPITALS.

the FISHermen are prePARing / for aNOTHer year OUT on the WAter // all aROUND the PORT / you can hear the SOUNDS of BOAT building / and SMELL fresh PAINT in the air.

6 Now you have a go! Practise saying the extract at natural pace.

REVIEW 5

1 Complete the text with one word in each space. Contractions like *don't* count as one word.

¹_____ you're looking for interesting places to go this summer, ²_____ panic! There are plenty of options to choose from. If you want something cheap and adventurous, and dream of the kind of holidays you ³_____ to go on when you were young, ⁴_____ you should try camping in Croatia. However, if you're the kind of person who ⁵_____ never sleep under the stars, then why ⁶_____ try a new city instead? Perhaps you ⁷_____ to think about a break in a capital you've never visited before. ⁸_____ to Chisinau in Moldova or Reykjavik in Iceland. You never know. They might be amazing!

2 Put the words in the correct order to make questions.

1 did / that / use / where / you / do / to

2 it / see / about / why / you / go / doctor / don't / and / a

3 do / what / it / you / happened / you / would / if / to /

4 what / think / about / I / you / ought / do / to / do / it

5 ask / it / should / you / think / I / do / who / about /

6 please / you / give / the / me / password / the / for / could / wi-fi

7 anywhere / you / would / could / where / world / go / go / the / if / in / you

8 the / did / stay / went / when / use / you / to / where / islands / to / you

3 Write replies to the questions in Exercise 2 to create short dialogues.

4 Choose the correct option.

1 I'm quite fit. I *usually / used to* go running after work. It helps me relax.

2 I *went / used to go* swimming last Friday.

3 *Not / Don't / Shouldn't / Not to* go to work if you're feeling ill.

4 Where *are / will / would* you recommend going?

5 I *won't / wouldn't* stay there if I *am / were* you. It was horrible the last time we visited.

6 I *wouldn't / won't* work weekends if I *hadn't to / didn't have to*.

7 They might do better if they *wouldn't be / aren't / wasn't / weren't* so expensive.

8 I *didn't never used to / usen't to / didn't use to / wasn't used to* like cheese when I was a kid, but now I love it.

5 ▶ 65 Listen and write the six sentences you hear.

6 Match the verbs (1–8) with the nouns they collocate with (a–h).

1 get   a your feet
2 brush   b my lip
3 settle   c out of breath
4 change   d your hair
5 wipe   e a deep breath
6 take   f a room
7 share   g my mind
8 bite   h your stomach

7 Decide if these words and phrases are connected to health problems or places to stay.

ache	an inhaler	the shower block
aspirin	the low season	sneeze
get a rash	a reduced rate	a temperature
the heating	serve breakfast	a wake-up call

8 Complete the sentences with the best prepositions.

1 I'm afraid we don't have any record _____ your booking.

2 Can you send someone _____ to have a look at the AC in my room, please?

3 Sorry. I've just got a lot _____ my mind at the moment.

4 I hate missing breakfast. I can't work _____ an empty stomach.

5 It's boiling in here. Can you turn the heating _____ a bit?

6 I'm not looking forward to the spring because I suffer _____ really bad hay fever.

7 That's a matter _____ opinion. I don't see it like that, personally.

8 I didn't see his face. He had his back _____ me.

9 Complete the email with one word in each space. The first letters are given.

We went camping for a week and it rained the ¹wh_____ time we were there. The night we arrived, there was a huge storm that ²la_____ for hours, so it was really hard to put up the ³te_____ . The next day, we realised the site was much more ⁴ba_____ than we expected: no shop, only one shared shower, horrible toilets! Awful! Then, to make ⁵ma_____ worse, I got really ill. I guess it was probably the flu. I had a really sore ⁶th_____ and a terrible ⁷he_____ that didn't stop for ages! Then I got an awful cough before finally I lost my ⁸vo_____ completely! I don't usually ⁹mi_____ camping holidays, but this was too much! Next time, I want a nice hotel that ¹⁰pr_____ meals and has free ¹¹wi_____ so I can connect to the web, and maybe even has a ¹²ba_____ service so we can get away from the kids for a night!

11

SCIENCE AND NATURE

IN THIS UNIT YOU LEARN HOW TO:

- talk about the weather
- discuss and respond to news stories
- talk about animals
- tell better stories
- talk about scientists and research
- understand newspaper headlines

SPEAKING

1   **Work in pairs. Discuss these questions.**

- Which of the words in the box describe the weather in the photo?

boiling	freezing	snow	sunny
a breeze	rain	a storm	windy

- Do you get weather like this in your country? When?
- Do you generally prefer cold weather or hot weather?
- What's your favourite / least favourite kind of weather? Why?
- What's the weather forecast for the next few days?

2   **Work in groups. Tell each other about a memorable experience connected to the weather in Exercise 1. Think about at least two of the following.**

- how you felt about the weather
- what temperature it was
- how strong the wind was
- how long the weather lasted
- how much rain / snow fell
- what problems you had because of the weather

DID YOU SEE THE NEWS?

VOCABULARY
Science and nature in the news

1 Complete the sentences with the verbs in the box.

ban	build	find	hit	launch
become	conduct	fund	investigate	spread

1 The forecast said that a huge storm is going to _____ the coast any time now.

2 They're not going to allow some researchers to _____ experiments on animals.

3 They're going to _____ five new nuclear power plants.

4 They said that if we don't do more to protect bees, they could _____ extinct.

5 It said in the paper that they expect to _____ a cure for depression soon.

6 I read that we're going to _____ a rocket into space next year.

7 The government is going to _____ more research into ways of improving mental health.

8 I read that they're going to completely _____ smoking next year.

9 Apparently, scientists are trying to create mosquitoes that don't _____ diseases.

10 A university is getting £5 million to _____ the effect of colour on memory.

2 Work in groups. Discuss whether you think each piece of news in Exercise 1 is good or bad. Explain your ideas.

3 Work in pairs. Try to think of:

1 two things that might happen when **a huge storm hits** an area.

2 two other things the government might **fund research into**.

3 two other animals / birds that could **become extinct** sometime soon.

4 two things they're still trying to **find a cure for**.

5 two other things you can **launch** – apart from a rocket.

6 two other things that governments sometimes **ban**.

7 two other animals that **spread diseases**.

LISTENING

4 ▶ 66 Listen to four short conversations about science and nature in the news. Which conversation mentions:

1 a discovery that might prevent deaths?

2 a government project to help the environment?

3 a problem with very negative effects?

4 a change in the weather?

6 Look at the sentences below. Decide which are reporting news, which are opinions / comments and which are suggestions. Write a suitable response to each.

1 They've opened a new park near my house.

2 Really? That's awful.

3 We should have a party to celebrate.

4 That's fantastic news.

5 They should do something about it.

6 They're conducting an experiment to investigate how the Big Bang worked.

7 It's going to be freezing tonight.

8 They should ban it.

PRONUNCIATION

7 ▶ **67** Listen to twelve different responses. Notice the intonation. Then listen again and practise saying the responses.

8 Work in pairs. Take turns saying the sentences from Exercise 6 and giving your own responses. Pay attention to your intonation.

CONVERSATION PRACTICE

9 You are going to have conversations like the ones in Exercise 4.

Student A: look at the news in File 5 on page 187.

Student B: look at the news in File 14 on page 191.

10 Take turns starting conversations about your news. Use the guide below to help you.

Student A	Student B
Did you see / hear ...?	
	No.
It said / It's ...	
	Really? That's ...
I know. It's ...	
	(make a comment – or a suggestion)
(agree)	

▶ 21 To watch the video and do the activities, see the DVD-ROM.

5 ▶ **66** Work in pairs. Decide which conversations these sentences are from. Explain your decisions. Then listen again and check your ideas.

a They're going to pull down a lot of the horrible houses they've built along the coast.

b Yeah, it said it could save millions of lives.

c It's been so wet and windy recently.

d It makes a change to hear some good news.

e They're all dying, for some unknown reason.

f They should do something – fund research or something.

g We need more green spaces.

h We should go out, then – go to the beach or somewhere.

DEVELOPING CONVERSATIONS

Responding to news and comments

When people tell us news that we haven't heard before, we often respond by saying *Really?* We then usually add a comment. Speakers can agree with comments by saying *Yeah* or *I know* and then adding their own comments.

A: *Really? That's bad news / awful / nice / great / interesting*, etc.

B: (*Yeah*) *I know. It's terrible / really good news / fantastic*, etc.

ANIMAL MAGIC

VOCABULARY Animals

1   Match six words in the box to the photos.

cow	fly	parrot	rabbit	shark
dog	lion	pigeon	rat	sheep

2   Decide if each animal in Exercise 1 could be described as a wild animal, a farm animal, an insect or a pet.

3   Work in pairs. Think of two more examples for each of the four categories in Exercise 2.

4   Work in groups. Discuss these questions.
   •   What pets do people you know have?
   •   Which of the animals in Exercise 1 can help humans? How?

READING

5   Read the stories about animals helping humans. Match each story (1–6) to a headline below. There is one headline you will not need.

Barking witness	Jail bird
Wedding goes with a 'woof'	Dinner not well done
Milk of human kindness	From zero to hero
Tips for birds	

6   Work in pairs. Discuss the following.
   •   What do you think each headline means?
   •   Do you think each story is nice, interesting, silly, surprising or boring? Explain why.
   •   One of the stories isn't true. Which one do you think is invented? Why?

7   Work in pairs. Discuss what you think the words in bold in the stories mean.

8   Work in groups. Discuss these questions.
   1   Which animals can you think of that have an amazing sense of smell / hearing / sight?
   2   Can you think of eight things that dogs are often trained to do?
   3   Which other animals are used to detect things?
   4   What advantages and disadvantages of having pets can you think of?

GRAMMAR

Past perfect simple

The past perfect simple is formed using *had / hadn't* + a past participle.

*These pets **had brought** the couple together.*

9 Look at these examples from the stories. Then choose the correct option to complete the rules below.

a *The World Wildlife Fund ... **had asked** the fishermen to let scientists have the body, but the fishermen **insisted** on using it.*

b *The parrots **had previously lived** in a cage ... . One day the owner ... **heard** the parrots copying his customers' requests and ... **trained** them to actually take orders.*

1 We use the past perfect to emphasise that something happened *before / after* another past action.

2 We *usually / don't usually* use the past perfect with other verbs in the past simple.

3 When we describe actions in the order that they happened in, we usually use the past *perfect / simple*.

(G) Check your ideas on page 179 and do Exercise 1.

10 Match the two parts of the sentences. Then work in pairs and compare your answers. Discuss why the past simple or past perfect is used in a–h.

1 The ground was wet
2 Someone had dropped a wallet
3 They took him to court
4 There was a huge traffic jam
5 I had to wait outside our house until my mum got back
6 I was very nervous
7 I was really shocked
8 My dog was going crazy when I got home

a because I'd forgotten my keys.
b because it had rained the night before.
c because I hadn't made a speech in public before.
d because there were roadworks.
e because he hadn't paid his bills.
f because I hadn't taken him for a walk all day.
g so I picked it up and sent it back to them by post.
h when I saw the rat in the kitchen!

11 Write endings to these sentence starters using the past perfect. Then work in pairs and compare your ideas.

1 I was hungry because _____ .
2 She was quite upset because _____ .
3 I was really tired because _____ .
4 I was quite nervous because _____ .
5 Before I was eighteen, I'd never _____ .

12 Work in groups. Discuss what you think happened before each of these events. Use the past perfect.

1 Guards caught and arrested a pigeon in a jail.
2 Fishermen found a pet dog on a desert island.
3 A pet rabbit saved his elderly owners.

13 Find out what actually happened by reading File 15 on page 191.

(G) For further practice, see Exercise 2 on page 179.

SPEAKING

14 Work in pairs. Choose one of the following.

a Have you heard any other animal stories in the news recently? Describe what happened.

b Do an internet search for animal stories in the news. Then tell your partner about the one you liked most. Who found the best story?

MAN'S BEST FRIENDS

1 When Andrew and Harriet Athay got married in the west of England, their dog Ed acted as the best man! Also present on the **big day** were their two female dogs, Humbug and Goulash. These pets had brought the couple together. Andrew and Harriet first met when they were walking their respective pets along a beach. They then started chatting while the dogs were playing with each other.

2 A megamouth shark, which is very rarely seen in the wild, was eaten by Filipino fishermen after they caught it in **a net** by mistake. The World Wildlife Fund, which wants to protect the sharks from extinction, had asked the fishermen to let scientists have the body, but the fishermen **insisted on** using it to prepare a traditional Filipino dish called *kinunot*.

3 A Japanese restaurant is employing two parrots as waiters. The parrots take drinks orders from customers and repeat them to a waiter at the bar, who then brings the drinks to the table. The parrots had previously lived in a **cage** in a corner of the restaurant. One day the owner, Mr Otusaka, heard the parrots copying his customers' requests and after that, he **trained** them to actually take orders.

4 Rats may have a bad reputation, but, says a spokesman for the charity HeroRats, they are saving hundreds of lives in Africa because of their incredible **sense of smell** and intelligence. The rats are trained to **detect** mines and bombs lying in the ground. Being so small, they don't cause the mines to explode when they stand on them. They can also **detect** some diseases in humans.

5 Researchers from Newcastle University have discovered that farmers can help to **boost** milk production by being friendly and talking to their cows. They found that when farmers gave their animals names, these cows produced over 300 litres more milk a year than those without names.

6 A dog called Scooby has appeared in court in a murder case. A neighbour had found the animal's owner dead in her flat and the family had asked for an **investigation**. Police brought Scooby, who had been in the flat at the time of death, into court to see how he would react to the **main suspect**. On seeing the man, Scooby barked very loudly. The police now need to decide if there is enough evidence to take the case further.

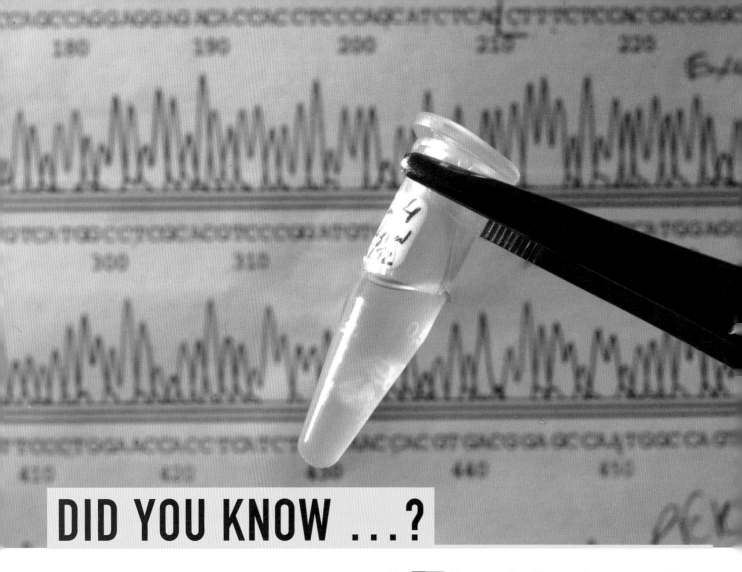

DID YOU KNOW ...?

SPEAKING

1 Work in pairs. Discuss these questions.

- Do you know much about science? Where did you learn what you know?

- Who are the most famous scientists in your country? What are they famous for?

- What TV or radio programmes about science do you know? Do you like them? What areas of science do they cover?

LISTENING

2 You are going to listen to a radio programme where a scientist answers questions from listeners. Work in pairs. Match each question (1–3) to a group of words (a–c). Explain your choices.

1 Are there 'crime genes'?

2 How do spiders walk on ceilings?

3 What is Graphene?

a hairs, atoms, electric charge, a balloon, attraction, weight

b a pencil, sticky tape, layer, to tear, be replaced, prize

c bananas, share, factors, violent, war, environment

3 ▶ 68 Listen to the radio programme and note down answers to the questions in Exercise 2.

4 Work in groups. Compare your ideas using the words in Exercise 2 and your notes.

5 ▶ 68 Listen again. Choose the correct option.

1 We share *15% / 50%* of our genes with bananas.

2 Some violent criminals share *a particular / a part of a* gene.

3 Violence and crime can *learn / be learned*.

4 Each hair is also covered in hundreds of thousands of *tiny / tidy* hairs.

5 The hairs and ceiling atoms are attracted *by / to* each other.

6 It's the world's thinnest material – it's just one atom *thin / thick*.

7 If you *pull / peel* this tape away, some layers of graphite come off.

8 It's an incredible discovery and it was *ordered / awarded* a Nobel Prize.

6 Work in pairs. Discuss these questions.

- Did you know any of the answers to the three questions before you heard them? If yes, where did you learn about them?

- Which answer was most interesting for you? Why?

- How do you think the different factors mentioned in the first answer can cause violent behaviour?

- Have you heard about any new genes scientists have discovered?

- What other things could you use Graphene for?

- How many other Nobel Prize winners can you think of?

GRAMMAR

Passives

When we use a passive sentence, we use a different word order compared to an active sentence. We make the object of an active sentence the subject of a passive sentence.

7 Look at the pairs of sentences and answer the questions below.

1 a *Two Russian scientists* **discovered** *Graphene.*

  b *Graphene* **was discovered** *by two Russian scientists.*

2 a *If that process* **is repeated** *a few times, it eventually* **leaves** *a layer one atom thick.*

  b *If you* **repeat** *that process, you're eventually* **left** *with a layer one atom thick.*

3 a *Could those things* **be replaced** *by Graphene?*

  b *Could Graphene* **replace** *those things?*

4 a *That stuff* **is called** *graphite.*

  b *We* **call** *that stuff graphite*

5 a *They* **awarded** *the discovery of Graphene a Nobel Prize.*

  b *It* **was awarded** *a Nobel Prize.*

1 Which verbs are active and which passive?

2 How are the passives formed?

3 Who does the action in each passive sentence? Do we know exactly?

G Check your ideas on page 180 and do Exercise 1.

8 Read the article below about a classic experiment. Choose the active or the passive form in 1–10.

In the 1950s Harry Harlow [1]*conducted / was conducted* a number of studies investigating the importance of love and contact between mothers and babies. In one experiment, young monkeys [2]*took away / were taken away* from their mothers and their mothers [3]*replaced / were replaced* by two models. The first model had a bottle of milk, but it [4]*made / was made* from wire and wood. The second model was like a soft toy. Even though the wire model provided food, the monkeys [5]*spent / were spent* much more time with the soft toy mother.

In another experiment, the monkeys [6]*put / were put* in a room with lots of strange things. If the soft mother was also in the room, the monkeys went straight to her. After they had been comforted by the mother, they [7]*explored / were explored* the whole room confidently. Where the monkey did not have the security of a mother or they had the wire mother, the monkeys were much slower to move round the room and some of the things [8]*didn't touch / weren't touched* at all.

These kinds of experiments [9]*don't allow / are not allowed* these days because removing baby monkeys from their mothers [10]*sees / is seen* as cruel.

In newspaper headlines, the verb *be* is often left out of the passive construction.

Rare shark eaten by fishermen

We do not leave out the verb *be* in normal sentences.

A shark that **is** *very rarely* **seen** *in the wild* **was eaten** *by Filipino fisherman after they caught it by mistake.*

9 Work in pairs. Look at the headlines. Discuss what you think each story is probably about.

1 DOG AWARDED MEDAL BY THE QUEEN

2 Man arrested after stealing 10 kilos of bananas

3 ROCKET LAUNCHED ON 100-YEAR JOURNEY

4 Cure for rare disease accidentally discovered

5 SCIENCE COMPANY OFFICES DAMAGED IN FIRE INVESTIGATED BY POLICE

10 Choose one of the headlines in Exercise 9 and write a short news report of 60–80 words.

G For further practice, see Exercises 2 and 3 on page 180.

SOUNDS AND VOCABULARY REVIEW

11 ▶ **69** Listen and repeat the sounds with /aʊ/, /ɔː/ and /ɒ/. Are any of them difficult to hear or say?

12 ▶ **70** Work in groups. Listen to eight sentences using the words below. Together, try to write them down. Then listen again and check.

allow	court	launch	power
bomb	dog	policy	storm

13 Work in teams. You have three minutes to write collocations / phrases for the words in Exercise 12.

not **allow** *smoking,*
be **allowed** *to keep pets,*
allow *the cat out at night*

12

ON THE PHONE

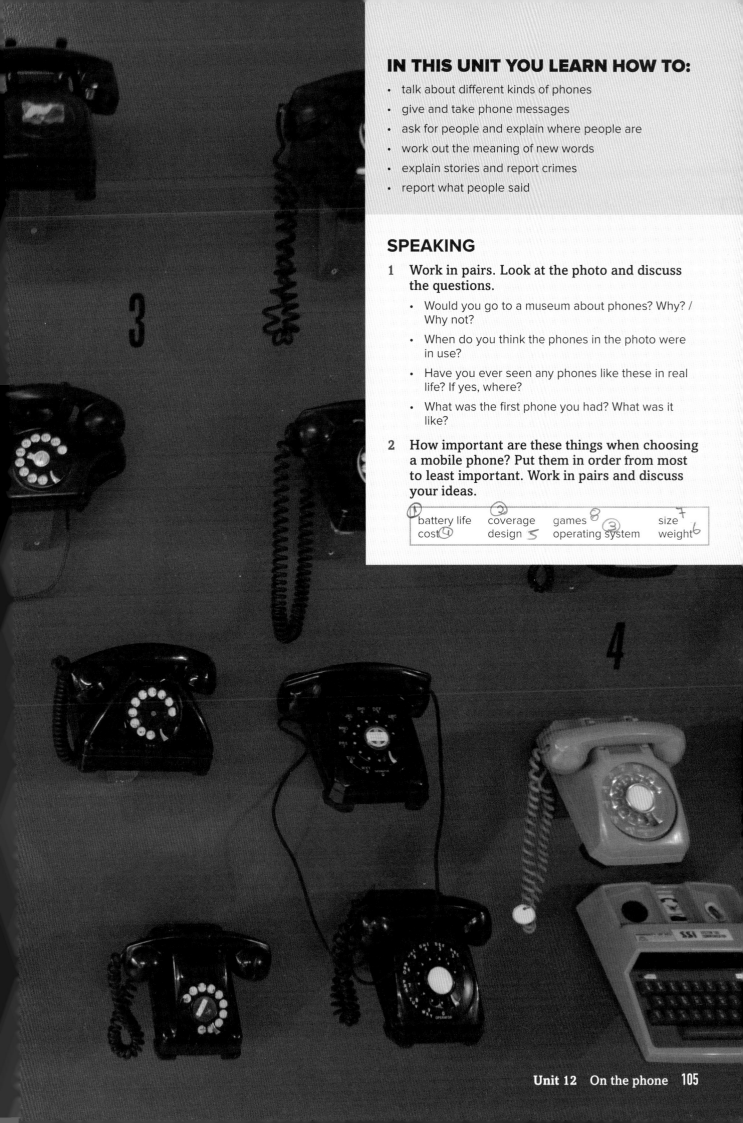

IN THIS UNIT YOU LEARN HOW TO:

- talk about different kinds of phones
- give and take phone messages
- ask for people and explain where people are
- work out the meaning of new words
- explain stories and report crimes
- report what people said

SPEAKING

1 **Work in pairs. Look at the photo and discuss the questions.**

- Would you go to a museum about phones? Why? / Why not?
- When do you think the phones in the photo were in use?
- Have you ever seen any phones like these in real life? If yes, where?
- What was the first phone you had? What was it like?

2 **How important are these things when choosing a mobile phone? Put them in order from most to least important. Work in pairs and discuss your ideas.**

battery life	coverage	games	size
cost	design	operating system	weight

CAN I LEAVE A MESSAGE?

VOCABULARY Using phones

1 **Match the words in bold in these sentences to the meanings a–h below.**

b 1 My son never answers his mobile when I call him. I always have to **text**.

e 2 When I called, I **was put on hold** for about 20 minutes with this terrible music playing.

f 3 I tried calling six times, but **the line was always busy**.

g 4 We couldn't finish our conversation because we **got cut off**.

d 5 Matt! Can I **call you back**? I'm having dinner.

h 6 The **coverage** isn't very good here. You might have to go outside to make a call with your mobile.

i 7 Sorry, I can't hear you very well. **It's a very poor signal**.

c 8 It was the wrong number, but she was very helpful and **put me through** to the right department.

a 9 We started to argue and I didn't want to hear any more, so I just **hung up**.

a put down the phone before the other person finished speaking

b send a written message

c pressed a button to connect me

d return your call later

e had to wait

f the person I wanted to speak to was on the phone to someone else

g lost the connection while we were on the phone

h the number of places it's possible to make phone calls from

i the connection on my phone isn't very good

2 **Work in groups. Discuss these questions.**

• Do you know anyone who never answers their phone?

• Do you usually text or phone more? Why? Does it depend who you're contacting?

• Do you know anywhere that often puts you on hold?

• Why might you get cut off during a phone call?

• Do you know anywhere with bad coverage?

• Have you ever hung up on anyone? Why?

LISTENING

3 ▶ **71** **Listen to two short phone conversations. Complete the messages written after each conversation.**

Brenda called.

Meet him at ² __7:00__ – not ³ __8:00__.

Diane ⁴ _Lincoln_ called. ⁵ _Price_ is fine.

Phone her to sort out ⁶ _details_

Mobile: ⁷ _07729651118_

Phone today – she's ⁸ ~~holiday~~ tomorrow.
    away on holiday

106

PRONUNCIATION

4 ▶ 72 Listen to these sentences from the conversation. Notice how only the key words are stressed.

No, he's <u>not</u> up yet. Is it <u>urgent</u>?

Just <u>tell</u> him we're meeting <u>earlier</u> – at <u>seven</u>, not <u>eight</u>.

5 Work in pairs. Look at the first conversation in audio script 71 on page 205 and underline the words you think are stressed. Then practise reading the whole conversation.

DEVELOPING CONVERSATIONS

Explaining where people are

We often explain where people are if they are not there when someone phones.

*Diane's **out** visiting a client.* (= she will return today)

*He's **away** on business.* (= he won't return for a day or more)

*It's her **day off**.* (= she doesn't work on this day of the week)

*He's **off sick**.* (= he's not at work because he's ill)

6 Complete the conversations with these words.

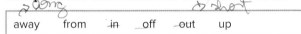

away	from	in	off	out	up

1 A: Hello. Is that Mary Williams?
   B: No, it's Jane. Mary's ___out___ . She's just gone to the shops. Is it urgent?

2 A: Hello, could I speak to Mr Haskell?
   B: I'm afraid he's ___away___ . He won't be back for a few days. Can I take a message?

3 A: Could I speak to Paul Philips? I phoned earlier.
   B: Of course. Hold the line. I'm afraid there's still no answer. He must still be ___in___ his meeting.

4 A: Hi. Frazer?
   B: No, it's actually Sylvia. I'm covering for Frazer. He's ___off___ sick today. How can I help?

5 A: Hi, is Jay there?
   B: Yes, but he's not ___up___ yet. Shall I wake him?

6 A: Hi, is Greg there, please?
   B: No, sorry. He's working ___from___ home today.

7 Work in pairs and practise reading the conversations in Exercise 6. Take turns to start. Continue each conversation with one or two lines each.

GRAMMAR

yet, already, still and just

These adverbs are often used with the present perfect or with other present tenses to emphasise the time something happened or when we expect something to happen.

8 Look at these sentences from the listening and match the adverbs in bold to the meanings (1–4) below. Which tense is used with each adverb?

a *He's not got up **yet**. Shall I wake him?*

b *I've **already** spoken to my boss and he's fine with the price.*

c *You've **just** missed him. He's **just** walked out of the door.*

d *I'm afraid there's **still** no answer. He must still be in his meeting.*

1 It shows the action is very recent.

2 It shows something happened before – often sooner than expected.

3 It shows something hasn't happened, but we expect it to happen. We also use it in questions.

4 It shows an action or situation continues unchanged.

G Check your ideas on page 181 and do Exercise 1

9 Choose the correct ending to each sentence.

1 Could you tell him I've already spoken to Brittany ...
   a so he doesn't have to email her now?
   b and we can't do anything until I have?

2 Tell him I'm still waiting for confirmation of the price ...
   a and it's better than we expected.
   b but I'll ring as soon as I get it.

3 Just tell him I don't have the money yet ...
   a and I'll send it to him right away.
   b but I'll definitely have it by Friday.

4 We've only just left the house ...
   a so could you tell her we're going to be late?
   b so tell her we'll be there earlier than expected.

5 Could you tell her we've already sorted out the problem ...
   a so there's no need for her to come over?
   b because I was out, but I'm dealing with it now?

6 I still haven't received the package ...
   a so can you ring and find out what's happened to it?
   b but I'm afraid it doesn't contain the parts I need.

10 Choose four of the sentence endings that were not correct in Exercise 9. Write a possible beginning for each sentence using *just*, *already*, *yet* or *still*.

CONVERSATION PRACTICE

11 You are going to have conversations like the ones you heard in Exercise 3. First write two messages you want to leave for different people. One should be more formal / a business situation, the other one should be for a friend.

12 Work in pairs. Roleplay four phone conversations. Take turns to start. Follow the guide in File 8 on page 189.

🎥 22 To watch the video and do the activities, see the DVD-ROM.

PHONE FOR HELP!

READING

1 In newspaper stories, the first sentence usually summarises what happened. Work in pairs. Read the first sentences (1–3) taken from three stories, then read the questions and discuss what you think the answers are.

  1 *A police force has launched a campaign against misuse of the emergency phone number.*

    a What's the emergency number?

    b How are people misusing the number?

    c What things are the police doing in their campaign?

  2 *A doctor in Australia has saved the life of a young boy using a domestic drill and a mobile phone.*

    a What happened to the boy?

    b What did the doctor use the drill for – and why a 'domestic' one?

    c Why did he need the mobile phone?

  3 *A chef has saved his own life, thanks to the photo of a rare spider that he took with his mobile phone.*

    a Where was the man?

    b What happened to him?

    c What was the spider like?

    d How did the photo save his life?

2 Now read the news stories on page 109 and answer the questions in Exercise 1. Work in pairs and compare your answers.

3 Work in pairs. Discuss what the words in bold in the stories mean. Then complete these sentences with the words.

  1 He had to pay a 100-euro _____ for speeding.

  2 He _____ because of the heat, but he was OK in the end.

  3 After my wallet was stolen, I _____ it to the police, but they said they couldn't do anything about it.

  4 He keeps phoning, _____ me telling him to stop.

  5 There are hundreds of _____ of animals that are becoming extinct each year.

  6 I phoned the main number and then I was _____ to the correct department.

  7 It was urgent, so we _____ him to the hospital.

  8 My hand was almost twice its normal size and I had to keep ice on it to reduce the _____ .

4 Work in pairs. Discuss the questions.

  • Which story did you find most interesting or surprising? Why?

  • Why do you think people make inappropriate calls to the emergency number?

  • Have you heard of any other true stories of emergency operations?

  • How do you feel about insects and spiders? Are there any poisonous creatures in your country? Do you know what you should do if they bite / sting you?

UNDERSTANDING VOCABULARY

Forming negatives

In the first article, you saw these words: *totally unnecessary; inappropriate calls*

We often form negatives of adjectives and adverbs by adding a prefix. The most common prefix is *un-*, but you will also see *in-*, *il-*, *im-* and *ir-*.

5 Write the opposites by adding or removing a prefix.

  1 a wise decision *unwise*

  2 it's illegal *legal*

  3 a fortunate result *un*

  4 very impolite *polite*

  5 a happy marriage *unhappy*

  6 totally expected *unexpected*

  7 a practical solution *impractical*

  8 very fair *unfair*

  9 a comfortable bed *uncomfortable*

  10 an uncommon name *common*

  11 a patient customer *impatient*

  12 an inconvenient time *convenient*

  13 completely possible *impossible*

  14 a natural product *unnatural*

  15 an irrational fear *rational*

  16 a very unpleasant man *pleasant*

6 Work in pairs. Discuss the questions.

  1 What happens if someone does something **illegal**?

  2 What does a person do if they are **polite**? And **impolite**?

  3 What else can be **uncomfortable**? What's the result in each case?

  4 What makes a **happy** or **unhappy** marriage?

  5 What's the most **common** surname in your country? Do you know anyone with a very **uncommon** one?

  6 What would you say on the phone to someone if it was an **inconvenient time** to talk?

7 Work in pairs. Take turns to explain an adjective or its opposite from Exercise 5. Your partner should try and guess the word.

SPEAKING

8 Choose one of the situations below. Spend a few minutes preparing to tell a story. It can be true or invented. Think about when it was, where you were, what you were doing at the time, the main events and how you felt.

  • a time you were really glad you had a mobile phone

  • an unusual phone call you made or received

  • a time you rang the police, fire brigade or ambulance service

  • a time you helped someone in a difficult situation

9 Work in groups. Tell your stories. Ask questions about the stories you hear.

IT'S AN
EMERGENCY

A police force has launched a campaign against misuse of the emergency phone number. Every day, the police in northern England have to answer three hundred 999 calls, but a third of them are totally unnecessary. Last year, the calls that police received included someone wanting a ride home, a man complaining about his TV not working and two people who **reported** lost cats. A number were also from young children who had accidentally dialled 999.

The police are sending leaflets to houses to explain the problem and have introduced £80 **fines** for those making inappropriate calls.

A doctor in Australia has saved the life of a young boy using a domestic drill and a mobile phone. Nicolas Rossi, a thirteen-year-old boy from a remote town in Australia, fell off his bicycle and hit his head. Although Nicolas initially seemed fine, his mother, a nurse, noticed a **swelling** on his head. She **rushed** him to the nearest hospital, where the doctor realised the boy was in danger of dying if he didn't have an operation to reduce the pressure on his brain.

Unfortunately, Doctor Carson had never done the operation, which required him to make a hole in the boy's head, and he only had a normal household drill. After cleaning the drill, he phoned a colleague in Melbourne, who explained where and how to make the hole.

The one-minute operation was successful and the boy was **transferred** by plane to a Melbourne hospital, where he has made a complete recovery. Carson described his actions as 'just part of the job'.

A chef has saved his own life, thanks to the photo of a rare spider that he took with his mobile phone. Matthew Stevens, 23, was bitten by one of the world's most poisonous spiders, the Brazilian wandering spider, in a pub in south-west England, while he was cleaning the kitchen. The spider probably came into Britain in a box of bananas.

After the incident, Mr Stevens took a photo of the twelve-centimetre spider with his mobile phone, but then went home, **despite** his hand **swelling** 'like a balloon'. At home, he **collapsed** with breathing difficulties and had to be **rushed** to hospital. Fortunately, he was able to show the picture on his phone. The photo was sent to a university, where they identified the **species** of spider and found a cure for the poison.

WHAT A NIGHTMARE!

SPEAKING

1 **Work in groups. Discuss these questions.**

- Can you think of three different ways people often lose their phone or bag?

- What would be the first thing you'd do if this happened to you?

- Have you ever lost – or has anyone ever stolen – your phone, your bag or another important piece of property? If yes, what happened? What did you do to sort things out?

Report to the police

LISTENING

2 ▶ **73** **Listen to three phone calls connected to a crime. Answer the questions.** *she was told*

1 What happened to Bettina? *bag* *Bank Police*
Lock company
2 What kind of company / organisation is each call to?
3 Why is she making each call? *Cancelled your card*
try to regain your bag

3 ▶ **73** **Listen again. Are these sentences true (T) or false (F)?**

1 a Bettina has to answer some questions before her request can be dealt with. *T*

   b Bettina's cards will be cancelled tomorrow. *F*

2 a Bettina was walking home when her bag was taken. *F* *Friends house*

   b She doesn't give a good description of the person that took her bag. *T*

   c The police promise to try to find the bag. *F*

3 a Bettina is calling from her apartment. *F* *Friends house*

   b She has no way of proving who she is. *T*

   c Bettina owns her apartment. *F* *rent*

4 **Work in pairs. Discuss:**

- what you would do if you were Bettina.

- what you'd do if you were the guy from Abbey Locks.

- if you would report this kind of incident to the police in your country and what they'd do.

- what you could do to avoid a similar situation to Bettina's.

5 ▶ **74** **Listen to another phone call one week later. Find out:** *Bank Kali* *bc the cards didn't arrive*

1 who Bettina is calling, and why.

2 what problem she now has. How do you think this happened?

GRAMMAR

Reporting speech

When we report things people said to us, we often use *said / told me* (*that*) + a clause. Reported speech usually moves one tense back from direct speech.

6 **Look at these two sentences from the conversations. The first is direct speech from Bettina's first conversation with the bank. The second is how she reported it. Answer the questions below.**

a *I've cancelled your cards and ordered new ones, and they'll be with you within three or four days.*

b *The guy I spoke to* **told me he'd cancelled them and that the new cards would be with me** *within three or four days ... but I still haven't received them.*

1 What tenses / structures are used in the direct speech in a?

2 What tenses / structures are used to report the speech in b?

3 How would you report someone saying *'I'm very sorry'*?

G Check your ideas on page 181 and do Exercise 1.

7 Look at this extract from an email that Bettina sent to a friend. The reported speech is in italics. Decide what you think the direct speech was.

I just couldn't believe someone could be using my card. I ¹*asked the guy how that had happened* and ²*he just said he had to speak to the manager*. I was then waiting for another ten minutes. Anyway, eventually I was put through to the manager ³*and she told me they had sent the cards to the wrong address*. ⁴*She said that there had been some security issues* and someone had probably hacked into my account and changed all my information before the cards were actually sent. Apparently, similar things have happened at other banks too! ⁵*She told me to change all my passwords* and ⁶*she promised the bank would repay any money I'd lost*.

8 Choose two of the following ideas. Spend a few minutes thinking about how you are going to report what was said. Then work in groups and tell your stories.

a A problem you had with a bank.

b A time you reported something to the police.

c The most surprising thing you can remember anyone telling you.

d Some promises someone in power made, and whether they kept them or not.

e A lie that someone told you, and how you found out it was a lie.

f An argument you had, and how it ended.

G For further practice, see Exercise 2 on page 181.

VOCABULARY Reporting crimes

9 Complete the sentences below with these pairs of words.

bought + got	hacked + stole
came + kicked	having + making
followed + threatening	hitting + kicking
grabbed + ran	texting + crashed

1 Two guys just walked up to me, _____ my bag and _____ off.

2 Someone _____ into my account and _____ most of my money!

3 I _____ home from work and found that someone had _____ my front door down.

4 I _____ something from a website that wasn't secure. I guess they _____ my bank details from there.

5 He just suddenly started _____ and _____ me for no reason.

6 This woman was _____ while she was driving, and _____ into the side of me.

7 It was really scary. This guy _____ me home and started _____ me.

8 Our neighbours are _____ a party and they're _____ a terrible noise!

10 You are going to roleplay a conversation between someone reporting a crime and a police officer. First, invent some details about the crime. Think about the following.

• what kind of crime it was

• if it affected you or if it was just something you saw

• where and when it happened

• what exactly happened and who was involved

• what you want the police to do now

11 Work in pairs. Roleplay the conversation. Use as much new language from the unit as possible. Then change roles and have another conversation. Start like this:

Police officer: *Yes Sir / Madam. How can I help you?*

Student: *Hi, I'd like to report a crime …*

SOUNDS AND VOCABULARY REVIEW

12 ▶ 75 Listen and repeat the sounds with /ʊə/ and /əʊ/. Are any of them difficult to hear or say?

13 ▶ 76 Work in groups. Listen to eight sentences using the words below. Together, try to write them down. Then listen again and check.

euro	hour	mobile	secure
home	insurance	photo	stolen

14 Work in teams. You have three minutes to write collocations / phrases for the words in Exercise 13.

*cost 30 **euros**, pay 100 **euros** a week, spent 50 **euros***

VIDEO 6

MEMORY MAN

1 Work in pairs. Discuss the questions.

- What's happening in the photo?
- Are you good at remembering these things?

| appointments | English words | numbers |
| books and films | jokes | your childhood |

- Why do you think you are good / bad at remembering these different kinds of things?
- Do you know anyone who has a really good memory? How do they do it?

2 ▣ 23 Watch the first part of the video (0.00–1.59) about an Italian man, Gianni Golfera. Complete the notes.

Examples of Gianni's good memory:

- *can remember and repeat [1]_____ in order and then backwards*
- *has memorised over [2]_____ books*
- *can also remember [3]_____*

Memory research

Malgaroli's memory research: wants to compare the genes of [4]_____ and _____

We know memory is coded in the hippocampus, but need research on:

- *how it's coded*
- *where [5]_____ and why there.*
- *why some people [6]_____*
- *why only a few people are like Gianni*

3 ▣ 23 Is a good memory mainly genetic or mainly a matter of learning and environment? Watch the second part of the video (2.00–end) to find out.

4 ▣ 23 Put the adverbs in bold in the correct places in the sentences. Then watch the whole video again to check your answers.

1 He practises to improve the power of his memory. **continuously**

2 He's memorised a series of historical books. **even**

3 Improving his memory has become like a full-time job. **almost**

4 He has a normal life. **relatively**

5 In other words, he's like other people. **just**

6 His genes are responsible for his great memory. **partly**

7 Researchers think it's because of his very hard work. **mainly**

8 Learning how to remember to remember. **basically**

5 Work in groups. Could you learn anything from Gianni? Make a list of ways to remember English vocabulary. Then put them in order from the most effective method to the least effective.

UNDERSTANDING FAST SPEECH

6 ▣ 24 Read and listen to this extract from the video said at natural pace and then slowed down. To help you, groups of words are marked with / and pauses are marked //. Stressed sounds are in CAPITALS.

if you really NEED // to USE your BRAIN caPAcity / to STORE / some kind of inforMAtion / you HAVE this / this abILity / AND you know // it's just a MAtter of EXercise

7 Now you have a go! Practise saying the extract at natural pace.

REVIEW 6

1 Complete the text with one word in each space. Contractions like *don't* count as one word.

I got my daughter her first pet for Christmas. She
[1]_____ wanted one for ages, so I decided to get
her one. I went to the dogs' home and was surprised
by how many questions they asked. They asked me
[2]_____ the dog would sleep, [3]_____ we'd had
a dog before, how old my daughter [4]_____ , all
kinds of things! In the end, I got a lovely Dalmatian for
her. The guy there [5]_____ me that the dog needs
to [6]_____ walked at least twice a day. My daughter
is [7]_____ finding that quite hard! In fact, I've
[8]_____ reminded her about it – again! It'll take time,
I can see!

2 Complete the second sentence so that it has a similar meaning to the first sentence, using the word given. Do not change the word given. You must use between two and four words including the word given.

1 In Canada, I saw snow for the first time in my life.

I _____ snow before I went to Canada. **NEVER**

2 I still haven't finished writing that report for work.

I need to get on with that report. I _____ . **YET**

3 They should ban smoking in all public spaces, if you ask me.

If you ask me, smoking in all public places
_____ . **BE**

4 I got home and then remembered my laptop was still in the office.

I got home and then I realised _____ my laptop at work. **LEFT**

5 Someone stole my car while I was away on a business trip.

While I was away on a business trip, _____ . **WAS**

3 Choose the correct option.

1 She *told / said* me that she'd be late.

2 They asked me if I *did want / wanted* the job.

3 When *did that happen / was that happened*?

4 *You've / You'd* just missed him, I'm afraid. He left for lunch two minutes ago.

5 I still *haven't received / don't receive* your email.

6 We wanted to find out *what / what did* our customers thought of us.

7 *I still wait / I'm still waiting* to hear back from my bank.

8 Most of what we sell *is imported / imports* from China.

4 ▶ 77 Listen and write the six sentences you hear.

5 Match the verbs (1–8) with the nouns they collocate with (a–h).

1	ban	a	an experiment
2	grab	b	the environment
3	conduct	c	the coast
4	spread	d	my bag
5	hit	e	the swelling
6	protect	f	smoking
7	reduce	g	a terrible noise
8	make	h	disease

6 Decide if these words and phrases are connected to science and nature in the news, phones or crimes.

become extinct	fund research	a poor signal
a busy line	get cut off	put on hold
crash	investigate the effect	run off
find a cure	pay a fine	threaten

7 Complete the sentences with the best prepositions.

1 Someone hacked _____ my bank account and stole all my money!

2 A strange guy just walked _____ to me and started screaming _____ me.

3 I bought something _____ a website that I guess wasn't very secure.

4 They kicked my door _____ and stole my TV and my computer!

5 This is the wrong number. I'll put you _____ to the right department now.

6 They launched a rocket _____ space a few years ago.

7 I'm afraid she's _____ a meeting at the moment.

8 I'm quite lucky because I can work _____ home one day a week.

8 Complete the text with one word in each space. The first letters are given.

I tried to call him at least ten times, but he never
[1]an_____ his phone! I then [2]te_____ him a
few times and eventually, he [3]ca_____ me back,
but at a really [4]in_____ time. I was driving through
the woods and the [5]co_____ there is terrible. To
make matters worse, there was a huge [6]st_____
and the [7]wi_____ was really strong. It was raining
too, so I couldn't hear him very well. To be honest, I just
find him quite an [8]unp_____ man – very rude and
aggressive. I think it'll be [9]im_____ to do business
with him. I really don't trust him. It's an [10]un_____
decision to work with him, if you ask me.

13

IN THIS UNIT YOU LEARN HOW TO:

- describe different kinds of films
- say what you have heard about things
- talk about how things make you feel
- talk about the film industry and culture
- discuss your favourite music, books or films
- ask how long people have been doing things

SPEAKING

1 Work in pairs. Look at the photo and discuss the questions.

- What do you think is happening in this photo?
- How do you think this photo is connected to film production? Why?
- What kind of films might the bears feature in?
- Would you go and see films like that? Why? / Why not?

2 Work in groups. Discuss the questions.

- What was the last film you saw?
- What kind of film was it?
- Who was in it?
- What was it like?

CULTURE

IT'S SUPPOSED TO BE AMAZING

VOCABULARY Films

1 Work in pairs. Think of an example for each kind of film below. Can you think of any other kinds of film?

an action movie	a musical
a comedy	a romantic comedy
a historical drama	a science-fiction film
a horror movie	a thriller
a martial arts movie	a war movie

2 Discuss which kinds of films might:

- have amazing special effects.
- have amazing costumes.
- have a happy ending.
- be set in space.
- have complicated plots.
- have car chases and explosions.
- be really scary.
- be quite predictable.
- be quite violent.
- be really boring.

LISTENING

3 ▶ 78 Listen to two friends discussing which film to go and see. Answer the questions.

1 What do you hear about these three films?

In the Heat of the Moment

The Cottage

It's a Love-Hate Thing

2 Which film do they decide to go and see in the end?

3 Where's it on?

4 What time does it start?

4 ▶ 78 Listen again and complete the sentences with three words in each space. Contractions like *don't* count as one word.

1 I was starting to fall asleep _____ .

2 Yeah, I'm thinking of _____ a movie.

3 Yeah, I've seen it already, actually. I saw it _____ .

4 Not bad, but not as good as _____ .

5 I got _____ with it after a while – and the ending _____ .

6 OK. _____ , I don't really like horror movies.

7 That sounds _____ ! Where's it on?

8 We could _____ a coffee or something first.

DEVELOPING CONVERSATIONS

supposed to

To report what we have heard or read about a film, a person, etc. we often use *be supposed to* + infinitive (without *to*).

It's a new horror movie. It's supposed to be really scary.

It's supposed to have great special effects.

116

UNDERSTANDING VOCABULARY

-ed / -ing adjectives

A small group of adjectives can end in either -ed or -ing. When they end in -ed, they describe people's feelings. When they end in -ing, they describe the thing or person that causes the feeling.

*I got a bit **bored** with it after a while.*

*What a **boring** lecture!*

8 Choose the correct option.

1 I got really *bored / boring* about halfway through.

2 The ending was really *surprised / surprising*.

3 I'm quite *excited / exciting* about the new Collocini film.

4 I just wasn't really *interested / interesting* in any of the characters.

5 The film was in English – with no subtitles – so I found it quite *tired / tiring* to watch.

6 It wasn't a bad film. I just found it quite *depressed / depressing*.

7 I must admit, I was quite *confused / confusing* by the ending.

8 The guy behind me was eating all through the film. It was really *annoyed / annoying*.

9 Write a sentence for each adjective that was not correct in Exercise 8.

CONVERSATION PRACTICE

10 Think of three films you would like to see. They can be new films or old films. Note down what you know about each film. Think about:

• what it's called.

• who directed it.

• who's in it.

• what kind of film it is.

• what it's supposed to be like.

11 Work in pairs. Roleplay conversations like the one you heard in Exercise 3. Student A starts, and Student B makes suggestions using the notes from Exercise 10. Discuss which film you want to go and see, where it's on and what time to meet. Then change roles and have another conversation. Begin like this:

A: *So what are you doing this afternoon? Have you got any plans?*

B: *I'm thinking of going to see a film. Would you like to come?*

A: *Maybe. What's on?*

B: *Well, there's a film called …*

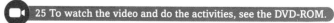

25 To watch the video and do the activities, see the DVD-ROM.

5 Match the two parts of the sentences.

1 I haven't seen *Hell Blood 3*,

2 I've never heard The Boredoms,

3 I've never tried Indonesian food,

4 I haven't been to the new shopping centre yet,

5 I've never seen him play tennis,

6 I've never been to Hawaii,

a but he's supposed to be really good at it.

b but it's supposed to be a violent film.

c but they're supposed to be quite strange.

d but it's supposed to be a beautiful place.

e but it's supposed to have a great selection of stuff.

f but it's supposed to be quite spicy.

6 Think of one example of each of the following things and say what each one is supposed to be like.

• a very famous film that you've never seen

• a new film that you haven't seen yet

• a famous book you've never read

• a group, singer or album you haven't heard

• a country you've never been to

• a kind of food you've never tried

7 Work in groups. Share your ideas.

MAKING MOVIES

SPEAKING

1 **Work in groups. Discuss the questions.**

1 Does your country have a film industry? How big is it?

2 How is the industry doing? Why?

3 Do most local films show at the cinema or do they go straight to DVD? Why?

4 What kind of films are most popular in your country?

5 What are the most important local films from recent years?

6 Who is the most famous director from your country?

7 Do you know how many films he / she has made?

8 Do you like his / her work? Why? / Why not?

READING

2 **Read the article on page 119. Work in pairs and discuss how the writer of the article might answer the questions in Exercise 1.**

3 **Match the verbs (1–8) with the words (a–h) they are used with in the article.**

1	reach	a	more ambitious
2	follow	b	Benin culture
3	give	c	a bad image
4	make	d	a middle-class cinema audience
5	be	e	a crossroads
6	steal	f	no money
7	promote	g	very similar plots
8	be aimed at	h	valuable works of art

4 **Compare your ideas with a partner. Can you remember who or what does each of the things in Exercise 3? Read the article again and check your ideas.**

5 **Work in pairs. Discuss the questions.**

• What similarities and differences are there between the Nigerian film industry and the film industry in your country?

• Would you like to watch any of the Nollwood films? Why? / Why not?

• Do you think people get a good image of your country from films? Why? / Why not?

• Have you heard of any similar stories to *Invasion 1897*?

• What films have made people more aware of an issue? What was the issue? Did it make a difference in real life?

• How do you feel about Hollywood movies? Are they popular in your country? Do you think they have more of a positive or a negative impact? Why?

GRAMMAR

Noun phrases

In the text you read: *you're likely to be offered **the latest DVDs from the Nigerian film industry**.*

The latest DVDs from the Nigerian film industry is an example of a **noun phrase**: a group of several words around a main noun. The main noun in this phrase is *DVDs*. All the other words add information about the DVDs.

6 **Look at these extracts from the article. Answer the questions below.**

a ***Nollywood films*** *are made for £20,000*

b *the **film cameramen** have to work in the streets*

c *stole many valuable **works of art***

d *make people aware of **the issue of stolen art***

1 Which is the main noun in each extract?

2 What is the singular and plural form of the main noun in each example?

 **Check your ideas on page 182 and do Exercise 1.**

7 **Make a noun phrase using the words.**

1 industry / the / fashion

2 a / director / famous / film

3 the / country / from / our / films

4 a / of / my / parents / photo

8 **Write a sentence using each noun phrase.**

PRONUNCIATION

9 ▶ **79** **Listen to how these compound nouns are pronounced and mark where the main stress is.**

cash machine

cash machine	film industry	success story
city centre	football boots	sunglasses
crossroads	heart disease	tennis court
flatmate	security system	traffic lights

10 **Spend two minutes memorising the compound nouns in Exercise 9. Then work in pairs.**

Student A: close your book.

Student B: act, draw or explain the compound nouns. See how many your partner can guess.

11 **Work in groups. Change one word in each compound noun in Exercise 9 to make a new compound noun. The first group to think of twelve new compound nouns wins.**

the film industry: *the **fashion** industry, a film **star***

G **For further practice, see Exercise 2 on page 182.**

NOLLYWOOD DREAMS

Sarah Walters reports on an African success story looking to the future

n many cities of the world, if you're stuck in a traffic jam, you'll find people trying to sell you drinks and food, but in Nigeria you're also likely to be offered the latest DVDs from the Nigerian film industry, known as Nollywood. Nollywood produces around 1,500 films a year, and is second only to India as the most productive film industry in the world. In just 25 years, and with no government support, it has grown from nothing to be worth around $7 billion a year. Nollywood now employs thousands and is one of Africa's great success stories, but it has also reached a crossroads, as profits have fallen recently and it's unclear what its future direction will be.

The majority of Nollywood films are made for around $30,000 and take ten days to complete. In comparison, making a top Hollywood movie can take a year and cost $200 million. Nollywood directors use very basic special effects, the actors sometimes write their own lines and the film cameramen have to work in the streets while real life continues around them. This low-budget approach has allowed Nollywood to grow very quickly, as almost anyone with talent can make films. However, it's also the source of several problems.

Low budgets often mean films are poor quality and there's no money to develop new talent. Films often follow similar plots and star the same actors, so have become too predictable. Typical Nollywood films are voodoo horror or gangster films; even stories about poor people becoming successful, or domestic dramas, contain elements of magic and violence. Some complain that this focus on black magic and crime gives a bad image of modern Nigeria.

Another problem is illegal copying. Films aren't usually shown in cinemas (there are currently less than 30 cinemas in a country of 150 million people), but are distributed as DVDs through market stalls and street sellers, so it's difficult to control copying. After two weeks, most films have been illegally copied and the producers make no more money.

However, Nollywood is changing, as seen in the work of its leading director, Lancelot Oduwa Imasuen. Imasuen has already directed around 200 feature films (Steven Spielberg at the same age had directed just fourteen!). His early films followed the Nollywood pattern – fast production and voodoo horror – but Imasuen's recent films are more ambitious. *Invasion 1897* had a budget of $1 million and tells the story of how the British invaded the kingdom of Benin, sent the king to prison and stole many valuable works of art, which are now in the British Museum in London. The film was first shown at several international festivals and many universities in Nigeria. As well as making a profit, it aims to promote Benin culture and make people aware of the issue of stolen art. Some think that films like this show a possible future direction for the Nigerian film industry because they are aimed at a more profitable middle-class cinema audience.

I'M A BIG FAN

VOCABULARY Music, art and books

1 Put each word in the box under the correct heading in the table.

album	crime fiction	painting
author	exhibition	poetry
comedy	instrument	portrait
composer	landscape	sculpture
concert	novel	singer

Music	Art	Books

2 Write six questions about music, art and books, using words from Exercise 1.

Do you like listening to music? *Who's your favourite* singer? *Why? What's your favourite* album? *Why?*

3 Now work in groups. Ask each other your six questions. Try to use these phrases in your answers.

I'm a big fan of ... .

It changes. I've been reading / listening to ... a lot recently.

She's got an amazing voice / style / technique.

I think my all-time favourite is a song / painting / novel by ... .

I don't know why I like it so much. I just do.

It's just really exciting / sad / beautiful, etc.

LISTENING

4 ▶ **80** Listen to four people talking about music, art and books. Match each speaker to one photo. Then work in pairs and explain your ideas.

5 ▶ **80** Listen again. Decide which speaker:

a has been a bit disappointed with something.

b escaped problems when they were a kid.

c has been studying a language.

d has changed their tastes recently.

e decided what kind of work they wanted to do a long time ago.

f is going to perform live.

g has travelled to see someone they're a fan of.

h is interested in politics and society.

6 Choose one of the following topics to talk about. Spend a few minutes thinking about what you want to say. Then work in groups and share your ideas.

• singing competitions
• art and music in education
• a film / TV series based on a book
• modern art

GRAMMAR
Present perfect continuous

7 Look at these sentences from the listening. Complete the rules in the Grammar box below.

a *For the last few weeks,* **they've been showing** *a series on TV based on the books.*

b **I've been learning** *Turkish since 2012.*

c **We've been rehearsing** *The Rite of Spring recently for a concert.*

d **I've liked** *her ever since then.*

e **I've known** *I wanted to be an artist since I was three.*

The present perfect continuous is formed using ¹_____ / has + ²_____ + the -ing form of the verb. It is used to talk about activities that started in the past and are unfinished.

To show the amount or period of time something lasted, use a time expression starting with ³_____ .

To show when something started, use a time expression starting with ⁴_____ .

Some verbs are generally not used in the present perfect continuous. We use them in the present perfect simple form. For example: *be, believe, hate,* ⁵_____ and ⁶_____ .

G Check your ideas on page 182 and do Exercise 1.

8 Respond to these comments by writing a *How long ...?* question. Use the verb in brackets in the present perfect continuous or simple.

How long have you been going there?

1 I'm a member of a gym. (go there)

2 They have their dance class on Tuesdays. (do)

3 She speaks English well. (learn)

4 I'm a drummer in a band. (play)

5 He's running in a marathon next week. (train)

6 Peter's my oldest friend. (know)

7 Franco is Violetta's boyfriend. (go out)

8 It's our wedding anniversary today. (be married)

PRONUNCIATION

9 ▶ **81** Listen and check your answers to Exercise 8. Notice that in normal speech *have* is usually pronounced /əv/ and *has* is pronounced /əz/. Then listen again and practise saying the sentences.

10 Work in pairs. Take turns asking and answering your questions from Exercise 8.

Student A: reply using *for.*

Student B: reply using *since.*

11 Change partners. Ask each other the questions below. If your partner answers positively, ask a follow-up *How long ...?* question and continue the conversation.

A: *Do you belong to any clubs?*

B: *Yeah. I'm a member of a cycling club.*

A: *Really? How long have you been doing that?*

B: *For quite a while. Since I was about 20 or 21, I guess.*

A: *And how often do you all meet?*

• Do you belong to any clubs?
• Do you go to any classes outside school / work?
• What hobbies or interests do you have outside school / work?
• What languages do you know?
• Do you play any musical instruments?
• Who's your oldest friend?

G For further practice, see Exercise 2 on page 183.

SOUNDS AND VOCABULARY REVIEW

12 ▶ **82** Listen and repeat the sounds with /h/. Are any of them difficult to hear or say?

13 ▶ **83** Work in groups. Listen to eight sentences using the words below. Together, try to write them down. Then listen again and check.

behind	halfway	historical	horror
habit	happy	hobby	rehearse

14 Work in teams. You have three minutes to write collocations / phrases for the words in Exercise 13.

*the guy **behind** me,*

*get stuck **behind** a big truck,*

*stand **behind** me*

14

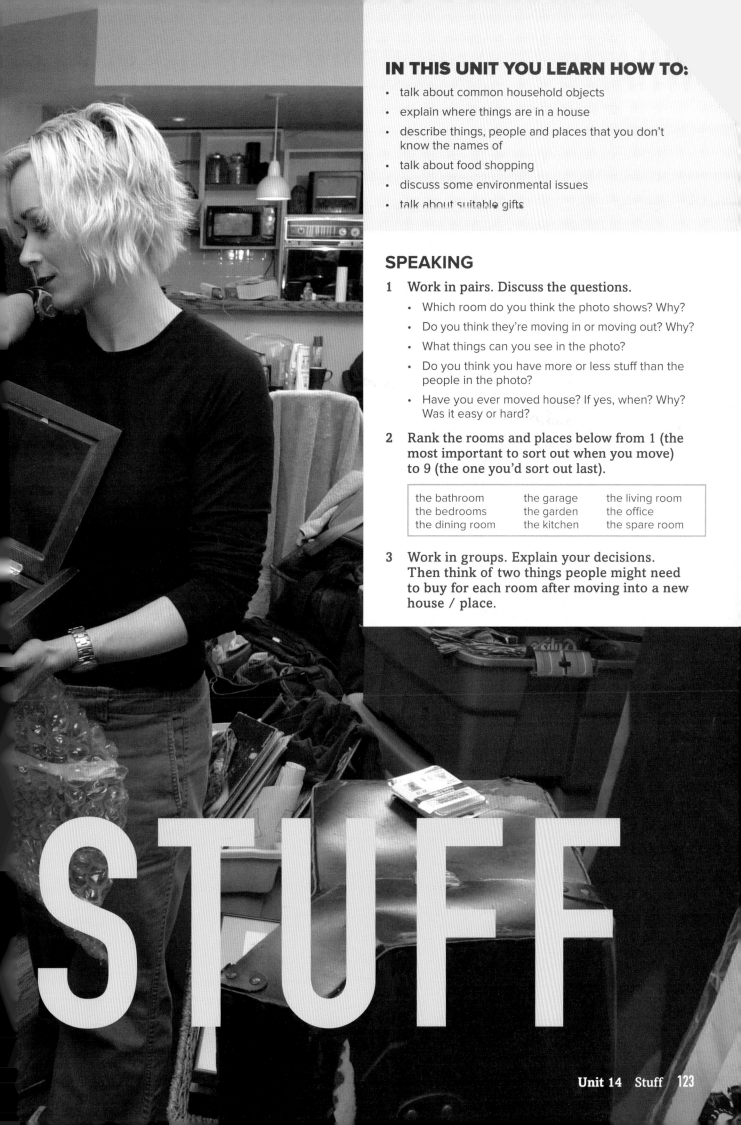

IN THIS UNIT YOU LEARN HOW TO:

- talk about common household objects
- explain where things are in a house
- describe things, people and places that you don't know the names of
- talk about food shopping
- discuss some environmental issues
- talk about suitable gifts

SPEAKING

1 Work in pairs. Discuss the questions.

- Which room do you think the photo shows? Why?
- Do you think they're moving in or moving out? Why?
- What things can you see in the photo?
- Do you think you have more or less stuff than the people in the photo?
- Have you ever moved house? If yes, when? Why? Was it easy or hard?

2 Rank the rooms and places below from 1 (the most important to sort out when you move) to 9 (the one you'd sort out last).

the bathroom	the garage	the living room
the bedrooms	the garden	the office
the dining room	the kitchen	the spare room

3 Work in groups. Explain your decisions. Then think of two things people might need to buy for each room after moving into a new house / place.

STUFF

LISTENING

1 ▶ 84 **Listen to three new flatmates planning a shopping trip. Decide which of the things in the picture they are going to buy – and what each of these things is called.**

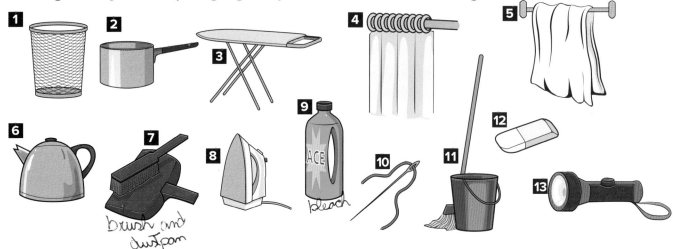

brush and dustpan

2 ▶ 84 **Listen again and complete the sentences with three words in each space. Contractions like *don't* count as one word.**

1 We'll have to give everything _____ and sort the place out.

2 Maybe we should go into town and _____ .

3 One minute. I'll get a pen and we can _____ .

4 When you use the brush, what _____ the thing that you use to get rubbish from the floor?

5 It's a kind of liquid that's really good _____ .

6 It's in the kitchen. In the cupboard _____ .

7 We should _____ for these things.

8 Oh yes, of course. A kettle! I _____ a kettle!

VOCABULARY Things in the house

3 **Which of these things can you see in the pictures?**

a bin	a hammer and nails	a pan	a stapler
a cloth	a mop and bucket ✓	a plaster	a torch
a desk	a needle and thread	a rubber	a towel

4 **Complete the sentences with words from Exercise 3.**

1 Have you got _____ I could borrow? I'd like to have a shower.

2 Have you got _____ ? I'd like to clean the table.

3 Have you got _____ ? I've just cut myself.

4 Have you got _____ ? I'll make us some soup.

5 Have you got _____ ? I need to go out into the garden and it's really dark out there.

6 Have you got _____ ? I need to put a button back on my shirt.

7 Have you got _____ ? I've spilt water everywhere.

8 Have you got _____ ? I need to join these bits of paper together.

5 **Work in pairs. Look again at the things in Exercise 3. Tell each other:**

• if there are any things you don't have.

• which things you use the most.

• if there are any things you never use.

• where exactly each of the things in the box are in your house.

DEVELOPING CONVERSATIONS

Explaining where things are

We often give two descriptions of where things are: one general, one more specific. Notice the prepositions used. For example:

*It's **in** the kitchen – **in** the cupboard **under** the sink.*

6 **Choose the correct prepositions.**

1 There's one at / *in* the bathroom *on* / at the shelf.

2 There's one *above* / down the sink in the kitchen.

3 There's one *on* / at the desk in my study.

4 There's one *at* / on the side – next to the sink.

5 There's one at / *in* the corner of the garage.

6 There's one *in* / at the cupboard down / *under* the stairs.

7 There's one *in* / at a drawer in the kitchen, the one up / *next* to the fridge.

8 There's one in the garage, in a box at / *by* the door.

7 **Work in pairs. Which things might be in the places in Exercise 6?**

A: *There could be a towel in the bathroom on the shelf.*

B: *Yes, or maybe different kinds of medicine.*

GRAMMAR Relative clauses

8 Work in pairs. How many of these things can you name? What do you call …

1 the thing in the kitchen that you can pull open and keep things like knives and forks in? *drawer*

2 something fixed to a wall which you put books and things like that on? *shelf*

3 the money which you borrow from a bank to buy a house or apartment? *mortgage* ✱

4 a person that lives next door to you, or upstairs or downstairs from you? *neighbour*

5 a man who owns the house or apartment that you rent? *landlord*

6 the place in the house where guests can stay or where you can store things? *balcony spare room*

7 the place near – or connected to – your house where you can keep your car? *garage*

8 the place just outside an upstairs window where you can stand? *spare room balcony*

9 Match the words in the box to the descriptions in Exercise 8.

balcony	garage	mortgage	shelf
drawer	landlord	neighbour	spare room

10 Work in pairs. Identify the relative clauses and pronouns in Exercise 8. Then complete the rules in the Grammar box.

We use relative clauses to add information about what a thing, person or place is / does. Relative clauses usually begin with a relative pronoun.

For things, we use _____ or _____ .

For people, we use _____ or _____ .

For places, we use _____ .

G Check your ideas on page 183 and do Exercise 1.

11 Complete the sentences with a relative pronoun.

1 An oven is a large piece of equipment *which or that* you use to heat and cook food in the kitchen.

2 A builder is a person *That / who* builds or repairs houses.

3 A building site is the place *where* a new building is constructed.

4 A deposit is the money *that* you pay when you start renting a place. You get it back when you leave.

5 A babysitter is a person *that* you pay to come to your house and look after your kids.

6 A shed is a wooden building in the garden *where that* you can store things.

7 A handle is the part of a door or a window *That / which* you use for opening it.

8 A lawn is an area of cut grass in the garden *where* kids can play.

9 A plumber is a person *that / who* installs or repairs pipes and things like showers, sinks and toilets.

12 Think of a thing, a job and a place that you don't know the words for in English, and write three *What do you call …?* questions. Then work in groups to ask and answer your questions.

G For further practice, see Exercise 2 on page 183.

CONVERSATION PRACTICE

13 Work in pairs. Imagine you are going on a picnic. You need to plan what to take.

Student A: look at File 9 on page 189.

Student B: look at File 16 on page 191.

Spend a few minutes thinking about how to describe each thing, using relative clauses.

14 Now roleplay a conversation with your partner. Take turns describing your objects.

▶ 26 To watch the video and do the activities, see the DVD-ROM.

WHAT A LOAD OF RUBBISH!

VOCABULARY Containers

1 Label the pictures of three families' shopping with the words in the box.

a bar of chocolate	a packet of biscuits
a box of cereal	a pot of yoghurt
a can of cola	a sack of rice
a carton of milk	a tin of tomatoes
a jar of honey	a tray of meat

2 Work in pairs. Decide if each container is usually made of metal, glass, plastic, cardboard or cloth.

3 Work in pairs. Discuss the questions.

- Which family do you think spends the most? 2
- Which family has the healthiest diet? 3
- Which family do you think causes the most damage to the environment? Why? 1
- How does your family's food shopping compare to these families'?

READING

4 Work in groups. Discuss the questions.

- Does your family shop at a supermarket? Which one? Why?
- What environmental issues are connected to shopping?

5 Read the article on page 127 about supermarket shopping and the environment. Find out four things you shouldn't buy. Explain why.

6 Discuss in pairs whether you think these sentences are true (T) or false (F).

1 100% efficiency is impossible. T
2 The writer lives in New Zealand. F
3 The writer doesn't recycle anything. F
4 Producing aluminium is very inefficient. T
5 Plastic bottles reduce transport costs. T
6 Tap water is better for the environment than bottled. T
7 The author eats a lot of meat. T
8 Eating a lot of cheese is bad for the environment. T
9 The sausages which were found were 30 years old. F

7 Work in groups. Discuss the questions.

- Based on what you read, what do you think the professor in the article would say to each of the families in Exercise 1?
- Do you do any of the things the professor suggests? Which ones?
- Is there anything in the article you don't believe? Why?
- Do you recycle any of the containers in Exercise 1?

8 Work in pairs. Read the fact file and discuss:

- if you find any of the facts surprising.
- what your country does to encourage recycling.

FACT FILE

- It's estimated it costs around $100 per tonne to dispose of rubbish and $1,000 a tonne to get rid of chemicals such as paint.
- Switzerland charges people for throwing away rubbish. People mustn't leave rubbish outside without a sticker on the bag to show they have paid.
- It recycles 50% of its waste and burns all the rest.
- Sweden heats 20% of its homes by burning rubbish.
- Estonia has the best record on rubbish in the EU. It wastes only 0.5kg per person per day.
- The airports in New York are built on top of rubbish.

126

RUBBISH FOOD

There are laws of nature that we can't ignore, like gravity and waste. We know what goes up must come down and, similarly, we can't avoid the fact that everything we produce and consume leads to waste. In the case of my supermarket shopping, there's loads of waste. Professor Liam Taylor, an expert on the environment, is trying to convince me I could waste less.

From my shopping basket, he picks up a polystyrene tray of six New Zealand kiwi fruits covered in clear plastic. 'These probably caused three tons of carbon dioxide by being flown twelve thousand miles. To make things worse, this kind of plastic is almost impossible to recycle. What's wrong with local apples?'

'Nothing', I weakly reply, 'I just prefer kiwis.'

'Hmm. Well, if you must have them, eat Italian ones – and buy them with no packaging.'

He looks at the bottles of water and cans of cola. Before he can say anything, I say, 'I'm always careful to recycle those.'

'Well, that's good, but the aluminium in those cans is bad. They have to mine four tonnes of rock to get one tonne of aluminium, and the transport costs of the cans and glass bottles are higher as they are heavier than plastic. Anyway, what's wrong with having tap water? It's much more efficient.'

'I … er … prefer … .' The professor's look stops me from finishing the sentence!

'If you must have soft drinks, buy them in recyclable plastic bottles and get the largest size, because they use less plastic than lots of small bottles. The same is true of those small boxes of cereal.'

The next problem is the amount of meat I've bought. He tells me the chicken is OK, but generally meat is bad for the environment. 'Firstly, cows and sheep produce a lot of natural gas which causes global warming. Secondly, they're an inefficient way to get food energy. Better to be vegetarian, especially if the vegetables are locally grown and you don't eat too many dairy products.'

I am becoming depressed as all my favourite things get crossed off my shopping list. 'What about those cakes?' I say. 'They were made in the supermarket bakery and the packaging is biodegradable, so they must be OK.'

He laughs. 'Well, I guess the cake is, but forget about biodegradable!' Apparently, a team of archaeologists recently investigated sites where rubbish had been buried. They found newspapers that were thirty years old, and which you could still read, next to perfectly preserved sausages!

I feel slightly sick and very, very guilty.

GLOSSARY

biodegradable: if something is biodegradable it means that it can be naturally changed by bacteria and can safely become part of earth or water.

GRAMMAR

must / mustn't

We use *must* to show something's essential, either because of a law or rule, or because we feel it's essential. *Mustn't* means it's essential not to do something. *Must* can also be used when we are guessing something is true. *Must* is often replaced by *have to*, but it's not always possible.

9 **Look at the extracts and decide if *must / mustn't* can be replaced by *have to / don't have to*.**

a *What goes up **must** come down.*

b *If you **must** have soft drinks, buy them in recyclable plastic bottles.*

c *The packaging is biodegradable, so they **must** be OK.*

d *People **mustn't** leave rubbish outside without a sticker on the bag.*

G Check your ideas on page 183 and do Exercise 1.

PRONUNCIATION

10 ▶ 85 **Listen to the examples of *must / mustn't* and notice how you often don't hear the final *t*. Then practise saying the sentences.**

11 **Complete the sentences with a form of *must* or *have to* and the verb in brackets. Sometimes both *must* and *have to* are possible.**

1 The new law means companies _____ waste by 10% in the next two years. (reduce)

2 You _____ chemicals down the sink. (pour)

3 You _____ annoyed you can't park your car at work now. How are you going to get here? (be)

4 We _____ to work or we won't finish everything. (get back)

5 I _____ to call Frank and tell him the meeting's cancelled. (remember)

6 You _____ to give me the key back. (forget)

7 Luckily, we _____ tax on rubbish, as I don't have much money. (pay)

8 If you _____ that stuff, can you go somewhere else. It smells disgusting. (eat)

12 **Write four laws to help improve the environment or reduce waste. Use *must / mustn't*. Work in groups to choose the best ideas.**

G For further practice, see Exercise 2 on page 184.

THANK YOU SO MUCH

SPEAKING

1 Work in groups. Discuss these questions.

- Can you think of a time you got a lot of presents? What did you get?
- Do you think people ever get too many presents? Why? / Why not?
- What was the last present you received? What was the occasion? Were you happy with it?
- What's the best present you've ever received / given? What was so good about it?
- Have you ever received any strange or bad presents? Who from? What was wrong with them?

LISTENING

2 ▶ 86 Listen to four people talking about presents they have received. Answer the questions for each speaker.

1 What presents did they get?

2 What was the occasion?

3 Were they happy with the presents when they got them?

3 Work in pairs. Take turns re-telling the whole stories using the words below.

1 loved the way / gave me clues / click the link

2 lived close / save loads / lose weight

3 kind of message / from then on / broke up

4 suddenly said / to be polite / blowing away

4 ▶ 86 Listen again. Did you miss anything from the stories?

5 Work in pairs. Discuss the questions.

- Which of the presents mentioned do you think is the best / worst? Why?
- What message do you think the third speaker's ex-boyfriend was sending her? Do you think she was right to break up? What would you do if something similar happened to you?

UNDERSTANDING VOCABULARY

Verbs with two objects

In the listening you heard *My big sister bought me my own website.* Some verbs, such as *buy*, can be followed by one or two objects.

*My big sister bought **a website.***

*My big sister bought **me a website.***

When there are two objects we usually say the person first and the thing second, but if we want to put the thing first, then the person is added in a phrase that begins with *for* or *to*.

*My big sister bought a website **for me.***

*She sent an email **to me** with the link in it.*

6 Complete the sentences with these pairs of words.

ask + a personal question	make + some tea
buy + a car	read + a story
cook + dinner	send + a card
lend + some money	tell + a secret

1 My parents don't give me presents any more – they just _send_ me _a card_ for my birthday.

2 Sorry about that. I couldn't talk earlier. I had to _read_ my kids _a story_ before they went to sleep.

3 I can't believe it! My dad has promised to _buy_ my brother _a car_ when he graduates! He doesn't even have a licence yet!

4 I'm going to _cook_ my flatmates _dinner_ tonight. I'm making a traditional dish from my country.

5 I've left my wallet at home. Can you _lend_ me _some money_? I'll pay you back tomorrow, I promise.

6 You must be exhausted. Come and sit down and I'll _make_ you _some tea_ – unless you'd prefer a coffee.

7 If I _tell_ you _a secret_, do you promise not to tell anyone else?

8 Do you mind if I _ask_ you _a personal question_? How much did you pay for it?

7 Work in pairs. Discuss the questions.

- Do you ever send cards / e-cards to people? Why?
- Do you ever cook dinner for people? When was the last time? What did you cook? What was it like?
- When was the last time someone cooked you dinner? What was it like?
- Have you ever lent someone some money? Did they pay you back?
- Who do you usually tell your secrets to? Why?

8 Complete the sentences. Add the words in brackets in the correct place.

1 We paid them so I expected something better. (a lot of money)

2 I sent presents for Christmas, but they haven't called. I wonder if they received them. (to all the family)

3 My husband made breakfast in bed on Valentine's Day. It's a shame he burnt the toast! (me)

4 My grandparents have been married for 40 years so we want to give them for their anniversary. (something special)

5 She cooked this amazing meal. Honestly, she should start her own restaurant. (for us)

6 It was a bit embarrassing because they brought some wine, but we don't drink! (us)

SPEAKING

9 Work in groups. Decide what is the best present to get in each of the situations below. Explain your ideas. Some of the expressions in the box may help.

> It depends *what they do / where they live / what kind of things they like*, etc. If ... then ...
>
> It's a safe choice.
>
> It's not very original.
>
> You want to get them something unusual like a ... .
>
> It's (not) the kind of thing a *teenager / elderly person,* etc. would *like / use / wear.*
>
> What would they do with it? Where would they put it?
>
> I think ... would be more appropriate.
>
> They can always take it back and change it.

1 It's your grandparents' golden wedding anniversary. They've been married for 50 years.

2 Your cousin turns thirteen next week and you want to buy her something special.

3 Some friends of yours – or of your family – have just had their first baby.

4 It's Valentine's Day next week and you want to get your boyfriend / girlfriend something romantic.

5 You've been invited to someone's house for dinner and you want to take something for them.

6 Someone where you work is retiring next month.

7 Some friends have moved into a new house and have invited you to a party there.

SOUNDS AND VOCABULARY REVIEW

10 ▶ 87 Listen and repeat the sounds with /e/, /ə/, /ɔː/ and /ɜː/. Are any of them difficult to hear or say?

11 ▶ 88 Work in groups. Listen to eight sentences using the words below. Together, try to write them down. Then listen again and check.

burn	chemical	environment	preserve
bury	drawer	present	store

12 Work in teams. You have three minutes to write collocations / phrases for the words in Exercise 11.

burn *my hand,*
burn *some rubbish,*
the dinner's **burnt**

VIDEO 7

OXFORD

1   **Look at the photo of Oxford. What do you know about this place? Think about:**
   - its location.
   - its history.
   - what it's famous for.
   - any literature / art / music that is connected to the city.

2   📹 **27 Watch the first part of the video (0.00–1.14). Decide if the sentences are true (T) or false (F).**
   1   Oxford is to the east of London.
   2   It was originally a place where farmers took their cows across the river.
   3   Oxford University is the oldest university in the English-speaking world.
   4   The university was founded in 1096.
   5   The university is made up of different colleges.
   6   The Harry Potter novels were written in Oxford.

3   📹 **27 Watch the second part of the video (1.15–end) and find out:**
   - how the author of *Alice In Wonderland* knew the girl that Alice was based on.
   - when the author used to tell kids the stories that became *Alice In Wonderland*.
   - two examples of how the *Alice* stories were possibly based on real people and places.
   - why The Eagle and Child pub was important.

4   **Choose the correct option. Then watch the whole video again and check your ideas.**
   1   Historians *know / have known* people *were teaching and studying / had taught and studied* here as far back as 1096.
   2   In recent years, the college building *has become / became* famous as a filming location.

3   He *took / was taking* them out on boat rides along the river and *told / had told* them many stories.
4   Dodgson *based / was based* the stories on situations, places and people that were familiar to the children.
5   The city *has also influenced / also influences* the writing of other great fantasy writers.
6   They *often met / were often meeting* at The Eagle and Child.

5   **Work in groups. Tell each other about:**
   a   other places you know that people visit because they're connected to books / films.
   b   any other famous universities you know about.
   c   what your home town / city is most famous for.
   d   any famous people from your home town / city.
   e   any films / TV series set in places you know well.

UNDERSTANDING FAST SPEECH

6   📹 **28 Read and listen to this extract from the video said at natural pace and then slowed down. To help you, groups of words are marked with / and pauses are marked //. Stressed sounds are in CAPITALS.**

   MANy beLIEVE the SHOP in the STOry / REPresents a SMALL SHOP / JUST aCROSS the ROAD from CHRISTchurch // In DODGson's TIME / the SHOPkeeper was an OLD WOman / with a SHEEP-like VOICE

7   **Now you have a go! Practise saying the extract at natural pace.**

REVIEW 7

1 Complete the text with one word in each space. Contractions like *don't* count as one word.

For the ¹_____ few weeks, they have ²_____ showing a series on TV ³_____ is all about the history ⁴_____ Africa. It ⁵_____ be good, because my son, ⁶_____ is never normally interested in that kind of thing, ⁷_____ watched every single episode. It's amazing! I've ⁸_____ known him to watch something so keenly. He keeps telling us we ⁹_____ watch anything else when it's on! We're not even ¹⁰_____ to suggest other things to watch! It's not open for discussion. This week, the show was about one of the cities ¹¹_____ white Europeans first landed – and what's happened to it ¹²_____ their arrival.

2 Complete the second sentence so that it has a similar meaning to the first sentence, using the word given. Do not change the word given. You must use between two and four words including the word given.

1 Things have become much more expensive over the last few months.

_____ has risen a lot over the last few months. **LIVING**

2 We got married ten years ago.

We _____ ten years now. **FOR**

3 The use of phones during the test is not permitted.

Remember: you _____ use your phones during the test. **TO**

4 I must remember to write and say thank you.

I _____ write and say thank you. **FORGET**

5 My brother has been reading lots of books about history recently.

My brother has started to develop _____ recently. **INTEREST**

6 I imagine you're quite hungry after all that travelling.

_____ quite hungry after all that travelling. **BE**

3 Choose the correct option.

1 I bought some amazing *leathers boots / boots leather / leather boots* in Mexico.

2 I've been going to Spanish classes *for / since / during* the start of the year.

3 We've *been knowing / known* each other for years. We went to school together.

4 That's the place *where / that* my dad used to work in.

5 *That / You / It* must be tired after such a long journey!

6 Be ambitious. You *don't have to / mustn't* be scared to dream big!

7 What do you call the place *where / that / which* you eat at school or in an office?

8 How many times have you *been seeing / seen / been seen* that movie now?

4 ▶ 89 Listen and write the six sentences you hear.

5 Write a sentence before or after the sentences you heard in Exercise 4 to create short dialogues.

6 Match the verbs (1–8) with the nouns they collocate with (a–h).

1	lend	a	the table
2	spill	b	a traditional dish
3	reach	c	a novel
4	promote	d	a personal question
5	read	e	the local culture
6	clean	f	money
7	ask	g	a crossroads
8	make	h	water all over the floor

7 Decide if these words and phrases are connected to films, things in the house, or music and art.

a carton	an exhibition	sculpture
a comedy	an explosion	special effects
a composer	a landscape	a stapler
costumes	a pan	a torch

8 Complete the sentences. Use the word in brackets to form a word that fits in the space.

1 It's a _____ drama set in England in the 12th century. (history)

2 I can't watch most horror movies. I find them too _____ . (scared)

3 It wasn't a bad film, but the ending was very _____ . (predict)

4 It's just a really _____ habit he's got. (annoy).

5 I don't read much _____ . I prefer novels and short stories. (poet)

6 Some really _____ works of art were stolen from the museum last night. (value)

9 Complete the text with one word in each space. The first letters are given.

We've recently moved house. To be honest, I found the whole process really ¹ti_____ . There was so much to do – and we had to buy a lot of new things as well. We needed a mop and ²b_____ so we could give the place a clean. The ³d_____ room was particularly dirty! Then my husband wanted to put up a big ⁴po_____ of his parents in the ⁵l_____ room, so we had to go and get a ⁶h_____ and nails to do that. Next, my son cut himself while he was playing, and we didn't have any ⁷pl_____, so it was another visit to the shops! Tonight I just want to stay in, watch a nice ⁸ro_____ comedy, eat my way through a ⁹p_____ of biscuits and relax!

15

IN THIS UNIT YOU LEARN HOW TO:

- talk about the economy
- use time phrases to say when things happen
- compare prices
- talk about money issues and problems
- say different kinds of numbers

SPEAKING

1 **Look at the photo. Discuss the questions:**

- Why do you think the illustration on this twenty-dollar bill was chosen?
- Do you know any other places or people that appear on American banknotes? If so, why do you think they were chosen?
- What illustrations are there on the banknotes in your country? Do you think they are a good choice? Why / Why not?
- Do you know of any other illustrations of different foreign notes?

2 **Work in groups. Imagine you are designing new banknotes. For each of the categories below, choose three illustrations. Explain your choices.**

- famous people
- buildings
- cultural images

MONEY

COST OF LIVING

VOCABULARY
The economy and quality of life

1 Work in pairs. Check you understand the situation in bold. Then think of one more consequence (good or bad) of each situation.

1 Our **currency is very strong**, so it's cheap for us to travel abroad.

2 Our **currency is really weak** at the moment. It's very expensive to import things from abroad.

3 A lot of people can't afford basic things because **the cost of living is very high**.

4 **Inflation is currently quite low**. Prices haven't changed much since last year.

5 **There's a lot of unemployment**. Around 25% of the working population don't have a job.

6 **Unemployment has fallen** a lot over the past year, so more people have work.

7 The **average salary is about $35,000 a year** there, so I can earn more than here.

2 Work in groups. Discuss the questions.

a How do the following things affect your quality of life?

- job security
- cost of living
- time off
- climate
- pace of life
- transport
- crime
- family

b Are there any other factors that you think are important for a good quality of life?

c Which things do you think are most important? Why?

LISTENING

3 ▶ 90 Listen to Aidan and Laima talking about life in Freedonia. Laima is on holiday there and Aidan works in a school. Find out:

1 what the quality of Aidan's life in Freedonia is like.

2 how well the economy is doing.

3 why he wants to leave.

4 ▶ 90 Listen again and choose the words you hear.

1 The economy's doing quite badly *at the / in this* moment.

2 I'm actually going back to Canada *in / for* a few months.

3 Unemployment has gone up quite a lot over the *last few months / rest of the month*.

4 I could get paid a lot more *back home / in Canada*.

5 Eating out is *twice / half* the price in my country.

6 That's true, but it used to be cheaper *in / at* the past.

7 Anyway, *in / at* the end, I miss my family and friends.

8 I don't mind the cold weather so much. You get used to it after a *time / while*.

5 Work in pairs. Discuss the questions.

- From what you heard, do you think Aidan is making the right decision? Why? / Why not?

- Apart from family and friends, what would you miss if you lived abroad – or, if you are living abroad at the moment, what do you miss?

GRAMMAR

Time phrases and tense

Some adverbs and time phrases are generally used with particular tenses. For example, *currently* usually goes with a present tense, especially the present continuous, whereas phrases starting with *since* more often go with the present perfect.

*Inflation **is currently** quite low. Prices **haven't changed** much **since last year**.*

*The economy **is currently doing** quite well.*

6 Look at the audio script for Track 90 on page 208 and find a sentence using each of the time phrases 1–6. Which tense or structure (a–d) is used with each time phrase?

1 in a few months
2 at the moment
3 over the last few months
4 in a years' time
5 in the past
6 over the last two years

a the present continuous
b the present perfect simple
c used to
d be going to / will

G Check your ideas on page 184 and do Exercise 1.

7 Complete the sentences with the correct form of the verbs (present continuous, present perfect, *be going to* or *used to*).

1 At the moment, the economy _____ quite well. (do)

2 Unemployment _____ over the last few months. (fall)

3 The cost of living _____ a lot in the last five years. (go up)

4 Eating out _____ a lot cheaper when I was a kid. (be)

5 There _____ an election in four months' time. (be)

6 The government _____ currently _____ popularity. (lose)

7 According to the government, inflation _____ over the next few months. (fall)

8 Crime _____ less of a problem when I was younger. (be)

9 Our currency _____ stronger at the moment. (get)

10 We _____ more job security in the past. (have)

8 Work in groups. Discuss which of the sentences in Exercise 7 are true for your country. Explain your ideas.

G For further practice, see Exercise 2 on page 184.

DEVELOPING CONVERSATIONS

Comparing prices

We often compare prices in different places and times:

*Eating out is **twice the price** in my country.*

*Milk is **much more expensive (now) than** it used to be.*

We often then give an example:

You can get a three-course meal for about $6 here. A meal back home costs $20.

You can't get a litre for less than a euro now. It used to be only 70 cents.

9 Complete sentences 1–4 with a word from the box and a price. Then write a similar follow-up sentence for 5–8.

can	laptop	packet	smartphone
kilo	litre	pair	suit

1 Clothes are much cheaper there than elsewhere. A designer _____ only costs _____ .

2 The crisps in here are four times more expensive than they are in the shops. A _____ here costs _____ .

3 Soft drinks there are twice the price they are here. You can't get a _____ for less than _____ .

4 Computers are much cheaper than they used to be. You can get a _____ now for _____ .

5 Petrol is a lot cheaper there. _____

6 Shoes are much more expensive there. _____

7 Electronic goods are much cheaper there. _____

8 Rice is much more expensive than it used to be. _____

10 Work in pairs. Take turns starting conversations and responding using the ideas from Exercise 9.

A: *Clothes are much cheaper there than elsewhere.*

B: *I know. A designer suit only costs about 1,200.*

11 Work in groups. Tell each other about very expensive / cheap places you know and give examples. Are there any things that have risen or fallen in price over the last few years?

CONVERSATION PRACTICE

12 You are going to roleplay conversations about life in different countries.

Student A: talk about the economy and quality of life in your own country.

Student B: read the role card in File 11 on page 190. Talk about the economy and quality of life in that country.

13 Now change roles.

Student A: read the role card in File 7 on page 189.

Student B: talk about your own country.

▶ 29 To watch the video and do the activities, see the DVD-ROM.

MY INHERITANCE

READING

1 Work in groups. You are going to read about a woman attending the reading of her father's will. A *will* is a legal document that says what should happen to a person's possessions after they die. Before you read, discuss these questions.

- Why do you think it important to have a will?
- What age do you think most people write their will?
- What are the most special or valuable things you have? Would you leave them to anyone in particular? Why? / Why not?
- Have you heard of any stories about wills in the news?

2 Read the story. Find out why the author was surprised.

3 Work in pairs. Discuss the questions.

1 Find the different sayings the author's parents had. What do you think they meant?

2 Based on what you read, what do you think the daughters enjoyed when they were growing up, and what do you think they complained about? Why?

3 How do you think the parents became rich?

4 Why do you think they didn't tell their daughters?

5 How do you think the daughters felt about it when they found out?

WILL POWER

None of us had any idea what was going to happen when we arrived at the lawyer's office. Dad had died two months earlier in his bed in the same two-bedroom house where we'd grown up. Apart from the house, we didn't expect Dad to leave anything of value. I mean, for years after my mum died, he'd gone to a neighbour's house to watch TV. I offered to buy him a TV once, but he just said, 'Never buy what you can borrow!' That was typical of him. I guess he liked his neighbour's company as well.

My mum had never worked and Dad was an insurance salesman. We assumed he wasn't successful because we were never bought toys and we wore second-hand clothes. We just thought he couldn't afford these things.

Dad used to find bits of wood and turn them into toy boats and dolls. Mum taught us to make and repair clothes, which we used to do together at night. They had funny little sayings that they'd repeat whenever we complained about things: 'Money's silver, but a needle and thread is gold!' 'Early to bed, early to rise, makes a man healthy, wealthy and wise'; 'Never buy what you can borrow, never throw away what you can repair.' We used to laugh at them, and sometimes invented our own silly sayings: 'A fool spends what the wise man saves'; 'A glass of water is worth all the tea in China.' We laughed, but having so little money was often annoying. I think we were the only family in our school without a TV; we never drank soft drinks, and sharing a room with two big sisters for sixteen years was difficult.

So we walked into the lawyer's office and sat down. We were serious, but not sad any more. Dad had had a good life. The lawyer started reading; I was hardly paying attention, really, but then the numbers seemed to continue without end. 'Wait, I'm sorry,' I said. 'How much did you say he had?' The lawyer smiled, 'Yes, I imagine it does need repeating. Two million, seven hundred and eighty-one thousand, six hundred and fifty three pounds and eighteen pence.'

> " We didn't know what to say! Nearly three million pounds! How? Why? We had so many questions, so many feelings. "

LISTENING

4 **▶ 91** Check you understand these sentences. Then listen to the rest of the story and decide if the sentences are true (T) or false (F).

1 Her father had won the money.
2 He bought shares in a company that doubled in value.
3 The daughters didn't receive all of the money.
4 She's still angry about the situation.
5 The money will help other people.
6 She's planning to spend the money on a holiday.

5 Work in pairs. Discuss the questions.

• How would you feel if you were in this situation?
• Do you agree that the parents did a fantastic thing? Would you do it? Why? / Why not?
• What would you do if you had a quarter of a million pounds now?

VOCABULARY Money verbs

6 Look at the story again and at the audio script for Track 91 on page 208. Find as many words as you can that are connected to money. Compare your ideas with a partner.

7 Complete the conversations with the correct form of the verbs in the box.

borrow	earn	invest	owe	win
buy	give	leave	save	worth

1 A: Sorry, can I _____ two euros? I don't have enough.
    B: Of course. Just take it. I _____ you three euros, anyway.

2 A: Why have you stopped going out so much?
    B: Well, I'm working more and I'm _____ for my university fees.

3 A: Hey, I've _____ ten euros on the lottery!
    B: Wow! Ten euros. What are you going to do with it? _____ it in shares? Buy a boat?
    A: There's no need to be sarcastic. I was going to _____ you a coffee actually, but maybe I won't now.

4 A: Would you like to _____ money to a children's charity each month?
    B: I'm sorry. I can't afford to. I don't _____ much in my job.
    A: It doesn't have to be much. Every little helps.
    B: I'm sorry. Not today. I'm in a hurry.

5 A: That's a nice painting. It looks quite old. Is it _____ much?
    B: I don't know. My granddad _____ it to me when he died. I don't know how valuable it is, but I'd never sell it.

8 Work in pairs. Answer the questions about the word *pay*.

1 What different ways can you **pay for** something?
2 What kinds of **bills** do people have to **pay**?
3 When do you have to **pay** a bank / someone **back**?
4 How and when do people **get paid**?
5 When do you have to **pay interest**?
6 Who do you **pay to do** something?
7 Where do people have to **pay attention**?
8 Say three things you might offer to **pay for**.

PRONUNCIATION

9 Work in pairs. How do you say these numbers from the story?

1 £2,000,000   5 £4.12
2 781,000   6 2.7
3 653   7 ¼
4 1965

10 **▶ 92** Listen and check your ideas.

11 **▶ 93** Listen and complete the sentences with the numbers you hear.

1 The minimum wage at that time was _____ an hour.
2 Inflation fell to _____ last month.
3 The government is going to invest _____ in schools.
4 _____ of the population own a car.
5 The new factory will create _____ jobs.
6 The house cost _____ .
7 We borrowed _____ from the bank.
8 We'll finally pay back the mortgage in _____ .

SPEAKING

12 Work in groups. Discuss the questions.

• What do you spend most of your money on? Are you any good at saving money?
• What are good things to invest money in? Have you ever invested in shares? Were they successful?
• In which jobs do you think people earn too much money? In which jobs do they earn too little? Why?
• Do you know anyone who's won any money? How?
• Have you ever lost money? How?
• Have you ever been left anything (e.g. in a will)? What?
• What charities have you given money to? What do they do?
• Does anyone owe you anything (money / a meal / a favour, etc.)? Why?

MONEY, MONEY, MONEY!

LISTENING

1 Work in groups. Discuss what money problems the people in these situations might have – and the best way of dealing with each problem.

   a a teenager living at home with parents

   b customers in a restaurant

   c young adults travelling cheaply round the world

   d a couple with two small kids

   e someone shopping in a second-hand / vintage store

   f someone unable to take money out of their bank account

2 ▶ 94 Listen to four conversations. Match each one to a situation in Exercise 1. Then work in pairs. Compare your ideas and discuss:

   • what problems were mentioned in each conversation.

   • how the problems were dealt with.

3 ▶ 94 Work in pairs. Complete the sentences with one word in each space. Then listen again and check.

Conversation 1

1 I'll get this. It's my _____ .

2 What's _____ ?

3 I've just realised I _____ my wallet in my other jacket.

Conversation 2

4 It's hard to find things like that in this _____ .

5 Look – there's a _____ here.

6 The best price I can _____ is 150.

Conversation 3

7 _____ have just gone up.

8 I haven't _____ to save much yet.

9 Maybe we can _____ some money from the bank.

Conversation 4

10 Your card was cancelled because of some _____ activity.

11 We _____ that your card was copied sometime last month.

12 Everything is covered by your _____ .

4 Work in groups. Discuss the questions.

   • Have you ever had any similar problems to the ones you heard about? If yes, when? What happened?

   • Which problem do you think was the most serious?

   • Who do you think should pay on dates: the man, the woman or both? Why?

   • Do you like vintage clothes? Why? / Why not?

   • Are you good at negotiating good prices in markets?

   • How much money do you think parents should give their children? Until what age?

   • Have you heard any stories about credit cards being copied – or about any similar crimes?

GRAMMAR

Time clauses

We start time clauses with words like *when, as soon as, before, after* and *until*.

5 Look at these sentences from the listening. Then work in pairs. Discuss the questions below.

   a *I'll pay you back **as soon as** I get paid.*

   b *You can pay half back **when** you have the money, OK?*

   c *You'll receive your new PIN number **after** you get the card.*

   1 What's the whole time clause in each sentence?

   2 Do the time clauses refer to the past, the present or the future?

   3 In what tense is the verb in each time clause?

   4 What tenses / structures are used in the main clause of each sentence?

G Check your ideas on page 184 and do Exercise 1.

6 Choose the correct option.

   1 I'm going to try and find a part-time job when *I'm / I'll be* at university.

   2 What *do you do / are you going to do* after you graduate?

   3 Call me as soon as you *arrive / will arrive*, OK?

   4 *I'm going to move / I move* back home before the recession here gets worse.

   5 You'll just have to save until *you have / you'll have* enough money!

   6 The software is really good. It'll really speed things up, but it might take some time before *you get / you'll get* used to using it.

   7 *I'll pay / I pay* you back when I get paid, OK?

   8 Can you two please finish arguing about the bill after *I leave / I'll leave*?

   9 *We'll support / We support* you until you graduate. After that, though, you'll have to start looking after yourself!

   10 I'm waiting for confirmation of the dates, but *I call / I'll call* you as soon as I hear anything.

7 Complete the sentences below using your own ideas. Then work with a partner and compare what you have written. Explain your ideas.

   1 When I get home today, I'm going to …

   2 As soon as I have enough money, I'm going to …

   3 After this course ends, I'll probably …

   4 Before I get too old, I'd really like to …

   5 I'm going to carry on studying English until …

 **G** For further practice, see Exercise 2 on page 184.

VOCABULARY Dealing with banks

8 Complete each pair of collocations with one verb from the box.

cancel	charge	open	take out
change	make	pay	transfer

1 ~ a savings account / ~ a joint account with my partner

2 ~ a mortgage / ~ a loan

3 ~ a complaint / ~ a payment

4 ~ some money / ~ my PIN number

5 ~ £1,000 from my current account to my savings account / ~ money to my son in Thailand

6 ~ money into my account / ~ bills by direct debit

7 ~ my credit card / ~ a cheque

8 ~ 5% interest / ~ me 30 euros

9 Spend two minutes memorising the collocations in Exercise 8. Then work in pairs and take turns to test each other.

Student A: read out each verb in the box.

Student B: close your book. Try to say the pair of collocations for each verb.

Then change roles.

10 Work in pairs. Discuss the questions.

1 When might you want to open a joint account?

2 Can you think of three reasons why people might take out a loan?

3 Can you think of three reasons why people might make a complaint to a bank manager?

4 Why might someone decide to change their PIN number?

5 Why might someone need to cancel their credit card?

6 Why might someone need to cancel a cheque?

SPEAKING

11 Work in pairs. Choose two of the following situations to roleplay. Decide which roles you are going to play. Spend a few minutes planning what to say. Use the audio script on page 208 to help you. Then roleplay the conversations.

1 Two friends are having lunch in a café. They try to decide how they are going to pay. One person realises he doesn't have any money. They work out what to do about it.

2 One person wants to buy a second-hand car. The seller asks a very high price. The buyer tries to negotiate a better price. The buyer points out problems with the car. They try to reach a deal.

3 A teenager wants her dad to buy her a new laptop. The father is worried about how much it will cost and how he will pay for it. He suggests alternative ideas. They try to reach a deal.

4 A customer is phoning a bank to find out why their credit card was rejected in a shop. The bank employee explains the situation and tells the customer what will happen next.

SOUNDS AND VOCABULARY REVIEW

12 ▶ 95 Listen and repeat the sounds with /ɪ/, /ɔɪ/, /ə/ and /əʊ/. Are any of them difficult to hear or say?

13 ▶ 96 Work in groups. Listen to eight sentences using the words below. Together, try to write them down. Then listen again and check.

average	currency	joint	owe
borrow	election	mortgage	unemployment

14 Work in teams. You have three minutes to write collocations / phrases for the words in Exercise 13.

*the **average** salary, the **average** age, increase the* ***average***

16

EVENTS

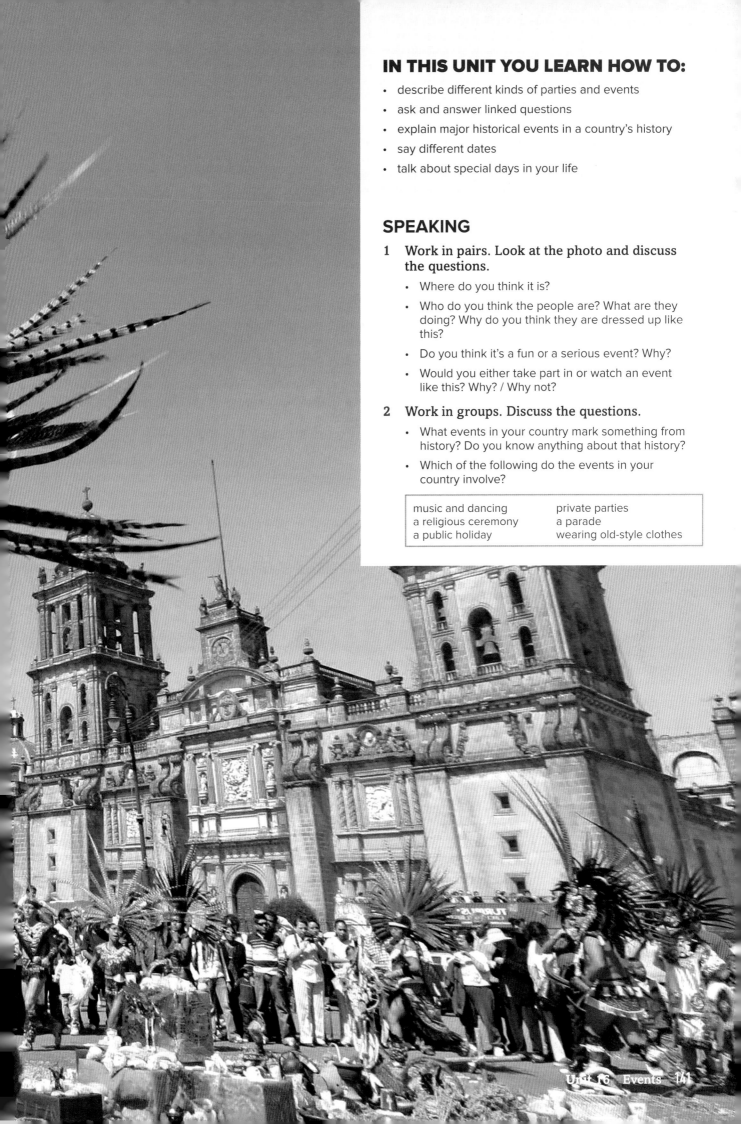

IN THIS UNIT YOU LEARN HOW TO:

- describe different kinds of parties and events
- ask and answer linked questions
- explain major historical events in a country's history
- say different dates
- talk about special days in your life

SPEAKING

1   **Work in pairs. Look at the photo and discuss the questions.**

- Where do you think it is?
- Who do you think the people are? What are they doing? Why do you think they are dressed up like this?
- Do you think it's a fun or a serious event? Why?
- Would you either take part in or watch an event like this? Why? / Why not?

2   **Work in groups. Discuss the questions.**

- What events in your country mark something from history? Do you know anything about that history?
- Which of the following do the events in your country involve?

music and dancing	private parties
a religious ceremony	a parade
a public holiday	wearing old-style clothes

HAVE A FEW FRIENDS ROUND!

VOCABULARY
Describing parties and events

1   **Complete the sentences about different kinds of parties with these words.**

| friends round | launch | surprise |
| housewarming | leaving party | wedding reception |

1   We've just moved to a new flat and we're having a _____ next week.

2   It's my last day in the office tomorrow and my colleagues have organised a _____ after work.

3   My brother's getting married in the summer and they've decided to have the _____ on a boat.

4   We've set up a new website and we've organised a big party to _____ it.

5   It was my birthday and I had a few _____ for dinner.

6   We're having a party for Keira on Friday, but don't tell her. It's supposed to be a _____ .

2   **Work in pairs. Tell each other as much as you can about the different kinds of parties:**

•   you have held.

•   you have been invited to.

3   **Match each question (1–5) to two answers (a–j). Check you understand the words in bold.**

1   What was the party like?

2   What was the place like?

3   What was the food like?

4   What was the music like?

5   What were the people like?

a   Everyone was great – really **warm and friendly**.

b   It was nice – not too loud. Just good **background music.**

c   It was fantastic. It's an amazing **venue** for a party.

d   A bit **cold** and **distant**, to be honest. No-one was really **mixing**.

e   It was nice. They had a **buffet** and everyone **helped themselves**.

f   Well, the first DJ was great, but the second guy completely **cleared the dance floor**.

g   It was great. I thought the organisation of the whole **event** was very **impressive**. They did a brilliant job.

h   It was great to begin with, but then there was a big argument and that **ruined** the rest of the evening.

i   Oh, it was OK. They just put a few **bowls of olives** and crisps and things on the tables for people **to pick at**.

j   It used to be a factory, but they **converted** it **into** an events venue a few years ago.

4   **Work in pairs. Think of one more way of answering each of the questions in Exercise 3.**

LISTENING

5   **▶ 97 Listen to three conversations about parties. Answer the questions for each conversation.**

1   What kind of party was it?

2   Whose party was it?

3   Where was it?

4   What was it like?

6 ▶ **97** In which conversations did you hear each of the adjectives below? Can you remember what each adjective described? Work in pairs and compare your ideas. Then listen again and check your answers.

easy to talk to	grilled	modern
full	impressive	spicy
gorgeous	lovely	typical

7 Work in pairs. Discuss the questions.

- What's the best kind of wedding reception to have? Why? How much do you think it's right to spend?
- Are there are any converted buildings in your area / town? Would they be good places to live / have a party?
- What different things might ruin a party?
- Do you prefer having friends round for dinner or eating out? Why?

DEVELOPING CONVERSATIONS

Linked questions

People often ask two questions together. A general *Wh-*question followed by a more specific *yes / no* question.

A: So *what did you do last night? Anything interesting?*

B: *Yeah, I had a little dinner party at my place.*

A: So *how did it go? Was it good?*

B: *Yeah, it was lovely. It was really nice to see everyone.*

8 Match the general questions (1–8) with the connected questions (a–h).

1 How was Michelle?
2 What was the weather like?
3 What time did the party go on till?
4 How did you feel when you found out?
5 Where did you have the party?
6 Who was there?
7 What's their new house like?
8 How was the launch party?

a Was it a bit of a shock?
b Anywhere nice?
c Was it late?
d Did everything go according to plan?
e Was she OK?
f Was it nice and hot?
g Is it big?
h Anyone I know?

9 Work in pairs. Take turns asking the questions in Exercise 8.

Student A: give positive answers.

Student B: give negative answers.

Continue each dialogue for one or two lines.

A: *How was Michelle? Was she OK?*

B: *Yeah, she was great. It was really good to see her again.*

A: *What's she doing at the moment?*

B: *What was the weather like? Was it nice and hot?*

A: *No, unfortunately. It was quite cold.*

B: *Oh dear. What a shame.*

CONVERSATION PRACTICE

10 You are going to have conversations about parties you have been to. First, think of three parties or celebrations you have been to in the last five years – or invent three. Think about the following questions:

- What kind of parties were they?
- What was the occasion for each?
- Where were they?
- What was the place like?
- Was there any food / music? If yes, what was it like?
- What were the other guests like?
- What time did the party go on till?

11 Imagine the parties / celebrations happened last night. Have conversations with other students. Start like this:

A: *So what did you do last night? Anything interesting?*

B: *Yeah, I did, actually. I went to …*

📹 **30 To watch the video and do the activities, see the DVD-ROM.**

A BRIEF HISTORY

VOCABULARY Historical events

1 Complete the fact file about Britain with the words in the box.

became	join	ruled	was killed
invaded	lasted	was established	won

FACT FILE: BRITAIN

London ¹_____ **by** the Romans around 2,000 years ago when they occupied Britain.

The Viking people from northern Europe first ²_____ Britain in 786. They eventually **occupied** half the country.

There was **a civil war** from 1642 to 1648 between Royalists (who supported the king, Charles I) and Parliament. Supporters of Parliament ³_____ **the war**, so in January 1649 **the king** ⁴_____ and England became a republic. **The republic** ⁵_____ **for** eleven years, until Charles II was made king.

Between the 16th and 20th centuries, Britain **established a huge empire** and at one stage it ⁶_____ **in** over a hundred countries, covering a quarter of the world. The United States **was once ruled by** Britain, but it ⁷_____ **independent** in 1776.

Britain was one of the countries that established the United Nations in 1945, but it didn't ⁸_____ **the European Union** (or EEC as it was then called) until 1973.

2 Work in pairs. How many of the words and phrases in bold in the fact file can you use to talk about cities and countries you know?

READING

3 You are going to read an article from a series called *Around the world in 300 words*. Read the introduction and discuss the questions in pairs.

1 Do you know anything about the country? What?

2 Why do you think people in the UK don't know much about it?

4 Read the rest of the article and answer the questions.

1 How long have people lived in Kazakhstan?

2 How has the Kazakh lifestyle changed?

3 When did the country finally become independent?

4 What's the main industry?

5 What's the most interesting information for you?

6 If you know about the country, is there anything important that isn't mentioned? Would you change anything in the text?

5 Work in pairs. Look at the prepositions in bold in the article. Underline the words that go with the prepositions. Then change the words before or after the preposition and write a new sentence.

People <u>have lived in the region</u> **since** the Stone Age.

Inequality has existed since the Stone Age. / People have lived in the region since **the 5th Century.**

GRAMMAR

Articles

There is no single clear rule for using articles (*a / an* and *the*). As a guide, we use *the* to show we think it's obvious which thing(s) we mean – there's nothing else it / they can be. We use *a / an* to show a thing could be one of several examples, and it's not important at this stage exactly which it is.

6 Work in pairs. Look at the sentences from the article. Explain why each article in bold is used.

1 *It's **the** ninth largest country in the world.*

2 *It's **an** exporter of many other natural resources.*

3 *They share **a** border.*

4 *Islam was introduced by **the** Arabs in **the** eighth century.*

5 *Kazakhstan became part of **the** Soviet Union.*

6 ***The** only thing they can say is we played them at football.*

G Check your ideas on page 185 and do Exercise 1.

7 Choose the correct option.

1 ***The / A* best day of my life was** *the / a* **day** I got married.

2 ***The / A* day I will never forget is** when I met President Putin.

3 **I've never seen** *a / the* whale in the wild, but I'd love to.

4 **I'd love to go to** *a / the* United Sates and see *a / the* Grand Canyon one day.

5 **I'm glad to say, I've never** broken *a / the* bone.

6 *The / A* left-wing party **won** *the / a* **last election** here. *The / A* party's leader is quite young.

8 Work in pairs. Take turns to say true sentences using the chunks in bold in Exercise 7.

G For further practice, see Exercise 2 on page 185.

SPEAKING

9 Work in groups. Discuss what should go in *Around the world in 300 words* for your country. Think about the following.

• What are the most important events?

• What places would you mention? Why?

• What would go under the headings *Place to visit, Big building, Special day* and *Firsts*?

AROUND THE WORLD IN 300 WORDS ...
KAZAKHSTAN

Ask most people on the streets of the UK what they know about Kazakhstan and the only thing they can say is 'We played them at football.' Ask where it is, and they may mention it's near Russia, but that's all. Yet Kazakhstan is huge – the ninth largest country in the world and the size of Western Europe. We think it's time people got to know it better. Oh, and yes, it is near Russia – they share a border and it's 6,846 kilometres long!

People have lived in the region **since** the Stone Age. The society was nomadic – different groups moved across the land to find grass and water for their animals, and places to grow food for the season. The name of Kazakhstan comes **from** a word meaning 'free spirit'.

However, some cities such as Talaz were established 2,000 years ago as part of the Silk Road trade route that went through the region.

Two key events had an important influence on the region: Islam was introduced **by** the Arabs in the eighth century, and Genghis Khan's Mongol army invaded in 1219. **Over** the next 200 years, the unique Kazakh language, culture and economy developed, based on nomadic life.

However, this traditional lifestyle changed **during** the 1800s, when the country was occupied by Russia. The population grew rapidly and there were political and economic problems. This resulted in food shortages and eventually led **to** fighting and a civil war in 1916.

In 1920, Kazakhstan became part **of** the Soviet Union. Over the following decade, the last Kazakh nomads were forced to live on farms or work in industry. Other people within the Soviet Union, including Germans, Ukrainians and Koreans, were sent to work there.

After Kazakhstan became independent on 16 December 1991, its economy grew rapidly. It's now the 11th largest producer of oil and gas in the world, as well as an exporter of many other natural resources.

A Kazakh family in their traditional yurt, a type of tent

The Pyramid of Peace cultural centre in Astana

POPULATION: 16.4 million

CAPITAL: Astana (changed from Almaty in 1997)

PLACE TO VISIT: The Charyn Canyon

BIG BUILDING: The Pyramid of Peace, Astana. The cultural centre aims to bring together all the great religions.

SPECIAL DAY: 22nd March. *Nauriz* celebrates Spring, friendship and unity. It was banned when the Soviets ruled.

FIRSTS: Humans here were the first to ride and use horses. The oldest rocket launch site in the world is Baikonur Cosmodrome. Russia rents the site for its space programme.

Next week KENYA

A DAY I'LL NEVER FORGET

SPEAKING

1 Work in groups. Discuss the questions.

1 When is your birthday? How do you usually celebrate?

2 When is the last day of term / of your English course?

3 When is the next public holiday? Do you have any plans for it?

4 Can you think of a date you always remember for personal reasons?

5 Can you think of a date with national or global significance?

LISTENING

2 ▶ 98 Listen and take notes on what day each person mentions – and why each day is special.

3 ▶ 98 Work in pairs. There are three words missing in each sentence. Can you remember what they are? Listen again and check your ideas.

1 a She fought for women's rights and _____ .

 b There's still some _____ , sure, but it's important to remember her life.

2 a My great-grandmother on _____ was Ukrainian.

 b I felt _____ with the place.

3 a It's _____ the day Michael Jackson died.

 b His death in 2009 was _____ .

4 a I climbed Mount Kinabalu in Malaysia, one of the highest mountains _____ .

 b We _____ just as the sun was coming up.

5 a It's the anniversary of the day that my _____ .

 b Amazingly, it worked, and _____ surgeon, I can now see my two kids.

4 Work in pairs. Discuss the questions.

• Which of the five days mentioned do you think is the most / least special? Why?

• Who do you think are the most important women from your country? Why?

• Do you know where your mother's and father's sides of the family come from originally?

• Can you remember where you were when you heard about the death of someone famous?

GRAMMAR

Verb patterns (*-ing* or infinitive with *to*)

When two verbs are used together, the second verb often takes the *-ing* form or the infinitive with *to*. The choice of form depends on the first verb. There are no rules for this. You just have to learn the patterns.

5 Work in pairs. Look at these verbs from this book. Which can be followed by the *-ing* form? Which can be followed by the infinitive with *to*?

agree	consider	finish	offer	promise
arrange	decide	hope	plan	recommend
avoid	enjoy	mind	practise	refuse
can't stand	fail	miss		

G Check your ideas on page 185 and do Exercise 1.

6 Complete these sentences with the correct form of the verbs from the box. Then look at the audio script for Track 98 on page 210 to check your answers.

be	buy	change	go	have	travel

1 She set up the country's first all-girls school and really helped _____ the country for the better.

2 My mum and I decided _____ on a trip to the village that she came from.

3 I really wanted _____ there, but I just couldn't afford _____ a ticket.

4 When I was 23 or 24, I spent six months _____ round South East Asia.

5 I agreed _____ this special new operation.

Some verbs can be followed by either the *-ing* form or the infinitive (with *to)* without any real change in meaning. There is also a small number of verbs that can be followed by both forms, but with these verbs there is a change in meaning when the *-ing* form or the infinitive (with *to)* is used after them.

7   For each pair of sentences, decide if the meaning of the words in italics is basically the same or different. If it's different, say why.

1   a   I *love going* for long walks in the countryside. I find it really relaxing.

    b   I *love to go* for long walks in the countryside. It helps me deal with stress.

2   a   I still *remember phoning* my dad and telling him I didn't want to go to university.

    b   It's her birthday today. I must *remember to phone* her later.

3   a   It *started raining* about halfway through the match.

    b   As we drove south along the motorway, it *started to rain* more.

4   a   I *stopped buying* their products when I found out how they're made.

    b   Sorry I'm late. I *stopped to buy* some food on the way.

5   a   I *hate exercising*, but I really need to lose some weight and get fit again!

    b   I really *hate to exercise*, but I love how it makes me feel afterwards.

8   Choose one of the following to talk about. Spend a few minutes preparing what you want to say. Then share your thoughts and feelings in groups.

• something you'll always remember seeing or doing
• something important you decided to do
• something you're hoping to do in the future
• something you really enjoy doing
• something important that you failed to do
• something you usually avoid doing if you can.

G   For further practice, see Exercise 2 on on page 185.

SPEAKING

9   Think of a special day that you have good memories of. Think about these questions.

• Where were you?
• Who were you with?
• What happened?
• How did you feel?
• Why was the day so special?

10   Work in groups. Tell each other about your special day. Who do you think had the most special experience? Why?

SOUNDS AND VOCABULARY REVIEW

11   ▶ 99 Lots of words contain consonant clusters (two or three consonants with no vowel sound between them). Listen and repeat the sounds you hear. Are any of them difficult to hear or say?

12   ▶ 100 Work in groups. Listen to eight sentences using the words below. Together, try to write them down. Then listen again and check.

background	discrimination	friend	spicy
clear	establish	impressive	traditional

13   Work in teams. You have three minutes to write collocations / phrases for the words in Exercise 12.

background music, from a poor background, from a rich background

VIDEO 8

COLUMBUS AND THE NEW WORLD

1 **Work in groups. Look at the monuments to Christopher Columbus. Discuss these questions.**

- Which of the monuments do you like best / least? Why?

- Why do you think there are so many monuments round the world to Columbus?

- Do you know any other places that have a Columbus monument? Which people are there lots of monuments to in your country? Why?

- How much do you know about the life of Christopher Columbus?

- How do you think each of the words below might be connected to his life?

spices	a new continent	parrots
a new route	Indians	the high point
three ships	Native Americans	disappointed
a month	gold	the Vikings

2 📹 **31** **Watch the video. Find out how the words in the box in Exercise 1 are connected to Columbus. Then work in pairs. Compare what you understood.**

3 📹 **31** **Watch the video again. Decide if the sentences are true (T) or false (F).**

1 By the 1400s, everyone had realised the world wasn't flat – it was round.

2 Columbus wasn't able to fund his voyage himself.

3 Columbus and his sailors almost gave up hope of finding land.

4 Columbus first landed in the country that is now known as El Salvador.

5 Columbus was confused about where exactly he was.

6 He never returned to the Americas.

7 Columbus didn't feel that his voyage had been a success.

8 Columbus died less than a decade after he set foot in the Americas.

4 **Choose the correct options to complete the sentences from the video.**

1 When he was a young man, he decided *studying / to study* geography.

2 Columbus wanted *finding / to find* a sea route from Europe to Asia.

3 He now knew that *the / an* earth was round.

4 Columbus persuaded King Ferdinand and Queen Isabella of Spain *giving / to give* him money.

5 After *the / a* month at sea, the sailors were very tired.

6 It was *the / a* small island in *the / a* Bahamas, probably *an / the* island known today as San Salvador.

7 People believed Columbus was *the / a* first European to reach America.

8 Columbus made 1492 one of *the / a* most important years in world history.

5 **Choose one of the following topics to talk about. Spend a few minutes preparing what you want to say. Then work in groups and share your ideas.**

- another famous journey – or famous explorer

- a historical figure who divides public opinion

- good and bad reasons why 1492 is so important

- a foreigner who's had a big impact on your country

- the advantages of studying geography or history

UNDERSTANDING FAST SPEECH

6 📹 **32** **Read and listen to this extract from the video said at natural pace and then slowed down. To help you, groups of words are marked with / and pauses are marked //. Stressed sounds are in CAPITALS.**

HOWever / ONE THING is CERtain // on ocTOber TWELFTH / FOURteen NINEty-TWO / the NEW WORLD / AND the OLD / CHANged for ALL TIME

7 **Now you have a go! Practise saying the extract at natural pace.**

REVIEW 8

1 Complete the text with one word in each space.

I ¹_____ to really enjoy playing computer games ²_____ I was younger. Obviously, games ³_____ the past were quite basic compared to what's available now. I mean, I remember ⁴_____ excited by one of ⁵_____ early online multi-player games. It was ⁶_____ war game – you had to kill your enemies – but it was really simple! One year, I ⁷_____ it almost every day – hour after hour! It's strange to think about, because these days I can't ⁸_____ playing computer games – probably because I have to use computers so much at work. When I ⁹_____ home, I don't usually want to do much: have a bath, maybe; read ¹⁰_____ book – just nothing involving technology!

2 Complete the second sentence so that it has a similar meaning to the first sentence, using the word given. Do not change the word given. You must use between two and four words including the word given.

1 I went swimming every day after school when I was a kid.

I _____ every day after school when I was a kid. **GO**

2 I don't want to say anything yet because I want to discuss things with my partner.

I don't want to say anything _____ things with my partner. **UNTIL**

3 Remind me to call my daughter later.

I _____ my daughter later. **REMEMBER**

4 The cost of living is lower than it was last year.

The cost of living _____ last year. **HAS**

5 Unemployment is higher than it was a couple of months ago – and it's going to get worse.

Unemployment is _____ . **MOMENT**

3 Choose the correct option.

1 I considered *take / to take / taking* the job, but in the end, I decided *wait / to wait / waiting*.

2 Inflation *falls / is falling / has fallen* quite a lot over the last few months.

3 I *go / have been / 'm going* to Morocco in two weeks' time.

4 My daughter really wants *to get / getting / get* a pet. She loves *a cat / cats / the cats*.

5 *I'll phone / I phone* you as soon as I *will have / have* more information.

6 Can you two please just stop *talking / talk / to talk* and pay *attention / an attention*!

7 I used to go there all the time *when I was a kid / the other week / at the moment*.

8 I don't have much money. I'm *a student / student*. It's hard to pay *bills / the bills*!

4 ▶ **101** Listen and write the six sentences you hear.

5 Write a sentence before and after the sentences from Exercise 4 to create short dialogues.

6 Match the verbs (1–8) with the nouns they collocate with (a–h).

1 open		a	the European Union
2 occupy		b	the dance floor
3 borrow		c	the minimum wage
4 join		d	a leaving party
5 earn		e	a war
6 win		f	an account
7 organise		g	a country
8 clear		h	money

7 Decide if the language in the box is connected to banks, historical events or parties.

an amazing venue	cold and distant
become independent	an empire
a buffet	establish a city
cancel my card	a housewarming
charge interest	a mortgage
a civil war	a republic

8 Complete the sentences with the best prepositions.

1 It used to be a church, but it was converted _____ flats a few years ago.

2 He made a lot of money by investing _____ property.

3 It was lovely. They had the wedding reception _____ a boat.

4 I pay all my monthly bills _____ direct debit.

5 She's really pleased because she won 100 euros _____ the lottery.

6 I had a few friends _____ for dinner on Friday, which was nice.

7 Hi there. I'd like to pay this cheque _____ my account, please.

8 I need to transfer £500 _____ my current account _____ my son in Peru.

9 Complete the text with one word in each space. The first letters are given.

Along with two of my friends, I've recently ¹s_____ up a company and we're thinking of organising a big party to ²la_____ it. The problem is, though, the ³ec_____ isn't doing very well at the moment and there's a lot of ⁴un_____ , so lots of people can't ⁵a_____ even basic things like food and rent. Even if people are working, there's less job ⁶se_____ than there used to be – and ⁷av_____ salaries are lower too. Because of all that, we don't want to spend too much on a party. It would be wrong! Instead, we'll have something small and friendly: nice ⁸ba_____ music, maybe a buffet, you know.

1 WRITING Organising ideas

SPEAKING

1   Think of the two best jobs you could have and the two worst jobs. Then work in groups. Compare your choices and explain your ideas. Try to agree on the two best and two worst jobs.

VOCABULARY Talking about jobs

2   Complete the sentences with the words in the box.

brilliant	lonely	satisfying	tiring
boring	part-time	technical	well-paid

1   My job's very _____ . I work very long hours and I work shifts, too.

2   My job's very _____ . The money's good.

3   My job's _____ ! I meet lots of people, the hours are good and I make very good money too.

4   My job's a bit _____ . I only make appointments – and coffee!

5   My job's very _____ . I sort out problems and help a lot of people.

6   My job's quite _____ . I install computer systems.

7   My job can be quite _____ sometimes. I don't mind the travelling, but I don't see my family very often.

8   I'm studying Design at college, so I can only do a _____ job.

3   Work in pairs and compare your answers. Do you know anyone with jobs like those described?

WRITING

4   You are going to read a text by Marta, describing how she feels about her job. First, work in pairs. Look at the photo of Marta and discuss how you think she might feel about her job, and why.

5   Check that you understand the five words in bold in Marta's text below. Then read the whole text and answer the questions.

- Did she mention any of the problems you thought of?
- What other problems does she mention? What reasons does she give for her feelings?

My job

Most people think my job's very interesting, but I don't really like it very much. Why? ¹_____ work on my own most of the time. It's a lonely job, because I don't have much contact with other people. ²_____ so much **pressure** in my job that I can never **relax** and ³_____ , because I often have to work very long hours to finish an **experiment**.

⁴_____ always get **impatient** if experiments take too long, so it's very **stressful**, and ⁵_____ , I really hate sitting in one place all day long. I'd really like a job where I could move about more and get a bit of exercise and a job that's a bit easier.

6 Complete the text with these expressions.

Thirdly, my bosses   what's more, it's tiring

finally,   Secondly, there's

Firstly, I have to

KEY WORDS FOR WRITING

Sequencers

To add ideas when you write an essay, use these sequencers (adverbs of sequence): *firstly* (for the first idea), *secondly* (for the second idea), *thirdly* (for the third idea), etc., and *finally* for the last idea.

You can also use *what´s more* and *in addition* to add ideas.

Sequencers are followed by a comma and then a clause.

Firstly, *I have to work on my own most of the time.*

7 Look at the photo of Luc. Work in pairs. Discuss how he feels about his job – and think of four reasons why he might feel like this.

8 Now complete Luc's text with your ideas.

I love my job! Why? Well, firstly, I like
1 _____ .
Secondly, I enjoy 2 _____ .
Thirdly, I really love 3 _____ .
What's more 4 _____ .
And finally, 5 _____ .

PRACTICE

9 You are going to write about your work or studies. You can write about what you actually do or you can invent details. First, think about how you feel about what you do. Think of as many reasons as possible for your feelings.

10 Work with a new partner. Tell each other about what you do. Your partner should ask you questions. This will give you more ideas for your text.

11 Write a plan for your text using these notes as a guide.

I'm a / I study _____ .
I _____ my job / studies. Why?
Firstly, _____
_____
Secondly, _____
_____
What's more / In addition, _____
_____
Finally, _____
_____

12 Now write your text. Use about 100–150 words.

2 WRITING Anecdotes

SPEAKING

1 Work in groups. Discuss the following.

- What is your favourite restaurant? Why?
- Describe the best restaurant you've ever been to.
- Describe the worst restaurant you've ever been to.

WRITING

2 Read this email about a visit to a restaurant and find out:

- what good things happened.
- what bad things happened.

To	stevieg@shotmail.com
From	kaori22@talk.com
Subject	A disastrous dinner!

Hi Stevie!

How are you? I hope you're well and that everything is OK with you and Dan.

Anyway, I just thought I'd write to let you know how my first few days at university are going. I haven't done much work yet, but I have met some very nice people. One guy, Scott, invited me out for dinner last night. ¹It was so funny!

²He took me to a very special fish restaurant, but unfortunately, when we got there, ³it was very crowded. I said I didn't mind waiting, so we sat in the bar. While we were waiting for a table, we had a great chat. Scott's from California and he told me a lot about his life there. In fact, during the two-hour wait, he told me ALL about ⁴it!

We finally got a table, and ordered our food. When it came, Scott's dish was OK, but ⁵mine was awful. I complained, and, luckily, they changed it really quickly. The new ⁶one was really nice. Unfortunately, during the rest of the meal, the musical 'entertainment' was playing right next to us, so we couldn't really continue our conversation without shouting. We decided not to have a dessert and left.

When ⁷they brought the bill, though, we noticed they'd charged us for all the dishes – including the ⁸one I'd sent back! Obviously, after that kind of service, we didn't leave a tip!

Anyway, I'll let you know how it goes with Scott!

Take care!

Kaori

KEYWORDS FOR WRITING

While, during and when

While, *during* and *when* show how two or more actions relate to each other in time.

While and *during* introduce a continuing action or a period of time in which another action happens.

While we **were waiting** for a table, we had a great chat.

... ***during*** the two-hour **wait**, he told me ALL about it!

When introduces a finished action.

When we **got** there, it was very crowded

When they **brought** the bill, we noticed they'd charged us for all the dishes.

You can use *when* instead of *while* for continuous actions, but *while* is more common.

3 Look at the examples in the box and in the email and complete the rules with *while*, *during* and *when*.

1 _____ is followed by a noun.

2 _____ is followed by a clause with past continuous.

3 _____ is followed by a clause with past simple.

4 Choose the correct option.

1 I fell in love with Bob *during / while* our last year at high school.

2 *While / When* I felt too tired to continue, I stopped studying and went to bed.

3 *During / When* the lunch break, I suddenly remembered that I hadn't called my mum.

4 *During / While* I was waiting to see the doctor, I read a magazine.

5 It started to rain *when / during* I was cycling to school.

6 There were no seats left *when / while* we arrived.

GRAMMAR

Pronouns

Pronouns are words that are used to avoid repeating nouns or noun phrases. A pronoun can be the subject of a sentence (*I, she, it*, etc.) or the object of a sentence (*me, her, it, us, them*, etc.).

Possessive pronouns (*mine, yours*, etc.) can replace *my, your*, etc. + noun.

Scott's dish was OK, but **mine** *was awful.* (*mine* = my dish)

To talk about two different things we can use *one / ones* to avoid repeating a noun. You can also use an adjective with *one / ones*.

This bag was a bit small, but I didn't have a **bigger one**.

We often use *they* to refer to groups or organisations when we don't know exactly who the subject is, or if it's very obvious.

They *arrested a pop star.* (*they* = the police)

5 Work in pairs. Look at the underlined pronouns in Kaori's email and say who or what you think they refer to.

6 Now read this description of a climbing trip. Replace the underlined nouns with pronouns.

My friend Ana had persuaded me to climb the mountain near the town, but as we walked towards ¹the mountain, I wondered if I could really climb ²the mountain. I'm very unfit and this was the first time I'd done anything like this.

We started climbing and I was really sweating and finding ³the climbing hard, but Ana kept encouraging me.

At midday, we stopped to have a sandwich, but I discovered that I'd left ⁴my sandwiches at home. Luckily, Ana was happy to share ⁵her sandwiches with me, and I had some sweets, so I shared ⁶the sweets with ⁷Ana!

After lunch, we continued to walk up and we finally reached the top! I couldn't believe ⁸we had finally reached the top. From there we could see all the way to the sea! ⁹Seeing all the way to the sea was beautiful. There were some other people up there too and they asked me to take a photo of them, and then they took a lovely ¹⁰photo of Ana and me. That photo is on my wall now. It's a day I'll never forget!

VOCABULARY

Adverbs of attitude

To show our feelings or opinions about something, we can use a range of adverbs, e.g. *unfortunately* or *luckily*.

He took me to a very special fish restaurant, but **unfortunately**, *when we got there, it was very crowded.*

I complained and, **luckily**, *they changed it really quickly.*

7 Choose the best adverb.

1 None of the students could answer the last question in the test. It was *obviously / luckily* too difficult.

2 I was going to go skiing, but *unfortunately / amazingly*, I broke my leg in a car accident the day before I was due to leave.

3 I was late for school, but *luckily / obviously*, the teacher was late too!

4 I usually get really nervous before an exam, but *amazingly / unfortunately*, this time I was very calm.

5 *Sadly / Stupidly*, Mike and Cristina have decided to get divorced. It's a shame.

6 *Stupidly / Fortunately*, I left the keys in the car, and someone stole it!

8 Look back at the description of the climb in Exercise 6, and add at least three adverbs to show how the writer feels.

9 Work in pairs. Compare your ideas. Did you use the same adverbs in the same places?

PRACTICE

10 You are going to write an email to a friend. Choose one of the experiences below and think about the things that happened.

- a particularly good or bad experience at a restaurant
- a particularly good or bad experience on a day out
- something you achieved

11 Work in pairs. Tell your partner about what happened to you. Ask each other questions to make sure you both understand the events properly.

12 Write an email of about 150 words. Use as much language from this lesson as you can.

3 WRITING A personal profile

SPEAKING

1 **Work in groups. Discuss the questions.**

- Have you ever had to write a profile of yourself for one of the following?
  - a CV
  - an application for a job or a course
  - an introduction to a blog or social media site
  - to introduce yourself to other people on a course or online forum
- Are there any other reasons you've had to write a profile of yourself?
- What kind of things might you talk about? Would they be different in each case?
- How do you feel about writing about yourself?

Hi there. I'm Bronwyn. I'm 23 and I'm from Wales. I finished University a year ago and moved here. At the moment I'm working in a coffee shop in Wood Green near where I live. I guess I'm doing the course because I've always loved languages and this will give me an opportunity to travel and live abroad. **As well as** speaking Welsh and English, I speak some Russian. I'm thinking of going to the Czech Republic next year (if I pass this course and can find a job)! In my spare time, I go running a lot and **also** play some basketball. **As well as** sport, I really love watching films and going to the cinema. One of my favourite directors is a Czech called Jan Svankmajer, which is another reason I want to go there.

2 **Read the profiles from two students doing the same online course. Answer the questions.**

1 What course do you think they are doing?

2 Do you think you would get on with each person? Why / Why not?

So, I'm Maureen. I was a journalist until recently, but I'm retired now. I mainly wrote articles for lifestyle magazines, but I was **also** lucky enough to write about tennis, because I'm a big fan. I'm married and have three children and two small grandchildren. My eldest daughter lives in the South of France and has a large house there. Now my husband and I are retired, we're going to move there. I'm doing this course because I might do some teaching out there to earn some extra money and meet some local people. I'm a bit nervous about teaching, but hopefully, this course will give me more confidence. I'm **also** having classes to improve my French. **As well as** playing and watching tennis, I like gardening and growing vegetables. I **also** still do some writing, but for my own pleasure, not work.

KEY WORDS FOR WRITING

as well as and also

We often use *as well as* and *also* to add ideas:

As well as *speaking Welsh and English, I speak some Russian.*

Hopefully this course will give me more confidence. I'm **also** *having classes to improve my French.*

3 Work in pairs. Look at the sentences in the box and in the profiles and discuss what you notice about:

1 the position of *as well as* and *also* in the sentence.

2 the kind of words that go before and after *as well as* and *also*.

3 the punctuation in the sentences with *as well as* and *also*.

4 Now complete sentences 1–6 using *as well as* or *also*.

1 I am a friendly, open person and I am _____ very responsible.

2 _____ playing video games, I like writing computer programmes.

3 I started writing this because I have always loved films and have seen thousands of them. I have _____ made a few.

4 I want to learn to play the drums better and _____ meet some new people.

5 _____ our two children, my husband and I share our apartment with our lovely dog, Shep.

6 _____ jazz, I love a lot of electronic music.

5 What kind of profile in Exercise 1 do you think each sentence in Exercise 4 comes from?

VOCABULARY

Sentence frames

It is often helpful to notice and learn whole sentences that you can adapt with your own ideas. For example, in the text Bronwyn said:

I guess I'm doing the course because I've always loved languages.

Look how you could adapt this when writing your own profile.

I guess I'm doing the course because I've always loved **films.**

I'm doing the course because I've always **been interested in history.**

I'm doing the course because I've always **wanted to become a nurse.**

I'm doing the course because **it's useful for my job**.

6 Look at these sentences from different profiles. Change them so that they are true for you.

1 Hi. I'm Kate and I'm 24.

2 I've always wanted to go travelling in India.

3 When I'm not working or looking after my baby, I like to go cycling.

4 In my spare time I watch TV a lot, but I also like gardening.

5 I mainly listen to pop music, but I sometimes also listen to elecronic music.

6 To be honest, the main reason I'm doing this class is because my work is paying for it.

7 I hope the course will give me the opportunity to develop my skills.

7 Work in groups and compare your sentences.

GRAMMAR

Verb agreement

Look at these examples from the text. You can join two verb phrases with *and* without repeating the subject.

I **finished** *University a year ago* **and moved** *here.*

My eldest daughter **lives** *in the South of France* **and has** *a large house there.*

I really **love watching** *films* **and going** *to the cinema.*

Notice how both verbs agree with the subject or follow the pattern after a shared verb (*love* + *-ing* form of the verb).

8 Complete the sentences with the correct form of the verb.

1 I really love golf and _____ round my local course most weeks. (go)

2 I spend most of my Saturdays cleaning the house and _____ the gardening. (do)

3 I left school when I was eighteen and then _____ to work in a paper factory. (go)

4 My wife is from a very big family in Tunisia and _____ six sisters. (have)

5 I have always loved travelling and _____ over 60 countries! (visit)

PRACTICE

9 Write a profile to introduce yourself to people in one of these situations.

- in your current class
- a pen pal website to look for friends to write to
- a course connected to a hobby

10 Work in groups. Share your profiles and discuss these questions.

- Is there anything new you learned about each other?
- Is there anything more you'd like to know about your partners?
- Do you think they are good profiles? How could they be better?

4 WRITING Describing places

SPEAKING

1 Work in pairs. Put the places in order from the best place to live to the worst, and explain why.

a big city	a farm	a seaside town
the capital city	a regional town	a village

VOCABULARY Describing places

2 Match sentences 1–6 with sentences a–f.

1 It's really green.
2 The climate's very hot and humid.
3 You find lots of modern buildings too, now.
4 It can be a bit noisy.
5 It's a very lively place.
6 The lake is a bit polluted.

a It's usually well over 25 degrees and you get a lot of storms.
b There are lots of parks and public gardens.
c Nobody swims there.
d There's a lot of traffic.
e The city is changing fast.
f There are lots of cafés and restaurants.

3 Complete the sentences with words from Exercise 2.

1 I love visiting cities with lots of _____ architecture. I find it fascinating.
2 The climate's so hot and _____ in Jakarta that I usually have three or four showers a day.
3 It's a really _____ city. There's always something happening!
4 The air is sometimes so _____ here that the TV stations tell us not to go outside.
5 Just close the window if it gets too _____ .
6 I live in a city, but I love nature. That's why I like living somewhere with lots of _____ areas.

WRITING

4 A student of English wrote a short description of her home town for her blog. Match the topics (a–d) to the paragraphs (1–4).

a Things to see
b What people like to do
c Nature
d Where I'm from

5 Work in pairs. Discuss these questions.

- Does the description make you want to visit Hanoi? Why? / Why not?
- In what ways is your home town / city similar to Hanoi?
- In what ways is it different?

SEARCH www.myhometown.blogspot.co.vn 🔍

THE CITY OF LAKES

Hanoi is a big city in the north of the country. I've lived there all my life, so I know it very well.

It's a beautiful city. It's really green. There are lots of parks, and you find trees and flowers everywhere. The climate is very hot and humid, so everything grows really fast.

The centre is very old and it has lots of historic buildings, but now you find lots of modern buildings, too, because the centre is changing fast. The city's very famous for the lake in the centre, called Hoan Kiem. It's a bit polluted, so nobody swims there, but it's nice to look at!

It always feels very lively. People spend a lot of time outside, talking to neighbours, eating, studying or just going around town. However, it can be a bit noisy at times, because so many people ride around on motorcycles.

4 The room can be _____ noisy at times. It's not too bad, but sometimes I have to close the window because of the traffic.

5 The country has a _____ amazing education system. Every child can read and write by the age of six.

6 The sea there is always _____ cold. People never swim there.

7 Add *very*, *really* or *a bit* to these sentences so they describe places you know. Then tell your partner about each place.

1 It's a fantastic place.

2 It's dirty.

3 The buildings are old.

4 The beaches are polluted.

5 It's noisy at night.

KEY WORDS FOR WRITING

because and *so*

We use *because* and *so* to join two parts of a sentence. Use *because* to talk about why something happens.

It can be a bit noisy at times, **because** *so many people ride around on motorcycles.*

Use *so* to talk about the result of something.

The lake is polluted, **so** *nobody swims there.*

8 Complete the sentences with *because* or *so*.

1 That part of the city is new, _____ you don't see any old buildings there.

2 People don't go out between 12 and 3 _____ it's really hot.

3 The city was very polluted, _____ I moved to the country.

4 Lots of tourists visit the museum _____ it's home to a lot of wonderful art.

5 I moved to the coast _____ I love walking on the beach and looking at the sea.

6 I love my home town _____ there are lots of parks, trees and lakes.

9 Change the second part of the sentences in Exercise 8 to describe places you know.

That part of the city is new **because** *the city has grown a lot / a lot of new companies have moved here.*

PRACTICE

10 Choose your favourite town or city to write about. Spend five minutes thinking about what the place is like. Write a list of the adjectives that you'd like to use.

11 Work in pairs and discuss your ideas. Tell your partner why you chose each adjective.

12 Plan an article to describe your town / city. Use the topics from Exercise 4, or choose other topics. Then write your article. Try to use some modifiers.

GRAMMAR

Modifiers

We use modifiers before adjectives to make them stronger or weaker. To make an adjective stronger, use *really* or *very*. To make it weaker, use *a bit*.

New York is a **really** / **very** *busy city so it's* **a bit** *difficult to find a taxi at times.*

Shanghai can be **a bit** *noisy, but it's* **really** / **very** *lively.*

When an adjective is already 'extreme', you can add *really*, but not *very*.

The weather is **really** (NOT ~~very~~) *excellent / fantastic / incredible / wonderful / freezing.*

6 Complete the first sentence in each pair with a modifier. Use the information in the second sentence to help you.

1 The river's _____ polluted. It will take years to clean.

2 The service at this restaurant is _____ wonderful. The people who work here are so helpful.

3 The roads can be _____ dangerous. You sometimes have to drive quite carefully, especially after it rains.

5 WRITING Postcards

WRITING

1 Work in pairs. Check you understand the words in the box. What kind of holiday are all these words connected to? Do you think this is a good kind of holiday for a honeymoon? Why? / Why not?

captain	movies	port	seasick	sights
galleries	parties	ruins	ship	tour

2 Read the postcards from a couple on their honeymoon. Answer the questions.

1 How do Sara and Bruce feel about their holiday? Why?

2 What do they have the same opinion about?

SPEAKING

3 Work in groups. Discuss these questions.

- What kind of holiday do you think Bruce prefers? Why?
- Does everyone in your family like doing the same things on holiday? What usually happens when you go on holiday together?
- Is it good for couples to have different tastes and interests?
- Do you know any couples who are quite different to each other? In what ways?

VOCABULARY

Postcard expressions

We use lots of fixed phrases when writing postcards. There's often no subject for the verb – and sometimes no verb at all.

Greetings from paradise.

Weather's great.

Writing this from a ship somewhere near Italy.

4 Put the words in order to make postcard expressions.

1 here / were / you / wish

2 all / you're / hope / well

3 to / wait / you / tell / can't / about / it

4 are / here / we / in / Panama

5 forward / soon / looking / to / you / seeing

6 from / greetings / Greece

7 in / this / writing / café / a

8 in / a / having / London / time / great / here

Hi Mum,

Well, here we are on our cruise. We get to a new port every two days and go on guided tours and see all the sights – cathedrals, ancient ruins, galleries, museums. It's a very full schedule!

Life on the ship is great – discos, parties, dinner with the captain (the food's great), even movies and concerts!

Weather's great, although the evenings are quite cool. Wish you were here.

Looking forward to telling you all about everything. (Have about 300 photos to show you!).

Lots of love,

Sara xxx

Charlotte Jenkins,

The Manor House,

Briardene,

Oxfordshire,

England OX6 4PC

Hi Mike,

Greetings from paradise! Writing this from a ship somewhere near Italy, although it might be Greece – everywhere looks the same to me! Ruins, cathedrals, and crowded art galleries and museums – non-stop sightseeing tours!

Despite trying hard to enjoy myself, I can't say I'm having a good time. What's more, although it's our honeymoon, we're never alone – there's always a crowd of 'friends' with us. The best thing is the food – amazing! Unfortunately, I sometimes get seasick, despite the good weather!

Can't wait to get back!

Hope you're well.

All the best,

Bruce

Mike Beardsley,

9 Shearer Way,

Toonton,

County Durham,

England

KEY WORDS FOR WRITING

although and *despite*

Although and *despite* both introduce contrasts – often something that shows the main statement is surprising or unlikely. Notice the different grammar after each word.

Although it's our honeymoon, we're never alone.

Weather's great, **although the evenings are** quite cool.

Despite trying hard to enjoy myself, I can't say I'm having a good time.

I sometimes get seasick, **despite the good weather**!

5 Complete the sentences with *although* or *despite*.

1 _____ the horrible weather, we had a great trip.
2 The beaches are fantastic, _____ you have to watch out for sharks.
3 I enjoyed the cruise, _____ I got seasick.
4 _____ getting very sunburnt, I enjoyed the holiday.

6 Complete the second sentence so that it has a similar meaning to the first sentence, using the word given. Do not change the word given. You must use between two and five words, including the word given.

1 We had a great time, although it rained a lot.
   We had a great time, _____ . **RAIN**
2 Despite the crowds, we enjoyed the concert.
   _____ , we enjoyed the concert. **CROWDED**

3 Despite being really tired, we stayed up all night and studied.
   _____ , we stayed up all night and studied. **WERE**
4 Although it was really sunny, it was still quite cold.
   It was quite cold, _____ . **BEING**
5 Although I had a headache, I still went skiing.
   I went skiing, _____ . **HAVING**

7 Complete each sentence in three different ways. Then compare your ideas in groups. Decide who has the funniest / saddest sentence.

• The holiday was great, although ... .
• We managed to catch our flight, despite ... .

PRACTICE

8 You are going to write a postcard to a friend or relative. Before you write, think about these questions.

• Where are you on holiday?
• What type of holiday is it?
• What things have you done?
• What are you doing at the moment?
• Are you enjoying yourself?

9 Write your postcard. Use 100–120 words. Use as much language from this lesson as you can.

6 WRITING Plans and schedules

SPEAKING

1 All the pictures below are from the same meeting. Work in pairs. Discuss these questions.

- What do you think is happening in each picture?
- What do you think the people are talking about?
- What is their relationship with the others at the meeting?

a

b

Figure 6

c

d

WRITING

2 Complete the email about a meeting with the words in the box.

begin	break	continue	is	feed back
gives	meet	move	present	starts

To: olga.williams@futuresforward.org
From: tom.petersen@futuresforward.org
Subject: Sales meeting in Oslo

Dear Olga,

I'm looking forward to seeing you at the Sales Managers' meeting in Oslo on Friday 13th July.

The meeting ¹_____ at the Clarion Royal Hotel.

Please find below the schedule for the day.

```
09.30-10.00
All managers ²_____ in the hotel
lobby.
The meeting ³_____ with coffee and
a short welcome from Liv Applund,
International Sales Director.

10.00-12.30
We ⁴_____ to the conference room
on the first floor.
Each national manager then ⁵_____
a presentation on this year's main
challenges and results.
Presentations ⁶_____ until
lunchtime.

12.30-13.30
Lunch in the hotel restaurant

13.30-15.00
We divide into small groups and
⁷_____ our brainstorming session.
Topic: sales strategy for the
coming year.

15.00-16.30
Groups ⁸_____ their ideas.
We then ⁹_____ on the presentations
until 16.30, when we ¹⁰_____
for coffee.

17.00-17.30
The final session begins at 17.00,
when Liv Applund answers any questions
and concludes the meeting.
```

Hope this is all clear.

Let me know if you have any questions.

All the best,

Tom

GRAMMAR

The present simple for timetables

3 Read the sentence from the email. Choose the best option (a, b or c) to complete the sentence below.

*The final session **begins** at 17.00, when Liv Applund **answers** any questions and **concludes** the meeting.*

The present simple is used in the email

a to describe possible future events.

b to describe events that happen all the time or regularly.

c to describe definite future events.

4 Work in pairs. Compare your ideas. Then check by reading the Grammar box.

We can use the present simple to talk about things in the future that are timetabled or scheduled.

*We **break** for coffee at 16.30.*

*The train **leaves** at 4.45.*

*What time **does** the meeting **finish**?*

---

5 Complete the sentences with the present simple form of the verbs.

1 When _____ the next regional sales meeting? (be)

2 My flight _____ at 13.30. (leave)

3 I _____ in Oslo until two o'clock in the morning. (not / land)

4 What time _____ your train _____ in Paris? (arrive)

5 We _____ for lunch at one. (break)

6 The lunch break _____ from 1.30 to 2.45. (last)

7 Remember – we _____ until eleven tomorrow. (not / start)

8 When _____ the meeting _____ ? (end)

KEY WORDS FOR WRITING

Time expressions

We use *then / after that* to show that one action follows another. They mean the same thing. However, *after that* usually begins a sentence or a clause.

At 10.00, we move to the conference room on the first floor.

*Each national manager **then** gives a presentation.*

***After that,** each national manager gives a presentation.*

To show the point in time when something will finish, we use *until*.

*Presentations continue **until** lunchtime.*

*She's in Britain **until** December.*

6 Complete the sentences with *then*, *after that* or *until*.

1 The hotel restaurant doesn't open _____ six.

2 The presentations finish at one. _____ , there's an hour break for lunch.

3 We start at ten with a brainstorming session, which continues _____ twelve.

4 I have a meeting _____ 12.45 but _____ I'll call you back.

5 I'm afraid you have to wait here _____ the room is ready.

6 The president gives her welcome speech at nine and _____ we divide into groups.

7 We don't break for coffee _____ 4.30, I'm afraid.

8 The restaurant is booked for one. We'll probably finish around 2.30 and maybe _____ we can find a quiet place to discuss Asia.

PRACTICE

7 You are going to write an email about a meeting at work, school or college. Work in pairs. Write a schedule for the meeting.

8 Now work on your own. Write an email to the people who are coming to the meeting. Use the present simple to talk about timetabled / scheduled events.

9 When you finish, check your work carefully and give it to your partner. Check each other's emails and make any changes or corrections you think are necessary.

7 WRITING Complaints

SPEAKING

1 Work in groups. Discuss these questions.

- Have you ever bought anything that didn't work?
- If yes, what did you do? Did you return it to where you bought it from? What was the result?
- If you have a problem with something you've bought, which of the things below do you usually do? Why?
  - go back to the shop
  - email
  - phone
  - search the internet

VOCABULARY Problems

2 Label the photo below with the words in the box.

button	headphones	screen	volume control

3 Complete the sentences below with the words in the box.

battery	damaged	properly	recharge
crack	faulty	received	slow

1 The screen has a _____ in it so you can't see the menu or video clearly.

2 The delivery service was very _____ . It took a long time to arrive.

3 The box that it was in was _____ .

4 The main button does not work _____ . It gets stuck and you cannot access the main menu.

5 I paid for it four weeks ago, but I still have not _____ it.

6 There is something wrong with the _____ . The player stops working an hour after you _____ it.

7 The headphones are _____ , so the sound is quite bad.

4 Work in pairs. Discuss whether each problem in Exercise 3 is very serious, quite serious or not very serious. Give reasons.

WRITING

5 Read the letter of complaint. Choose the options that are best for formal writing.

> The Manager
> Electronics Biz
> Banbury
> OX15 1LN
>
> B Tarlon
> 45 Doone Street
> Adderbury
> OX17 3AZ
>
> 4th August 2016
>
> Dear Sir / Madam,
>
> [1]*Further to* / *After* my email of 26th July, I am writing to [2]*ask* / *enquire* where my replacement MP4 player is, and to make a formal complaint about the quality of service that your company provides.
>
> On 15th June this year, I [3]*purchased* / *bought* an MP4 player from your store in Banbury. However, I soon realised it was faulty and returned it on 19th June. At this time, I [4]*asked for* / *requested* a replacement and a member of staff there promised to send one the following day, but it never arrived.
>
> After [5]*numerous* / *loads of* phone calls to your call centre, I then sent an email last week, describing the problems I was having. In the reply I [6]*received* / *got*, I was told that a brand new player had already been sent. However, I still have not received it. I am [7]*really unhappy about* / *not at all satisfied with* the quality of the after-sales service you provide.
>
> If I do not receive the MP4 player by next Monday, I shall take this matter to Consumer Affairs.
>
> [8]*All the best* / *Yours faithfully*,
>
> *Brad Tarlon*
>
> Brad Tarlon

6 Work in pairs. Discuss these questions.

- Where do the two addresses and the date go in formal letters?
- Is this the same when you write formal letters in your language?
- Why do you think the letter starts with *Dear Sir / Madam*?
- What kind of information does each of the four paragraphs contain?
- Why does the letter end with *Yours faithfully*?

7 Cover the letter of complaint in Exercise 5. Try to complete these sentences with three words in each space. Then look at the letter again and check your answers.

1 I am writing to ... make a _____ the quality of service that your company provides.

2 On 15th June this year, I purchased an MP4 player _____ in Banbury.

3 A member of staff there promised to send one _____ , but it never arrived.

4 I then sent an email last week, describing the problems _____ .

5 In the reply I received, I was told that a _____ had already been sent.

6 I am not at all satisfied with the quality of the _____ you provide.

8 Work in groups. Discuss these questions.

• What would you do if you were in Mr Tarlon's situation?

• Which of these adjectives do you think describe Mr Tarlon? Why?

reasonable	impatient	stupid

• In your country, do you have a government office like Consumer Affairs that protects the rights of shoppers? What do you know about it? Is it effective?

KEY WORDS FOR WRITING

but and *however*

But and *however* both connect two opposing ideas, or introduce surprising information.

But connects two clauses in one sentence and starts the second clause.

*A member of staff there promised to send one the following day, **but** it never arrived.*

However connects two sentences and usually comes at the beginning of the second sentence, or sometimes after the subject.

I was told that a brand new player had already been sent. ***However***, *I still have not received it.*

We phoned to complain. The woman at the call centre, ***however***, *said we had to send our complaint in writing.*

9 Complete the sentences with *but* or *however*.

1 The camera was damaged when I bought it, _____ the company won't give me a new one.

2 I have asked for my money back. _____ , the company say that I caused the damage to the camera.

3 I have tried to speak to your sales manager three times. The line, _____ , is always busy.

4 The shop says I dropped the box, _____ I didn't.

10 Complete the sentences with your own ideas. Then compare your sentences with a partner.

1 I called your company to complain, but _____ .

2 I bought the book from your online store over three weeks ago, but _____ .

3 I received the camera yesterday, as promised. However, _____ .

4 You stated the total cost would be £15. However, _____ .

PRACTICE

11 Work in pairs. Think of a situation that requires you to write to complain about something. Your complaint could be about something you bought or something you are trying to organise. Discuss:

• the situation and why you are writing.

• the problem and what has caused it.

• what action you now want from the person / company.

• what you will do next if you don't receive a response that you're happy with.

12 Write an email or letter of complaint. Write 100–150 words. Use as much language from this lesson as you can.

'If she doesn't get well, do I get a refund?'

SPEAKING

1 Make a list of events, receptions or parties in the last year that:

- you have been invited to.
- you have invited other people to.

2 Work in groups. Compare your lists. Explain:

- what the events were.
- who held each event and why.
- why you were invited – or who you invited.
- if the events were successful or not.

WRITING

3 Read the two emails. Decide if you would accept each invitation or not. Then explain your decisions to a partner.

To: Salma.Abad@ozmail.com
From: Carlos66@ozmail.com
Subject: Housewarming!

Hi Salma!

How're you? It's been so long since we last talked! What's new with you? I've just moved into a new flat in Bondi. It's really great to live so near the beach.

I'm having a housewarming party next Saturday. I hope you can come. Bring your brother if you like – he's really funny! Unless it rains, we'll have a barbecue in the garden! I'm going to make some salads, and there'll be drinks, but I'm asking people to bring something to cook on the barbecue, if that's OK.

Send me an email and let me know if you can come. It'd be great to see you.

Love,

Carlos

4 One email is more formal and the other is more informal. Decide if the following show formality or informality:

1 contractions (*I'm*, *he's*, etc.)
2 longer, more complex sentences
3 dashes (–) and exclamation marks (!)
4 direct questions
5 more passives

5 Work in groups. Discuss these questions.

- How do you show different levels of formality in your language?
- Do you think it's OK:
  - to ask guests to bring food to a party?
  - to ask people to give to charity instead of giving a present?

To: Marketing@BLTLtd.com
From: BMarchant@ BLTLtd.com
Subject: Reception for Simone Lacroix

Dear colleagues,

You are invited to a reception to mark the retirement of our business manager, Simone Lacroix.

The reception will take place in the main boardroom on the first floor at four o'clock on Friday afternoon. Drinks and snacks will be served.

Simone has been with us for the last fifteen years and has helped us through some difficult times. I am sure you would like to join us in giving her a proper goodbye as she returns to her native France.

If you are able to attend, I would be grateful if you would respond to this email so that we can confirm numbers.

Simone has asked if people could make a donation to the charity Southern Cat Rescue rather than give her a leaving present. If you wish to donate, please contact Ken in Sales.

Yours,

Ben Marchant

Communications Director

VOCABULARY

Formal and informal language

Some vocabulary such as *attend* or *Yours* (to end an email) sounds quite formal. A less formal way to say these things is *come* and *All the best*. Recognising and learning more and less formal ways of expressing ideas will improve your writing.

6 Mark each of the following MF (more formal) or LF (less formal).

1 if you are able to

2 Dear Mr Parker

3 Hiya

4 if you can

5 if you like

6 Dear Pete

7 Love

8 Give me a call

9 Respond by email

10 We look forward to seeing you

11 Cheers

12 If you wish

13 Kind regards

14 We're having some friends round

15 Yours sincerely

16 It'd be great to see you

17 Let us know

18 Please contact us on 020-7034-5019

19 We are delighted to announce

20 I would be most grateful if …

7 Work in pairs. Compare your ideas. Which five phrases might come very near the beginning of an invitation? Which phrases can you use already?

KEY WORDS FOR WRITING

if, *when* and *unless*

We can talk about the future using *if*, *when* and *unless* + the present simple.

If shows something will possibly or probably happen.

When shows we expect something to happen.

Unless means *if … not*.

Bring your brother **if you like**.

Give me a call **when you have** time.

Unless it rains, we'll have a barbecue in the garden!

8 Match the two parts of the sentences.

1 If the train is late,

2 Unless there's a problem,

3 I'll give you a call

4 You can bring the kids

5 John says he'll come to the party,

6 Give me a call

a unless he has to work late.

b when you've got a minute.

c when I get to my hotel.

d we'll give you a call and let you know.

e there's no need to reply to this invitation.

f if you think they might enjoy it.

9 Complete the sentences with *if*, *when* or *unless*.

1 Give me a call _____ you arrive and I'll open the gate for you.

2 _____ you would like us to arrange collection from the station, please send us details of your train and arrival time.

3 You may bring a guest _____ you wish.

4 I am afraid I will be unable to attend, _____ I can change the date of my flight.

5 We're going to have a party _____ we finish our exams.

6 We'll go swimming in the river in afternoon, _____ it's too cold.

PRACTICE

10 You are going to write two email invitations to a reception or party. The first is an informal invitation to something you are organising. The second is an invitation to a formal event in a school or company. Work in pairs. For each invitation, think of:

• the reason for the reception / party.

• where it will be and when.

• if guests should bring anything.

• anything else special about it.

11 **Student A:** write the informal invitation.

Student B: write the formal invitation.

12 Check each other's invitations. Discuss anything you think should be written differently in each invitation.

GRAMMAR REFERENCE

1 JOBS

PRESENT SIMPLE AND PRESENT CONTINUOUS

Present simple

We use the present simple to talk about something that is generally true, a habit or a permanent state.

The present simple is the infinitive form of the verb (without *to*). The third person form ends in *-s*.

We **live** above the shop.

She **runs** her own company.

We form negatives with *don't / doesn't* + the infinitive (without *to*).

I **don't** really **mind** the travelling.

He **doesn't** really **get on** with his boss.

We form questions with *do / does* + the subject + the infinitive (without *to*).

Where **do** they **work**?

What **does** she **do**?

The present simple is often used with adverbs such as *usually, generally, normally, often, sometimes, never*, etc.

I **usually come** down to London every two weeks.

I **often do** a sixty-hour week.

Present continuous

We use the present continuous to talk about actions we see as temporary and unfinished.

The present continuous is a form of the auxiliary verb *be* + the *-ing* form of the verb.

She**'s working** in Canada this month.

They**'re building** a new sports stadium.

He**'s chatting** to his mum. (for most verbs ending in a vowel + consonant, double the last letter)

He**'s using** my car while I'm away. (remove the final e before adding *-ing*)

We form negatives with *am / is / are* + *not* + *-ing*.

I**'m not working** at the moment.

He's unemployed, but **he isn't / he's not looking** for a job.

We form questions with *am / is / are* + subject + *-ing*.

What **are** you **studying**?

Where**'s** she **going**?

We often use the present continuous with *at the moment, this month, this week*, etc.

I**'m working** in Scotland **at the moment**.

She**'s doing** nights **this week**.

Exercise 1

Choose the correct form.

1 A: So *what do you do? / what are you doing*?
   B: I work for a bank.

2 A: *How does your job go? / How's your job going at the moment*? OK?
   B: Yeah, fine, but we're very busy. *We work / We're working* on a new project this month.

3 A: What time *do you start / are you starting* work?
   B: Eight – and my office is on the other side of town, so *I usually leave / I'm usually leaving* the house around seven and *am getting / get up* around six.

4 The business *does / is doing* well at the moment.

5 I'm unemployed at the moment. *I'm looking / I look* for a job, but it's difficult.

6 I usually work in Padstow, but *I do / I'm doing* a training course in Hendon this week.

DID YOU KNOW?

These verbs are not generally used in a continuous form. They are used in the present simple, even to describe unfinished or temporary states.

agree	depend	like	own	suppose
believe	hate	need	seem	taste
belong	know	owe	sound	want

Exercise 2

Decide which four sentences are incorrect then correct them.

1 Is your friends staying in a hotel or with you?

2 I'm sometimes cycling to work.

3 I hate my job at the moment.

4 Karen knows the guy who is owning that restaurant.

5 We don't get much work at the moment, unfortunately.

6 They're building a new shopping centre near here.

PRESENT SIMPLE AND PRESENT CONTINUOUS FOR THE FUTURE

Present continuous for talking about the future

We sometimes use the present continuous to refer to arrangements with other people in the future. We usually add a time phrase.

I**'m meeting** a customer **at twelve**.

I**'m giving** that presentation **next week**.

Are you going to that training session **on Friday**?

What time **are we having** dinner?

We're going to Spain **in the summer** for our holiday.

My friend Petra **is having** a party **on Saturday night**. Do you want to come?

Present simple for talking about the future

Some verbs and phrases like *have got (have), have to, need, there's*, etc. are not used in the present continuous when talking about the future.

I**'ve got** an appointment with the dentist at one (or **I have** an appointment at one).

I**'ve got** a test tomorrow (or **I have** a test tomorrow).

I **need to** leave at eight.

I **have to** go to a meeting later.

There's a training session on time management on Friday.

We also use the present simple to talk about future events connected to a fixed timetable, but you can use the present continuous for this too.

What time **does** your **train** leave tonight?

What time **is** your train **leaving** tonight?

Exercise 1

Make dialogues using the ideas in 1–5 and the present simple or continuous. The first one is done for you.

1 A: What / you / do / Saturday?
   What are you doing on Saturday night?
   B: meet / a friend for dinner. Why?
2 A: your boyfriend / come / the party tomorrow?
   B: No, he can't. have to / work late.
3 A: be / you / busy / afternoon?
   B: Yes. have got / several appointments / clients
4 A: We / go / Italy / the summer
   B: That's nice. How long / stay there?
5 A: be / a meeting / later about the new computer system. you / go?
   B: No. I / not need / go. I know about it already.

Present tense after *depend* and *hope*

We also use the present tense to refer to the future after *depend* and *hope*.

A: *Are you going out tonight?*
B: *It depends what time I finish work.*
B: *It depends how I'm feeling.*
B: *It depends if my girlfriend wants to.*

I hope I pass my exam.
I hope I get paid tomorrow.
I hope he likes his birthday present.

Exercise 2

Use your own ideas to complete each comment with three different endings.

1 A: Are you going away during the next holiday?
   B: Maybe. It depends … .
2 I'm starting a new job next week. I hope … .
3 What time are you coming home tonight?
   It depends … .
4 I'm working at a music festival this weekend, so I hope … .

You will learn more about present tenses and the future in Unit 5, Plans and arrangements; Unit 7, *will / won't*; Unit 15, Time clauses.

2 SHOPS

PAST SIMPLE

Regular verbs

To make the past simple add *-ed* to the infinitive (without *to*). Note the spelling with some verbs.

delay – delayed	last – lasted	work – worked
advise – advised	organise – organised	use – used
apply – applied	cry – cried	try – tried
fit – fitted	stop – stopped	travel – travelled

Irregular verbs

Many of the most common verbs in English are irregular.

be – was / were	get – got	say – said
break – broke	give – gave	see – saw
bring – brought	go – went	sell – sold
buy – bought	have – had	spend – spent
catch – caught	keep – kept	take – took
choose – chose	know – knew	tell – told
come – came	leave – left	teach – taught
cost – cost	lose – lost	think – thought
cut – cut	make – made	wake – woke
do – did	meet – met	wear – wore
drive – drove	pay – paid	win – won
eat – ate	put – put	write – wrote
fall – fell	read – read	
find – found	run – ran	

Questions and negatives

What		*you*	*do?*
Where		*he*	*buy it?*
Who	*did*	*she*	*go with?*
When		*they*	*arrive?*
How long		*it*	*take?*

		you	*enjoy it?*
	Did	*he / she / they*	*go?*
		it	*take long?*

I		*hear you.*
You		*say anything.*
He / she		*come.*
It	*didn't*	*cost much.*
We		*do anything.*
They		*win.*

Where	*was*	*he / she / it?*
	were	*you / they?*

	Was	*it / she / he*	*OK?*
	Were	*you / they*	

I		*happy.*
He / she	*wasn't*	*interested.*
It		*very good.*

We		*sure.*
You	*weren't*	*here.*
They		*very helpful.*

Exercise 1

Complete the sentences with the correct form of the verbs.

1 A: What [1]_____ yesterday? (you / do)
   B: Nothing much. I just [2]_____ at home. What about you? (stay)
   A: I [3]_____ the day tidying the house. Some friends are visiting. (spend)

2 A: [1]_____ anything nice? (you / get)
   B: Yeah, I [2]_____ this top. (buy)
   A: That's really cool. I love the design. [3]_____ any others like that? (they / have)
   B: Not exactly the same, but there [4]_____ lots of nice things. (be)

3 A: [1]_____ a nice weekend? (have)
   B: Yeah. It [2]_____ my birthday so we [3]_____ out for dinner. (be, go)
   A: Where [4]_____? (you / go)
   B: Gambino's. That Italian place on the High Street.
   A: Really? [5]_____ expensive? A friend [6]_____ me it is. (it / be, tell)
   B: I don't know. My girlfriend [7]_____ for everything and she [8]_____ . The food [9]_____ great though. (pay, not say, be)

DID YOU KNOW?

Instead of repeating a past verb phrase we often replace the verb with only *did* or *didn't*.

A: *Did you speak to him about changing class?*
B: *Yes, I **did** and he said it was fine. (**did** = spoke to him)*
A: *I went shopping yesterday.*
B: *So **did** I. (= I went shopping too.)*
*They thought the film was really good, but I **didn't**. (**didn't** = didn't think it was really good)*

Exercise 2

Decide which nine sentences are incorrect then correct them.

1 I didn't saw anything I liked.
2 I love your earrings. Where you got them?
3 What he say? I didn't hear.
4 She told me not to say anything, so I didn't.
5 He complained and I do too, but it didn't make any difference.
6 I breaked a glass and cut my finger.
7 It started to rain five minutes after we leaved the house.
8 Why wasn't you in class yesterday?
9 A: I didn't buy anything in the end.
   B: No, neither do I.
10 It was broken when I taked it out of the box.

You will learn more about verb forms to talk about the past in Unit 3, Past simple and past continuous; Unit 4, Present perfect simple; Unit 11, Past perfect simple; Unit 15, Time phrases and tense.

COMPARATIVES

-er, -ier or more

We add -er to the end of adjectives / adverbs of one syllable. Notice the spelling changes are similar to past simple forms.

smart – smarter   warm – warmer
nice – nicer   large – larger
big – bigger   hot – hotter

With one- or two-syllable words ending in -y, we change the -y to -ier.

pretty – prettier   easy – easier   dry – drier

We use *more* before two- or three-syllable adjectives / adverbs.

expensive – more expensive   complicated – more complicated

much and a bit

To say there's a big difference, use *much* or *a lot*. To say there's a small difference, use *a bit*.

It's **a lot more expensive** here than in Brazil.
I'm **a bit taller than** my brother – maybe two centimetres.

Negative comparisons

Make negative comparisons using *not as* + adjective / adverb.

I never go to Bonds. I shop at Costsave. The quality is**n't as good** but it's **not as expensive**.

With adjectives of two syllables or more you can also use *less*.

It's less expensive.

Better and worse

Remember the comparative for *good / well* is *better* and the comparative for *bad / badly* is *worse*.

Exercise 1

Choose the correct option.

1 A: I like this top. Have they got it in a *more large / larger* size?
   B: I don't think so. I can ask, though.
2 A: What do you think of this coat? It's a bit *more thick / thicker* than the other one.
   B: Hmm – it's nice – it fits *more well / better* too.
3 A: Do you want to sit inside? it'll be *more comfortable / comfortabler*. There's a sofa which is free.
   B: It's *nicer / more nicer* out here, isn't it?
4 A: I prefer shopping online – it's *more convenient / more easy*.
   B: Absolutely, and it's often not as *expensive / cheap*.
5 A: What time shall we leave? Eight? Eight thirty?
   B: I think it's *better / more good* to leave a bit *more early / earlier*. Say seven thirty. The traffic isn't *as heavy / as light*.

DID YOU KNOW?

Both *quieter* and *more quiet* are commonly used. People also say *more friendly* or *friendlier*. You may see other two-syllable words in either form.

Comparing two things in a sentence

To compare things in the same sentence, use comparative + *than* ... and *not as* + adjective / adverb + *as*.

Costsave is much **cheaper than** the other supermarkets.
Their selection of clothes is **less varied than** at Harrods.
I don't usually finish **as late as** this. I normally finish at six.

Exercise 2

Write sentences comparing the two things. Use the ideas in brackets.

1 The market / the supermarket (much / cheap)
2 My new job / my old one (well paid)
3 This school / my local one (much / good)
4 People here / people in my country (not / friendly)
5 The shop / last year. (do badly)
6 The design of your phone / mine (not / nice)

3 GETTING THERE

PAST SIMPLE AND PAST CONTINUOUS

Past simple

We use two or more verbs in the past simple in a sentence to show that the actions were completed one after another. We often link these actions with *and (then)*, *before*, *after* or *when*.

*I **checked in** online **and printed** my boarding pass.*
*We **got** to the airport **and checked** the departures board.*
***When** the plane **landed**, everyone **stood up**.*

Past continuous

We form the past continuous with *was / were* + the *-ing* form of the verb.

I / He / She	**was**	**going** home.
It	**was**	**snowing**.
We / You / They	**were**	**leaving**.
It	**wasn't**	**raining** very hard.
They	**weren't**	**listening**.
What	**were** you	**doing**?
Where	**was** he	**going**?

The past continuous shows an action started, but was incomplete when another action (or other actions) happened. We often link sentences with *when* or *while*. We often use the past continuous at the beginning of the story to show the general situation / background.

1 ***When** I **got** to the train station, **they were doing** repairs on the line.*
   (The repairs started before I got to the station and weren't finished.)
2 ***When I woke up**, the **woman** from the airline **was walking away** from the gate.*
   (The woman started walking away before I woke up, and I could still see her walking away.)
3 ***I was reading** the last few pages **when I suddenly heard** the last call for my flight.*
   (I started reading the last pages before I heard the call, and I still had some pages left to read.)

Exercise 1

Choose the correct option.

1 I fell asleep when I *got on / was waiting* for the train and I slept all the way to London.
2 I got to the airport very early, so I *bought / was buying* a few things while I was waiting.
3 I *was still packing / packed* when the taxi arrived so he had to wait fifteen minutes.
4 My parents *met / were meeting* on a bus in Chile when they were both living there. They live back in the States now.
5 I *drove / was driving* back home from the office and a dog ran in front of my car. I tried to stop, but I couldn't.
6 Where *were you going / did you you go* when I *saw / was seeing* you yesterday?

Verbs not used in the continuous form

The following verbs are not generally used in the past continuous.

agree	believe	belong	cost	depend
hate	know	like	need	owe
seem	sound	suppose	taste	want

DID YOU KNOW?

We sometimes use a phrase starting with a preposition (*on, in*, etc.) instead of the past continuous.

I was going to work.	*I was **on my way** to work.*
She was coming home.	*She was **on her way** home.*
They were having a meeting.	*They were **in a meeting**.*
He was sitting next to us.	*He was **at the table** next to us.*

Exercise 2

Complete the stories with the past continuous or past simple form of the verbs.

1 A few years ago, I [1]_____ (go) to Singapore to visit some friends. They [2]_____ (offer) to let me stay in their flat, but I [3]_____ (decide) to stay in a hotel instead. One day, I [4]_____ (have) breakfast in the hotel restaurant when suddenly Jackie Chan [5]_____ (walk) in and [6]_____ (sit) down next to me. I couldn't believe it!

2 I [1]_____ (do) something really stupid last month. I [2]_____ (write) an essay for college and I [3]_____ (start) to feel tired, so I [4]_____ (go) to the kitchen and [5]_____ (make) a cup of coffee. I [6]_____ (put) the coffee next to my computer and [7]_____ (start) working again. Then the phone [8]_____ (ring) and I [9]_____ (jump) up to answer it – and [10]_____ (spill) coffee all over my computer! It's going to cost a fortune to repair it.

You will learn more about the past simple and past continuous in Unit 15, Time phrases and tense.

QUANTIFIERS WITH COUNTABLE AND UNCOUNTABLE NOUNS

Quantifiers are words we use before nouns to show quantity.
Many and *a few* are only used with plural countable nouns such as *people, sheep, animals* and *trains*.
Not **many planes** can fly over France.
Quite **a few flights** are cancelled.

Much is only used with uncountable nouns such as *accommodation, advice, anger, chaos, help, information, luggage, news, progress, traffic, water* and *work*.
There's not **much hope** of a deal.

A bit of is usually used with uncountable nouns. It can be used with some singular countable nouns.
Expect **a bit of trouble** there.
Expect **a bit of a wait** there.

Some, any, a lot of, plenty of and *no* go with both plural countable and uncountable nouns.
There were **some cows** on the line. (countable)
This follows **some** heavy **rain** in the area overnight. (uncountable)
There aren't **any** more **problems** on the A6. (countable)
It wasn't **any help**. (uncountable)
There are terrible problems in **a lot of places**. (countable)
Come on! We don't have **a lot of time**. (uncountable)
There are **plenty of flights** to choose from. (countable)
Relax! We have **plenty of time**. (uncountable)
There are **no trains** today, I'm afraid. (countable)
There's **no parking** in or around the ground. (uncountable)

In negatives, use *any, much* or *many*.
I **didn't** book **any accommodation** before I left.
We **didn't** take **much luggage** with us.
There **weren't many cars** on the road.

DID YOU KNOW?

Any is used in positive sentences to mean 'it's not important which one or how little'.

Any passengers *who are flying in the next few days should ring their airline.*

In formal written English, *many* and *much* are also used in positive sentences.

Many town planners *believe that we should limit car use.*

*There is **much talk** about creating more cycle lanes.*

Exercise 1

Complete the sentences with one word in each space.

1 There are _____ places to stop on the way, but not very _____ .

2 Let me give you a _____ of advice: avoid the underground at night. It's not safe.

3 The stop's just over there. Take _____ bus. They all go into the centre.

4 There are usually _____ of buses. They come every ten minutes or so.

5 I don't have _____ information yet – just the time of the flight. I need to speak to a _____ people first and find out what's happening.

6 There's a _____ of anger about the train strike.

7 I usually only have hand luggage. I don't like to have _____ bags to check in.

8 I waited for ages, but there were _____ taxis. In the end, I decided to walk!

DID YOU KNOW?

To express negative ideas, we often use *too many, too much, too few* and *too little*.

*There are **too many motorbikes** on the road. It's crazy!*

*There's **too much traffic**. They need to do something about it.*

*There are **too few buses** after ten at night. We need more.*

*There's too much to do – and **too little time** to do it in!*

Exercise 2

Complete the second sentence so that it has a similar meaning to the first sentence. Use one word in each space.

1 There weren't many people on the train this morning.
   There were only _____ _____ people on the train this morning.

2 There's too much traffic on the roads.
   There are _____ _____ cars on the roads.

3 There weren't any places to park.
   There were _____ places to park.

4 There's too little time! I need more hours in the day.
   There are _____ _____ hours in the day. I need more time!

5 Most drivers are fine, but there are some who drive really badly.
   Most drivers are fine, but there are _____ _____ who drive really badly.

6 You can park there. There's plenty of space.
   You can park there. There's a _____ _____ space.

---

4 EAT

PRESENT PERFECT SIMPLE

The present perfect is *have / has* + past participle. The past participle is usually the same as the past simple form, but look at the present, past simple and past participle forms of these verbs:

is – was – been	forget – forgot – forgotten
break – broke – broken	give – gave – given
choose – chose – chosen	go – went – gone / been*
come – came – come	know – knew – known
do – did – done	run – ran – run
drink – drank – drunk	see – saw – seen
drive – drove – driven	take – took – taken
eat – ate – eaten	wake – woke – woken
fall – fell – fallen	write – wrote – written

The present perfect is often used to start a conversation and find out about other people's experiences. You do NOT have to use the present perfect in the reply. Look at these different answers to A's question

A: *Have you ever tried horse meat?*

B: *No, I don't like the idea of it.*

   No, but I'd like to.

   Yeah, we eat it quite a lot in our country.

   Yeah, I ate it when I was in France a few years ago.

   I've had it a couple of times, but I don't really like it.

Don't use the present perfect with a past time phrase such as *yesterday* or *a few years ago*. Use the past simple.

~~Have you gone out~~ Did you go out **last night**?

~~We've had~~ We had dinner there **the other day**.

~~I've spoken~~ I spoke to him **two minutes ago**.

~~We have never eaten out~~ We never ate out **when I was a kid**.

You can make the present perfect negative with *not* or *never*. *Never* means 'not in my life'.

I've never heard of it. Where is it?

I've never tried snake. What's it like?

We often use *haven't / hasn't* with *still* and *yet* to mean 'not before now, but probably in the future'.

*You **still haven't seen** my new apartment. Why don't you come round for a coffee?*

A: *Sorry I'm late, I was waiting for the bus for ages.*

B: *Don't worry. We **haven't ordered** anything **yet**. Here's the menu.*

DID YOU KNOW?

The past participle of *go* is sometimes *been* when we want to say *went **and** came back*. When the person hasn't come back, we use *gone*.

*I've **been** to that restaurant several times.*

*Ben's not here. He's **gone** for lunch.*

Exercise 1

Choose the correct option.

1 A: We *went / have been* to a Thai place on Grove Lane yesterday. *Did you go / Have you been* there?
   B: Yeah, lots of times. We often *have got / get* a takeaway from there during the week too.

2 A: *Have you had / Did you have* anything to eat yet?
   B: Yes thanks. *I've made / I made* myself a sandwich before I left home.

3 A: Have you ever *eaten / ate* snake?
   B: Yeah. I *have had / had* some on holiday last year. It *tasted / has tasted* a bit like fish.

4 A: *Are you visited / Have you visited* Romania before?

   B: No, this *is / has been* my first time. It's great.

5 A: Sorry I'm late. I *was / have been* stuck in the office sorting out a problem.

   B: Never mind. I *was / have been* late too and James still *hasn't arrived / didn't arrive* either.

DID YOU KNOW?

You can use *have / haven't*, etc. on it's own to avoid repeating the whole verb.

*I haven't been to that restaurant, but Javi **has** (been there).*

A: *Have you talked to Karen recently?*

B: *No, I **haven't** (talked to her). **Have you** (talked to her)?*

We also use the present perfect simple with some verbs to talk about the duration of events that are still not finished now.

A: *How long **have you lived** here?*

B: *Not long. We moved here in February.*

Exercise 2

Complete each pair of sentences with the correct form of the verbs in bold. Use the present perfect in one sentence and the past simple in the other.

1 **lose**

   a I _____ my mobile two weeks ago, so I'm in a mess! It had all my contacts on it.

   b My brother _____ his mobile about five times.

2 **have**

   a I love your car. How long _____ you _____ it?

   b I _____ a car for years, but then I decided It was too expensive to run.

3 **try**

   a I _____ never _____ coffee. I don't like the smell.

   b I got these jeans on holiday, but I _____ (not) _____ them on and they don't fit very well.

4 **see**

   a _____ you ever _____ that film *Babette's Feast*? It's on tonight.

   b _____ you _____ the news last night? I was on it!

5 **know**

   a I _____ Ken for years. We're really good friends.

   b We _____ each other at all before we started working here, but we get on great.

6 **go**

   a Luigi _____ to the meeting, but I didn't.

   b I _____ there, but I think Steffie has, so ask her what it's like.

Exercise 3

Write present perfect questions using the prompts (1–6). Then match the answers a–f to the questions.

1 you / be / here before?

2 you / ever / eat / chicken feet?

3 you / try / that new restaurant round the corner?

4 Dave / speak / to you about tonight yet?

5 you two / be introduced?

6 how long / she / live / there?

a Yeah, I had them once when I was in Hong Kong.

b Yeah, we've met before actually.

c Yeah, I came on holiday here a few years ago.

d No, but I've had my phone switched off.

e About six years now.

f No, but I'd like to go there. It looks nice.

You will learn more about the present perfect in Unit 12, *Yet, already, still* and *just*; Unit 13, present perfect continuous and *how long*; Unit 15, Time phrases and tense.

TOO / NOT ... ENOUGH

too, too much, too many

Use *too* + adjective / adverb when you want / need less of something. It is often followed by the infinitive with *to* to show something is not possible as a result.

*I'm **too lazy to cook** for myself.*

*He was driving **too fast to stop** in time.*

*Is the music **too loud**?*

Use *too much* + uncountable noun or *too many* + countable noun (see also Unit 3).

*My doctor says I'm eating **too much sugar**.*

*I don't feel well. I think I had **too much ice cream**.*

***Too many people** these days eat fast food.*

*I can't go out tonight. I have **too many things to do**.*

not ... enough

Use *not* + adjective / adverb + *enough* when you need more. It is also often followed by the Infinitive (with *to*).

*My daughter helps me cook, but she's **not old enough to be left on her own** in the kitchen.*

*You did**n't** cook it **long enough**. It's still raw in the centre.*

Use *not enough* + noun (either uncountable or countable).

*They're closing down the restaurant on the corner, because it doesn't make **enough money**.*

*The match was cancelled because we didn't have **enough people** to make a team.*

Questions

You can use *enough* in questions. It means 'is it OK or is more needed?'

A: *Do you have enough food?*

B: *Yes thanks.*

*Are you **comfortable enough**?*

Exercise 1

Complete the sentences with *too, too much, too many* or *enough*. Then match the sentences with the responses a–h.

1 Do you have _____ chairs for everyone?

2 It's been cooked _____ long. Look, it's almost burnt!

3 Are you warm _____ ?

4 Have you had _____ dessert?

5 I think we made _____ food. People haven't eaten a lot.

6 Are you sure you're not _____ hot in here?

7 Wow. That's a big portion. I think we've ordered _____ dishes.

8 Is the volume loud _____ ?

a Yes thanks. It was lovely. Shall I help you clear the table?

b Actually, no. Could we sit inside instead?

c You're probably right. Shall we ask the waiter to cancel a couple?

d We don't actually. Could you bring a couple of folding ones?

e It is very warm. Could I open a window?

f Not really. Could you turn it up?

g Oh yes. Shall I ask the waiter to change it?

h I know. Would you like to take some home with you?

COMMON MISTAKES

Enough goes after an adjective / adverb, but before a noun.

*I am not ~~enough patient~~ **patient enough** to be a teacher.*

*I don't have ~~money enough~~ **enough money** to eat out every week.*

Don't use *too* to describe positive feelings. *Too* means you want *less*. Use *really / very / so* or an adjective like *great, fantastic* or *amazing!*

I love my Mum's cooking ~~too much~~. She's ~~too~~ good. I miss it now I live on my own.

*I **really** love my Mum's cooking. She's **fantastic**.*

You don't need *for* before an infinitive with *to*.

*Leave it to cool down. it's **too hot** ~~for~~ **to eat** now.*

Exercise 2

Decide which five sentences are incorrect, then correct them.

1 The restaurant we went to for my birthday was great value. The food was delicious and it was too cheap.
2 Have you put salt enough in that soup? Just check.
3 It tasted disgusting. They put too much chillies in it for my liking.
4 I find it too bitter for to drink If I don't add any sugar.
5 It didn't taste too bad, but it wasn't spicy enough for my taste.
6 I don't think this pan is enough big to cook pasta for everyone. I might need two pans.

5 RELAX

PLANS AND ARRANGEMENTS

We can use both *be going to* + infinitive (without *to*) and the present continuous to talk about future plans and arrangements. To talk about definite personal plans for the future, we generally use *be going to*.

*I'm not going to do anything tonight. I'm just **going to take** it easy.*

*I'm **going to go** for a walk after dinner.*

To talk about definite arrangements with other people – usually in the near future – we generally use the present continuous. However, *be going to* is also possible.

A: *What **are** you **doing** this weekend?*

B: *Well, I'm playing / I'm going to play basketball on Saturday. What about you?*

A: *Some important clients are coming / are going to come so I need to go to the airport to meet them.*

To talk about possible plans in the future that are not fully decided, use *might* + infinitive (without *to*) or *be thinking of* + *-ing*.

*I **might go** shopping in the morning.*

*I'm **thinking of leaving** quite early.*

Note that *might* is not usually used in questions. Instead, we often use *be thinking of*.

A: *I **might go** out somewhere later tonight.*

B: *Oh, OK. Where **are** you **thinking of going**?*

DID YOU KNOW?

When we talk about possible future plans, we sometimes use *may* instead of *might*. In this context, it means the same thing.

*I **may go** shopping in the morning.*

*I'm not totally sure yet, but I **may leave** quite early.*

*I **may go** out somewhere later tonight.*

Exercise 1

Complete the sentences with the correct form of the verbs in the box.

do	get	have (x2)	hire
meet	see	play (x2)	watch

1 A: I'm going _____ the Madrid–Malaga match at a place in town.
   B: OK. What time are you going _____ there?
   A: Quite early, so I can get a seat. Seven?
2 A: What _____ you _____ later?
   B: We _____ Gary and Sam to go to the cinema – would you like to come?
   A: Yeah, that sounds good. What are you going _____ ?
   B: *Juniper Love* – the one that won the Oscar.
3 A: We're thinking of _____ a party to celebrate finishing school.
   B: That's a good idea. Are you thinking of _____ it at your house?
   A: I don't know. We might _____ a room somewhere. It depends how expensive it is.
4 A: Simon and Matt told me to tell you they _____ tennis tomorrow if you're interested.
   B: What time are they going _____ ?

Exercise 2

Write positive sentences (+), negative sentences (–) or questions (?) using the ideas below and the structures in brackets.

1 I / call you later. (might / +)
2 What / you / do. (be going to / ?)
3 We / have / a meeting about it. (be thinking of / +)
4 I / go on holiday this year. (be going to / –)
5 I / be in class tomorrow. (might / –)
6 Where / you / stay. (be thinking of / ?)
7 I / go fishing this weekend. (be going to / +)
8 What / you / go / to see. (be thinking of / ?)
9 I / come. It depends how I feel. (may / –)

SUPERLATIVES

In general, we use *most* with two- or three-syllable adjectives or adverbs.

*Football is **the most popular** game in the world.*

*Moscow is one of **the most expensive** cities in the world.*

*It was one of **the most boring** matches ever!*

We add *-est* to adjectives or adverbs of one syllable.

*That's **the longest** film in the series.*

*She's **the youngest** person to ever win an Olympic medal.*

*He's **the oldest** person to ever play for his country.*

With two-syllable words ending in *-y*, the *-y* changes to *-iest*.

*The basic rules are among **the easiest** to grasp of any sport.*

*I can't stand him. He's **the laziest** player ever.*

Note that for some short adjectives – *big*, *fit*, *sad*, etc. – we double the final consonant when we add *-est*. *Wimbledon is probably* **the biggest** *competition in tennis*. Also note that some two-syllable words can take either *-est* or *the most*. *Two o'clock is our* **quietest / most quiet** *time of the day.*

DID YOU KNOW?

We usually use *the* before superlatives, but sometimes we can use *my*, *his*, etc.

My best *time for running a kilometre is four minutes twenty.*

Exercise 1

Complete the sentences with the superlative form of the adjectives.

1 It's _____ film ever! (bad)
2 It's freezing outside so wear your _____ coat. (thick)
3 My mum's probably _____ person I know. (generous)
4 We're usually _____ in the afternoons, so ring in the morning. (busy)
5 Personally, I like cricket. It's _____ sport there is! (interesting)
6 My cat died last week. It was really awful – _____ thing ever! (sad)
7 I tried it, but it was _____ thing ever! (disgusting)
8 Deano's has _____ selection of clothes in town. (wide)

Superlatives + present perfect

Superlatives often go with the present perfect.

It's **the best** *book* **I've (ever) read** *in my life.*
I think this is **the fittest I've ever been.**
He's **the most successful** *striker who's* **ever played** *for us.*
That's **the most exciting** *match* **I've seen in a long time.**

Exercise 2

Write sentences with a superlative + the present perfect.

It / long time / he / be / away from home.
It's the longest time he's been away from home.

1 He / nice person / I / ever meet.
2 It / exciting race / I / take part in.
3 That computer / reliable / we / ever have.
4 This / complicated game / I / ever play.
5 It / funny book / I / read / in a long time.
6 That / smart / I / ever see / you look.

6 FAMILY AND FRIENDS

QUESTION FORMATION

When we make questions and negatives, we use different auxiliary verbs. There are only three: *be*, *do* and *have*.

Normal verbs

(Question word)	Auxiliary	Noun / pronoun	Verb
Present simple			
	Do	you	work?
	Do	they	live near here?
What	does	he	do?
Past simple			
	Did	you	speak to him?
	Did	your friends	get home OK?
Why	did	he	go there?
Present continuous			
	Is	she	just visiting?
	Are	they	driving here?
Where	are	you	staying?
Present perfect			
	Has	she	decided yet?
	Have	your parents	met her before?
How long	have	you	been here?

Be

(Question word)	Be	Noun / pronoun	Adjective, adverb or noun
Present			
Who	is	your favourite	singer?
	Are	your parents	OK?
	Is	your sister	married?
How	are	you?	
Past			
Why	weren't	they	there?
	Were	you	very annoyed?
	Was	he	OK last night?
Where	was	the party?	

DID YOU KNOW?

We DON'T usually use full sentences or auxiliaries to answer questions.

A: *How old are you?*
B: *23. (NOT I am 23)*
A: *Do you like learning English?*
B: *Not really, but I need it for my job. (NOT I don't really like it, but ...)*

Exercise 1

Complete the questions with the correct auxiliary verb or write X if no auxiliary is needed.

1 A: Where _____ she work?
   B: In a café in the centre of town.
   A: Oh, OK. _____ she worked there long?
   B: No. She started quite recently.

2 A: _____ you like football.
   B: Yeah. I'm a Leeds fan. You're a Milan fan, aren't you?
   A: No, who told you that?
   B: The guy in class with the long hair. So who _____ you support?
   A: Fiorentina.
   B: Oh, OK. _____ they play last night?
   A: Yes. We lost … to Milan!

3 A: What _____ you do?
   B: I'm a student.
   A: Oh right. What _____ you studying?
   B: Civil engineering.

4 A: I'm going to Brazil in May.
   B: Oh really? How long _____ you going for?
   A: Two weeks.
   B: OK. _____ you been there before?
   A: No, it's actually the first time I've ever been abroad.

Questions without auxiliaries

Did you notice this question in Exercise 1 above?

Who told you that?

We sometimes ask questions without an auxiliary because we want to know who or what did an action (the subject of the verb). These questions usually start with *who*, but sometimes other question words are used.

*Who **organised** it?*

*Who **took** that photo?*

*Who **told** you to come here?*

*What **happened**?*

*Which one**'s** better?*

Exercise 2

Cross out the auxiliary where it is not needed.

Who ~~did~~ told you that?

1 What did you buy?
2 Which battery do lasts longer?
3 Who did gave you this?
4 Who was at the party last night?
5 Who did you speak to? Maybe I can talk to them.
6 What did happened to you? You're really late.
7 Why did it happen? It normally works fine.
8 Who do wants coffee? Put your hand up.
9 Who's moved my bag? It was here a moment ago.

Questions with *how* or *what*

We sometimes use *how* and *what* with other words when we ask questions.

We use *how* with an adjective or adverb.

How old is he?

How far is it from here?

We use *what* with a noun.

What kind of films do you like?

What time did you get home?

Exercise 3

Write *How …?* or *What …?* questions using the words in brackets. The first is done for you.

1 A: _____ ? (old / be / your gran)   *How old is your gran?*
   B: 83.

2 A: _____ at the weekend? (kinds of things / you / do)
   B: I always play tennis on Saturdays. Apart from that, I go to the cinema, watch TV, nothing much.

3 A: _____ last Friday? (film / you / see)
   B: *Forever*. It's a romance. My wife wanted to see it.

4 A: _____ here? (long / you / live)
   B: About six months now. We moved here in January.

5 A: _____ in the exam? (questions / they / ask)
   B: *How old are you? Where do you live?* Things like that.

6 A: _____ tomorrow morning? (time / you / leave)
   B: Four o'clock! Our flight's at seven and it'll take at least an hour to get to the airport.

7 A: _____ to get to work? (far / you / travel)
   B: It's 50 minutes by train and then a ten-minute walk.

8 A: _____ in your class? (many students / there)
   B: There are twelve of us, I think.

SIMILARITIES AND CONTRASTS

Number

Both and *neither* refer to two people or things.

All and *none* refer to three or more.

neither and *none*

We use *neither* and *none* to show that the people / things are the same in <u>not</u> doing / being something. We don't follow *all* or *both* with negatives.

Neither of them take no for an answer.

~~Both of them don't take no for an answer.~~

None of us want to take over the business.

~~All of us don't want to take over the business.~~

both of, *all of*, etc.

If *both*, *all* etc. is before the pronoun, we have to use *both of*, *all of* etc. Then we use the pronouns *us*, *you* and *them*.

Look at the ways of saying the same thing.

We both work as waiters.   **Both of us** work as waiters.
They're all very confident.   **All of them** are very confident.
They're both quite short.   **Neither of them** are very tall.
We all hate to sit still.   **None of us** like to sit still.

whereas

Whereas has a similar meaning to 'but'. Use it to show a contrast – how people / things are different.

*My dad's quite religious, **whereas** my mum isn't.*

*Neither of my parents speak English, **but** I do.*

Exercise 1

Complete the sentences with one word.

1 I've got two brothers and a sister and we're _____ doctors.
2 I see my two grans a lot because they _____ live nearby.
3 My girlfriend and I often play tennis together. _____ of us are very good, but we enjoy it anyway.
4 Although they're twins, they're _____ quite different.
5 Both _____ you, can you stop screaming and shouting?
6 My family are all very friendly, but none of _____ like going out very much. We're happy with our own company.
7 I didn't know any of my grandparents. They _____ died before I was born.
8 He had six children but none of _____ were interested in taking over the business.

either and any

We use *either* or *any* after a negative form of the verb instead of *neither* or *none*.

I **don't** get on very well with **either** of my neighbours.
He had five exams and he **didn't** pass **any** of them.

Exercise 2

Choose the correct option.

1 I've got two older sisters, but I'm not very close to *either / both / none* of them.
2 *Neither / Either* of my parents speak *any / none* foreign languages at all.
3 Can you believe it? *Any / None* of my brothers or sisters remembered my birthday.
4 I don't know *both / none / any* of the people in my street.
5 I don't talk to *either / both / none* of my ex-husbands anymore!
6 I never really see *any / both / neither* of my cousins anymore. They live too far away.
7 *Neither / Either / Any* of my brothers are very fit. They hardly ever do *none / any* exercise.
8 I hate networking and managing people. I'm no good at *either / both / none* of them.

7 YOUR PLACE

HAVE TO, DON'T HAVE TO, CAN AND CAN'T

have to

To talk about rules or things that are essential or necessary to do, use *have to / has to* + infinitive (without *to*)
We **have to pay** a month's deposit before we can move in.
I **have to walk** about ten minutes to get to the train station.
Do you **have to do** much housework?
My brother **has to help** my dad run the family business.

don't have to

To talk about things that are not essential or necessary, but that you can do if you want to, use *don't have to / doesn't have to* + infinitive (without *to*).
I **don't have to do** any housework, but I like to do the cooking.
It's Sunday tomorrow, so I **don't have to get** up early!
It's OK for her! She **doesn't have to** work evenings!

can

To show something is possible and you are free to do it if you want, use *can* + infinitive (without *to*).
I live near the river and you **can walk** along the banks, which is nice.
Can we stay with you when we come to Berlin?

can't

To show something is not possible and you have no choice, use *can't* + infinitive (without *to*).
I **can't help** you, I'm afraid.

Exercise 1

Choose the correct option.

1 I *have to / don't have to / can* share a room with two other students! Luckily, we all get on OK.
2 *Do you have to / Can you* travel far to work?
3 You *can / have to / don't have to* tell me if you don't want to. It's your choice.
4 Unfortunately, we *can't / don't have to / has to* use the pool that's connected to the block of flats.
5 I think she *can / has to / doesn't have to* pay about 100 euros a week rent.

6 I *have to / don't have to / can* always talk to my flatmates if I have a problem.
7 *Do you have to / Can you* have friends to stay in your flat?
8 We *have to / don't have to / can't* do military service. We *have to / can / don't have to* choose to do social work or community work instead if we want to.

DID YOU KNOW?

To talk about ability / inability at a particular time, we sometimes use *be (not) able to* instead of *can / can't*. It's usually used in more formal contexts and in written English.

Exercise 2

Rewrite the sentences using *is / are (not) able to* + verb.

1 I'm afraid we can't help you with that.
2 It's not a palace or anything, but at least I can pay the rent!
3 We have five bedrooms, so we can invite friends to stay, which is nice.
4 I think there's some kind of problem because I can't enter the site.
5 She can't sleep at the moment because she has very bad pain in her leg.
6 You're lucky you can stay with friends. It saves you a lot of money!
7 The clients called earlier and said they can't make the meeting today.
8 He has to work overseas, but he can visit four times a year.

Exercise 3

Correct the mistake in each sentence.

1 We have to telling our landlord three months in advance if we want to move out.
2 My sister cans stay with my uncle whenever she visits the capital.
3 My friend Juan have to find a new place to live.
4 You doesn't have to do it if you don't want to.
5 If you want, I can to drive you home.
6 I'd love to get my own place, but I don't can afford it.

WILL / WON'T

We use *will / won't* + infinitive (without *to*) to talk about future actions or give opinions about the future. We often use *will / won't* as an immediate response to situations / things people say, and to talk about now or the immediate future.

Offers
A: *Can I use the washing machine?*
B: *Oh, **I'll do** it for you, if you like.*
A: *Is it OK if I have a shower in the morning?*
B: *Of course. **I'll get** you some towels in a moment.*

Opinions about the future
You're welcome to watch TV. Although **you'll probably have to** watch repeats of The Big Bang Theory as that's all my son Theo seems to watch.
A: *He's sixteen.*
B: *Oh yes? Like my baby brother. **He'll remind** me of home.*
A: *I think **you'll be** warm enough but I can get you a blanket, if you want.*
B: *Oh no. **I'll be** fine.*

Decisions (made at the time of speaking)
A: *And here?*
B: *Oh that's Oliver's study, but **we won't go** in there. It's a mess!*
A: *The dog's very friendly*
B: *I'm sure, but maybe **I'll go out** the front next time.*

Promises

A: *Your dog scared me.*
B: **He won't bite** *you. I promise. He's very friendly.*
A: *Do you have your homework?*
B: *No, but* **I'll give** *it to you tomorrow.*

Questions

Most questions with *will* are about opinions, and they often use *do you think*.

Do you think you'll be warm enough?
Do you think Spain will win tonight?
What time **do you think you'll** be here?

Exercise 1

Complete the dialogues with *'ll* or *won't*.

1 A: I need to wash these clothes.
   B: OK. Leave them there. I _____ do them with the rest of the washing.
2 A: Maksim. Can you hear me? I need to use the bathroom.
   B: Oh, OK. I _____ be long.
3 A: Do you mind if I use your computer?
   B: Of course not. I _____ just save and close what I was working on.
4 A: Do you think you _____ be home for dinner?
   B: I don't think so. I probably _____ finish till late and we _____ probably eat near there.
5 A: Shall I do the washing up?
   B: No, it's OK. I _____ do it. Just leave the dishes in the sink.
6 A: Have you seen my keys?
   B: No, but I _____ lend you mine if you like. I'm going to be at home all day.
   A: Are you sure? I promise I _____ lose them!
7 A: Be careful, and call me if you need any help.
   B: I _____ ! But, don't worry. We _____ be fine.
8 A: Do you think you _____ go to the party later?
   B: Probably not, to be honest. We probably _____ get back in time and I'm sure we _____ be too tired anyway.

DID YOU KNOW?

When we give opinions, we use *will / won't* to show we're certain. However, if we're less certain, we often add words like *I doubt, I don't think, I'm not sure, it's possible* and *probably*.
I doubt *I'll go.*
I'm not sure *I'll have time.*
It's possible *I'll finish early.*
I **probably** *won't see you before I go, so I'll say goodbye now.*

WIll and other future forms

Remember that when we talk about plans and arrangements we have made, we use *be going to* + infinitive (without *to*) or the present continuous. We also sometimes use *be going to* for opinions about the future.

Exercise 2

Choose the correct form.

1 I can't meet you tonight. A friend of mine *will come / is coming* to my house for dinner.
2 I need to give you an injection. *It won't hurt / it's not hurting.*
3 A: What are you doing tonight?
   B: Nothing. *I'm just going to go / I'll just go* home and have an early night.
4 Our oldest son *is getting / will get* married next month.
5 That looks hard. *I'll help / I'm helping* you if you want.

6 A: I need to send some letters sometime today.
   B: *I'll go / I'm going* into town later, so *I'll post / I'm going to post* them for you if you want.

You will learn more about *will / won't* in Unit 2, Developing conversations (page 20); Unit 8, First conditionals; Unit 15, Time phrases and tense.

8 EDUCATION

FIRST CONDITIONALS

First conditionals are sentences of two parts – one part to talk about possible future situations or actions and the other to talk about the results of those actions.

The *if*-clause

The *if*-clause refers to possible future situations or actions, but it uses present tenses. Don't use *will / won't* here to refer to the future. The *if*-clause doesn't have to start the sentence.
If I ~~will get~~ **get** *the grades I want …*
… if you ~~won't~~ **don't start** *working harder.*

The result clause

We can talk about the result of the possible future action using *will / won't* + infinitive (without *to*). *Will / won't* shows you are certain about the result.
Well, if it all goes well, I'll have two more years.
You **won't pass** *if you don't start working harder!*

You can use *will probably* or *might (possibly)* to show you are less certain.
If I get the grades I want, **I'll probably** *do a Master's.*
I'll probably go *out later if I finish all my homework.*
If I can't find a job here soon, I **might go** *abroad somewhere.*

Questions

Look at the ways of asking questions.
Where **will she live** *if she gets into university in England?*
What **will you do** *if that happens?*
What if *you don't get into university?*

Exercise 1

Match the two parts of the sentences.

1 If you copy anything directly from the internet,
2 If I do well in the entrance exam,
3 I'll give you a hand with that
4 If the bank won't lend me money,
5 I'll graduate next December
6 We'll be late for the lecture
7 If you go to room 605,
8 I'll probably do some research for my project today,

a you'll find the finance department. Ask there.
b they'll then ask me to go for an interview.
c if I don't fail any of my finals.
d you'll get 0%.
e if you want.
f I might need to borrow some from you.
g if I'm not too busy with everything else!
h if we don't hurry up!

DID YOU KNOW?

If we start a sentence with the *if*-clause, we use a comma after it. If we start with the result clause, we don't usually use commas.
If I save enough money, **I'll take** *a few months off.*
I'll take *a few months off* **if I save** *enough money.*

Exercise 2

Decide which four sentences are incorrect, then correct them.

1 If I'll go to England, my English will get better.
2 You don't do well at the interview tomorrow if you don't look smart enough.
3 I'm sure your tutor will help if you ask her to.
4 If I find the website address, I send it you later.
5 If I'm still feeling bad, I won't come to class.
6 If I won't go to university, my parents will be really upset.

HAD TO / COULD

had to

Use *had to* + infinitive (without *to*) to talk about things that were necessary to do. Use *did* + *have to* + infinitive (without *to*) in questions.

*Sometimes we just **had to copy** from the book.*

***Did you have to** have extra Spanish lessons?*

didn't have to

Use *didn't have to* + infinitive (without *to*) for things that were not necessary to do.

*We **didn't have to do** much homework in England – a bit of reading or something.*

could

Use *could* + infinitive (without *to*) for things in the past that were possible – that you had a choice about.

*My wife and I **could organise** our holidays to be at home with the kids most of the holiday.*

couldn't

Use *couldn't* for things that were not possible because:
(1) you didn't have the ability; (2) because of a rule / law; or (3) because of a problem.

1 *I **couldn't understand** very much. It was horrible.*
2 *We **couldn't take** mobile phones with us to my school.*
3 *I **couldn't see**, because there were people in front of me.*

Exercise 1

Choose the correct option.

1 I *could / couldn't* go home for lunch when I was at school, but now I'm working, I don't have time.
2 I *had to / didn't have to* get up early when I was at school, but at university the classes start later.
3 When I was living at home, I *had to / didn't have to* cook, but now I'm on my own, I *had to / have to* make my own dinner.
4 When I was at school, we *couldn't / could* call a teacher by their first name. We *had to / have to* call them 'Sir' or 'Miss'.
5 Go now if you want to. You *don't have to / didn't have to* wait for me.

DID YOU KNOW?

Must has no past form. Instead, we use *had to*.

*She's not here because she ~~must~~ **had to go** and see someone.*

be able to

To talk about ability / inability at a particular time in the past, we sometimes use *wasn't / weren't able to* instead of *could / couldn't*.

*I **wasn't able to understand** very much in the class!*

*We **weren't able to see** much because we were at the back.*

Exercise 2

Decide which six sentences are incorrect, then correct them.

1 We can't come yesterday because of the bad weather.
2 I'm going to the bank. I have to get some money.
3 We don't have to study English when I was at school.
4 I'm sorry I weren't able to come to class last week. I was ill.
5 When I was at school, we always must stand up when the teacher came into the classroom.
6 Could you move, please? I can't see the board.
7 He has to retake the test twice before he passed.
8 The question was so difficult, I couldn't to answer it.
9 In the past, teachers were able to organise the course how they wanted.

9 MIND AND BODY

GIVING ADVICE

The most common way of giving advice – to say what you think is the best thing to do – is *should* + infinitive (without *to*). We often soften advice by adding *maybe* at the beginning of the sentence. It's also common to say *I think you should*.

Should is a modal verb. With modal verbs we use the same form for all persons, we do not add *-s* for the third person. We do not use *do / does* in questions, or *don't / doesn't* in negatives. The negative form is *shouldn't*.

***Maybe you should go** home and get some rest.*

***You shouldn't worry** about it. It'll all be fine.*

***What should I do** if the medicine doesn't work?*

What do you think I should do?

Two other common ways of giving advice are *why don't you* + infinitive (without *to*) and *ought to* + infinitive (without *to*). They basically mean the same as *should*.

***Why don't you get** some sunglasses to protect your eyes a bit?*

*(Maybe) you **ought to try** it.*

Exercise 1

Rewrite the sentences using the words in brackets.

1 You should go on a diet. (why)
2 You ought to put some cream on that rash. (should)
3 What do you think we should do? (ought)
4 You should phone and make an appointment. (don't)
5 Anyone taking drugs to improve their performance should be banned. (to)
6 Why don't you drink less coffee? (maybe)

Exercise 2

Complete the sentences with *should / shouldn't* and the verbs in the box.

do	eat	go	ignore	miss	watch

1 You _____ so much! You'll get fat if you're not careful!
2 I'm not surprised your eyes are sore. You _____ less TV!
3 If it hurts, you really _____ and see a doctor about it. You _____ just _____ it. It might get worse.
4 The government _____ more to sort the problem out.
5 I know you're busy, but it's an important appointment. You really _____ it if you can help it.

IMPERATIVES

We use imperatives to:

1 give instructions: **Take** *twice daily with food.*
2 give an order: **Be** *quiet.*
3 give advice: **Go** *and see your doctor if you're worried.*
4 encourage: **Come on!** *You can do it!*
5 make an offer: **Have** *a seat.*
6 warn: **Don't buy that one.** *It's bad quality.*
7 reassure: **Don't worry.** *It'll be fine.*

Structures with imperatives

We often use imperatives in conditional sentences, especially when giving advice.

Don't worry if you find *it difficult. (= you shouldn't worry)*
If you need *anything, just* **email** *me.*
If you can't *sleep,* **try** *counting backwards from 100.*

We often use *will* after imperatives.

Hurry up *or we***'ll** *miss the train.*
Have *a seat. I***'ll** *stand.*
Don't worry *about cleaning up. I***'ll** *do it.*
Don't make *so much noise. You***'ll** *wake the baby!*

We sometimes use imperatives as requests when talking to friends, but it's better to use *could you / can you* because imperatives can sometimes sound rude and too direct with people we're not close to. However, in all the examples above, imperatives sound fine.

Pass *the salt.* (with friends)
Could you pass *the salt, please?* (more polite, less direct)

DID YOU KNOW?

We often use *so* + adjective after negative imperatives.
Don't be so lazy!
Don't be so rude!

Exercise 1

Correct each pair / group of sentences by making one of the imperatives negative.

1 Panic. Stay calm.
2 Whisper. Speak up. We can't hear you.
3 Be careful. Slip.
4 Just sit there. Do something.
5 Take your time. Rush.
6 Be quiet. Make so much noise.
7 Get up. Be so lazy.
8 Wait for me. Go ahead. I'll catch you up.

DID YOU KNOW?

We can use imperatives to give advice to friends – instead of using *maybe you should / ought to ...*
Phone *them and* **make** *an appointment.* (with friends)
Maybe you should / ought to phone *them and* **make** *an appointment.* (more polite, less direct)

Exercise 2

Rewrite the sentences using *could* for requests and *should* for advice.

1 Pour me some water, please.
2 Try talking to someone about it.
3 Bring me the bill.
4 Help me carry these bags to the car.
5 Don't drive if you're taking that medication.
6 Don't call him now. It's too late.

10 PLACES TO STAY

SECOND CONDITIONALS

Second conditionals are sentences of two parts. We use them to talk about imagined situations or things that are unlikely or impossible.

The *if*-clause

In the *if*-clause, use the past simple to talk about imagined situations. It refers to now or the future.

... **if she ate** *a nut by mistake.*
(She doesn't plan to eat one, but imagine her eating one.)
... if I could.
(I can't move anyone, but imagine the situation is possible.)

The result clause

Use *would* + infinitive (without *to*) to talk about imagined results or further actions.

She'd be *ill if she ate a nut by mistake.*
(She isn't ill now, only because she hasn't eaten a chocolate with nuts in.)
I would move *them if I could.* (I want to move them, but I can't.)

might

You can replace *would* with *might* to show less certainty about the imagined result.

They **might attract** *more people if they weren't so expensive!*
(= maybe they would attract more people)

Exercise 1

1 Match the two parts of the sentences.

1 The company wouldn't have these problems
2 I'd be more willing to try camping
3 It's a nice hotel, but it'd be better
4 I think that if they opened a branch in Brighton,
5 I suppose if I had a lot of money,
6 If something like that happened to me,

a if the rooms were a bit more child-friendly.
b I'd complain. I'd be really angry about it!
c if they employed staff who spoke better English!
d I might stay in a top hotel, but there are other things I'd prefer to buy.
e if the weather here was a bit better.
f it'd be a big success.

2 For each sentence above, say what the real situation is now.

The company has problems because the staff don't speak good English.

Advice

We often use a second conditional to give advice.

If I were you, I'd book *online. It'd be cheaper.* (I'm not you!)
If I was / were *in your situation, I'd complain.*

Note that we often only say the *would* part, because the situation is obvious.

A: *Do you think I should say something to the manager.*
B: **I would.** *He was quite rude to you.* (= I would, if I were you).

Exercise 2

Choose the correct form.

1 I might think about staying there if it *was / would be* nearer the beach.
2 I'd / I'll pick you up from your hotel if it *was / wasn't* so far from the centre of town!
3 If I *am / were* you, I *wouldn't / don't* have the hotel breakfast. *I'll / I'd* eat somewhere else instead.
4 *It'd / It's* be better if the website *was / will* be more user-friendly.
5 I'm having a good time here, but it *was / would be* even better if it *wasn't / wouldn't be* raining all the time!
6 If we *was / were* earning more money, we *can / could* stay in nicer places.

USED TO

To talk about past habits, we can use either *used to* + infinitive (without *to*) or the past simple.
*They **used to take** us on day trips.*
*We **went** swimming all the time.*

We also use both *used to* + infinitive (without *to*) and the past simple to talk about past states.
*My parents **used to own** an apartment on the beach.*
*It **was** so strict.*

The most common way to form the negative of *used to* is with *never*.
*It sounds dull, but **I never used to** get bored.*

You can also form the negative of *used to* like this:
*It sounds dull, but **I didn't use to** get bored.*

Note that when we talk about actions that only happened once in the past, we use the past simple. We cannot use *used to*.
*We once **made** cornflake cakes.*

There is no present form of *used to*. It is only used to talk about the past. For habits in the present, use the present simple (see page 166).
*My son usually **spends** his summers like this.*

Exercise 1

Complete the sentences using *used to, never used to* or *usually*.

1 We moved to Zagreb this year. We _____ live in quite a small place on the coast.
2 I _____ go to the beach every day, but now I'm working I can't.
3 We _____ go to the cinema because the nearest one was 60km away!
4 Now that I'm in Madrid, we _____ go out three or four nights a week.
5 Although there weren't many facilities, we _____ get bored, because we _____ make our own entertainment at home.

DID YOU KNOW?

When we use the past simple, we often add time phrases. However, when we use *used to* we often leave the time phrases out.
*My parents **lived** in Holland **in the 80's**.*
*My parents **used to live** in Holland.*
*I **didn't like** vegetables **when I was younger**.*
*I **never used to like** vegetables, but I love them now.*

Exercise 2

Decide which five sentences are incorrect, then correct them.

1 Last week, I used to have to study for my exams.
2 Before I started working here, I used work as a researcher for a drug company.
3 He's lost a lot of weight. He used to weigh 100 kilos.
4 I didn't never used to have lunch at school. I always had lunch at home.
5 I didn't use to like swimming, but I go quite a lot now.
6 Most Sundays, me and my kids use to watch a DVD at home together.
7 When I was a kid, we usually go to the mountains during the summer.
8 My grandparents usually come to stay with us at Christmas.

11 SCIENCE AND NATURE

PAST PERFECT SIMPLE

We use the past perfect simple to show that something happened before another past action. The past perfect is often used after the verbs *realise, find out, discover* and *remember* to refer to an earlier event. It is usually used with other verbs in the past simple.
*I realised **I'd made** a mistake and changed the answer.*
*I suddenly remembered I **hadn't bought** any food for my dog.*

When we describe actions in the order that they happened in, we usually just use the past simple.
*One day the owner **heard** the parrots copying his customers' requests and **trained** them to actually take orders.* (First he heard them, then he trained them.)

Exercise 1

Complete the sentences using the past perfect simple form of the verbs.

1 That's it! We met at Mina's party! I knew I _____ you somewhere before. (see)
2 I suddenly remembered I _____ to bring my homework. (forget)
3 When I got home, I realised I _____ my keys in the office. (leave)
4 We found out we _____ at university at the same time, but we _____ . (be / not meet)
5 When we arrived at the hospital, they were ready to operate, but there was a problem. Because they _____ me not to, I _____ breakfast that morning. (not tell / eat)
6 To begin with, they were surprised he _____ so well in his exams, but then they discovered he _____ ! (do / cheat)

Exercise 2

Decide which actions happened first and change the verb to the past perfect.

1 After they had one date, he asked her to marry him.
2 I rang you as soon as I heard the news.
3 I never went on a plane until I went to Japan.
4 They had an argument before I arrived, so there was a bad atmosphere. It was quite uncomfortable.
5 I was fed up after I found out I didn't get the job.

PASSIVES

To make passive sentences, use a form of the verb *be* + a past participle.

See Unit 4 page 170 for more on past participles.

	Subject	*be*	Past participle	
Present simple	*The process*	*is*	*repeated*	*several times.*
	She	*is*	*employed*	*by the government.*
	You	*are*	*left*	*with a very thin layer.*
	Mice	*are*	*used*	*in experiments.*
	We	*are*	*taught*	*French in school.*
	I	*am*	*paid*	*1,000 euros a month.*
Past simple	*Graphene*	*was*	*discovered*	*by two Russian scientists.*
	He	*was*	*arrested*	*for drink driving.*
	I	*was*	*born*	*in Berlin.*
	We	*were*	*asked*	*to leave.*
	They	*were*	*told*	*about it.*

	Question word	*be*	Subject	Past participle
Present Past	*Who*	*are*	*you*	*employed by?*
	Where	*were*	*you*	*born?*
		Was	*he*	*arrested?*

Modals

Passives after *can / could / should* use *be* + past participle.

*Experiments on animals **should be banned**.*

***Could** those things **be replaced** by Graphene?*

Who or what does the action

The most common reasons for using passives are because we don't know exactly who does an action, or because it's unimportant who does it.

However, you can introduce who or what does the action in passive sentences using *by*.

*Graphene was discovered **by two Russian scientists**.*

*We were stopped **by the police** when we were walking home.*

Avoiding passives

Passives are used a lot in formal writing. In speech, we often use *you* or *they* as a general subject to avoid using passives.

*Experiments on animals **should be banned**.*

***They should ban** experiments on animals.*

Exercise 1

Rewrite the sentences using passives.

They told me I couldn't work in there.
I was told I couldn't work in there.

1 You repeat the test a number of times
2 They send me junk emails all the time.
3 You usually make it with lamb, but you can use beef.
4 You could use Graphene in mobile phones.
5 They introduced new stricter limits on pollution last year.
6 They arrested two men after they found a bomb in their car.

DID YOU KNOW?

In passive sentences adverbs usually go between *be* and the past participle.

*This dish **is usually served** with rice.*

*I **wasn't badly hurt** when I fell – just a few small cuts.*

Exercise 2

Complete each pair of sentences with the verb given. Use one passive form and one active.

1 fund
  a I think the government should _____ more research into Graphene.
  b The study _____ by the company who made the product, so I'm not sure you can trust the results.
2 catch
  a The government wants fishermen to _____ fewer fish.
  b Their head scientist _____ lying about the results of their research.
3 break
  a I _____ my arm when I was taking my dog for a walk.
  b To test its quality, the stone _____ into tiny pieces.
4 wake up
  a _____ you _____ by that storm last night?
  b I've been in a rush all morning because I _____ late.
5 allow
  a We _____ not _____ to use the internet at work.
  b You heat the metal to a very high temperature and then _____ it to cool.
6 give
  a My gran _____ me some socks for my birthday.
  b It _____ to me as a leaving present.

Intransitive verbs

You can only make passives with verbs that take an object. The verbs below don't take an object and can't be used in the passive form. Verbs like these are often marked with an [I] in dictionaries. This means they are intransitive.

appear	come	exist	happen	progress	seem
behave	disappear	go	last	rise	sleep

Exercise 3

Decide which four sentences are incorrect, then correct them.

1 How was the accident happened?
2 The internet didn't exist when I was at university.
3 A dog was suddenly appeared in front of me.
4 Fortunately, none of us badly was hurt.
5 Prices in the shops have risen a lot recently.
6 Those batteries weren't lasted very long.

12 ON THE PHONE

JUST, ALREADY, YET, STILL

Just, *already* and *yet* are often connected to the present perfect (although they can be used with other tenses). *Still* is sometimes used with a negative present perfect, but is more common with other present tenses.

just

Just + the present perfect simple shows an action is recent. It often goes with *only*.

A: *Is Gary here?*
B: *You've **just** missed him. He's **just** walked out of the door.*

A: *Sorry, I'm late*
B: *Don't worry. I've **only just** got here.*

already

Already + the present perfect shows something happened before, often sooner than expected. It's usually in positive sentences.

*I've **already** spoken to my boss and he's fine with the price.*
*I can't believe you've **already** finished those biscuits.*

yet

Yet + the present perfect in a negative sentence shows something hasn't happened, but we expect it to happen. We also use it in questions.

*He's not got up **yet**. Shall I wake him?*
*Have you seen the latest Almodóvar film **yet**? You'll love it.*

still

Still shows an action or situation continues unchanged.
*I'm afraid there's **still** no answer. He must **still** be in his meeting.*
*He's 45, but he **still** lives with his parents.*

DID YOU KNOW?

When *yet* and *still* are used with present perfect negatives, they both have a similar meaning but the position in the sentence is different.
*I **still** haven't got through to him. I'll ring him again.*
*I haven't got through to him **yet**. I'll ring him again.*

Exercise 1

Write sentences with *just*, *already*, *yet* and *still* using the prompts below.

1 you / speak / the bank yet?
2 I / have / time yet. I'll do it tomorrow.
3 she / only just / graduate.
4 she / still / try / to decide / what to do with her life.
5 I'm afraid he / be / back yet.
6 don't worry! I / already / sort out / everything.
7 she / just / hand / the work to me this second. I'll put it in the post now.
8 he / already / make $1 million / and he's only 26!

REPORTING SPEECH

When we report what people said, we often move 'one tense back'.

present simple → past simple
present perfect → past perfect
past simple → past perfect
will → would
can → could

Direct speech:	***I've cancelled** your cards.*
Reported speech:	*The guy I spoke to told me **he'd cancelled** them.*
Direct Speech:	*They**'ll be** with you within three or four days.*
Reported speech:	*He said the new cards **would be** with me within three or four days.*
Direct speech:	***I'm** very sorry.*
Reported speech:	*He said **he was** very sorry.*

Note that the time phrase may also change.
'This week' → *Last week / That week*
'Today' → *Yesterday / That day*

Exercise 1

Complete the reported speech sentences.

1 'We're installing a new computer system.'
   → I phoned last month and the man I spoke to told me you _____ a new system. Why is it still so slow?
2 'We've tried to deliver the order twice this week.'
   → The man I spoke to on Friday said you _____ to deliver my order twice that week, but that's impossible! I was at home all last week.
3 'According to our records, the package arrived in the country on May 1st.'
   → The last time I called, I was told that the package _____ already _____ in the country – and now you're saying it hasn't!
4 'Your cards will be with you by Friday at the latest.'
   → I called two weeks ago and was told that my cards _____ with me within a couple of days, but I still haven't received them.
5 'We can offer you a full refund.'
   → Last time I called, the guy told me you _____ me a full refund, but now you're saying there's nothing you can do!

DID YOU KNOW?

When we report questions that start with a question word, we don't use *do / does / did*. The word order becomes subject + verb.
'Where do you live?' → *She asked me where **I lived**.*
'How old are you?' → *He asked me how old **I was**.*

For *yes / no* questions that start with *do, can, would*, etc. add *if*.
'Can you hear me?' → *He asked **if I could** hear him.*
'Have you seen it before?' → *She asked me **if I'd seen** it before.*

Exercise 2

Complete the reported questions.

1 'Why do you want to work for us?'
   → They asked me why _____ .
2 'What are your career goals?'
   → They asked me what _____ .
3 'Who did you speak to last time you called?'
   → They asked me who _____ the last time I called.
4 'Where did you go to school?'
   → They asked me where _____ .
5 'Have you had many other interviews?'
   → They asked me _____ .
6 'Is there anything you want to ask?'
   → They asked me _____ .

13 CULTURE

NOUN PHRASES

These are some common patterns for noun phrases. The main noun is in bold. Notice its position in the two patterns.

noun + noun (compound nouns)	a Nollywood **film** a **film** cameraman the film **industry** a traffic **jam**
noun + preposition + noun	a **work** of art the **issue** of stolen art the latest **DVDs** of the Nigerian film industry an **interest** in modern art

Plurals

We usually only make the main noun plural.
*You get a lot of **traffic jams** in the city.*
*The **cameramen** work very long hours.*
*We are dealing with the **issues** around illegal copying.*

DID YOU KNOW?

There are no clear rules about when you can make a compound noun and when you have to use a prepositional phrase.

a **gym member**	OR	a **member of a gym**
the **film industry**		~~the industry of film~~
~~life quality~~		**quality of life**.

You just have to notice common patterns and follow the rules above.

Exercise 1

1 Match the noun phrases in the box with the correct group of words below.

bookshelf	life guard	university gym
cookery book	member of a gym	war film
friend from university	quality of life	world war

1 watch a / make a / a long _____
2 experience a / fight in the / end the _____
3 improve my / a good / reduce the _____
4 work as a / have a / call the _____
5 put up a / be on the / fall off the _____
6 write a / buy a / a useful _____
7 Join the / go to the / do exercise in the _____
8 become a / be a / a regular _____
9 meet a / an old / visit a _____

2 Make the noun phrases from the box above plural, if possible.

's / '

To show that something belongs to a person, animal or organisation, we generally use *'s* after a singular noun (*Andrew's*) or irregular plurals (*children's rights*) and *'* after a plural noun (*my daughters' school*). We use a noun with *'s* or *'* instead of *his, her, their,* etc.

*I met **Andrew's / his** parents yesterday.*
***Bigelow's / Her** best film is The Hurt Locker.*
*It's against **Google's / its** policies.*
*I need to tidy the **children's / their** room.*
***My daughters' / their** English is very good.*

Exercise 2

Look at the student's text and write the correct noun phrases (1–7). The first one is done for you.

I'm very interested in the [1]~~industry of fashion~~ because my oldest sister is [2]~~a shoes designer~~. [3]~~The shoes of my sister~~ are very beautiful. I often watch the [4]~~channel fashion~~ on TV. I love the beautiful models. I have been to a few [5]~~show of fashion~~ with my sister because she sometimes gets invitations. I also go shopping for clothes every week. Really, I spend too much money because the [6]~~clothes cost~~ is quite high here and I always have a big [7]~~bill of card of credit~~ at the end of the month.

1 *fashion industry*
2 _____
3 _____
4 _____
5 _____
6 _____
7 _____

PRESENT PERFECT CONTINUOUS

The present perfect continuous (*have / has + been + -ing*) is used to talk about activities that started in the past and are unfinished.
***We've been rehearsing** The Rite of Spring recently for a concert.*
*I think she's just tired because **she's been working** so hard.*

for and since

For is used to give an amount of time.
*I've been playing the trumpet **for ten years now**.*
***For the last few weeks**, they've been showing a series on TV based on the books.*
Since is used to say when the period of time started.
*I've been learning Turkish **since 2012**.*
*I've been playing the violin **since I was about twelve**.*
*We **met at school and** we've been good friends **since then**.*

Verbs not in present perfect continuous

Some verbs are generally used in the present perfect simple – not the present perfect continuous, e.g. *be, believe, hate, like* and *know*.

Exercise 1

Write sentences in the present perfect continuous or simple with *for* or *since*, using the prompts below.

1 I / learn Chinese / I was eight.
2 I / go to the gym every day / the last two months.
3 They / be together / quite a long time.
4 The Social Democrats / be in power / the last election.
5 He / live there / last year.
6 I / try to find / a job / months.
7 She / make amazing films / quite a while now.
8 I / not really like / much of her work / her first album.

DID YOU KNOW?

We use the present perfect continuous to talk about how long – and to focus on the activity. We use the present perfect simple to talk about how many – and to focus on finished achievements in the time up till now. Compare:
*I've **been phoning** him all morning, but he's not answering. (= how long)*
*I've **phoned ten** shops, but none of them had the book! (= how many)*
*They've **been meeting** since April to discuss the project. (= how long)*
*We**'ve met** several times before. (= how many)*

Exercise 2

Choose the correct option.

1 El Sistema is a social programme in Venezuela. It aims to help children from poor backgrounds avoid problems like crime and drug addiction by teaching classical music. It has been running [1]*for / since* over 30 years and it [2]*has been producing / has produced* several international stars, including the conductor Gustavo Dudamel. He [3]*is conducting / has been conducting* the National Youth Orchestra for the last ten years. Since 2007, Scotland [4]*has been having / has had* a similar scheme and many other countries are also considering adopting the idea.

2 Henning Mankell [1]*has been writing / is writing* since the late 1960s. He [2]*has started / started* by writing plays, but then became internationally famous through his crime novels. He [3]*has been winning / has won* several awards for his books. In 1985, he founded a theatre in Mozambique and [4]*for / since* then, he's been working there part-time.

3 I've always [1]*loved / been loving* the Eurovision Song Contest. It's great. I've been watching it [2]*for / since* I was eight, when a rock band from Finland won. Apparently, they [3]*have been showing / have been shown* it on TV every year since 1956 and it is one of the longest-running TV programmes in the world. Abba and Celine Dion were both past winners.

14 STUFF

RELATIVE CLAUSES

We use relative clauses to add information about nouns. The relative clause usually comes immediately after the thing / person / place it describes.

I have a friend **who lives near there**. *It's a book* **that upset a lot of people when it came out**.

Relative clauses begin with a relative pronoun.

For things, we use *that / which*.

For people, we use *that / who*.

For places, we use *where*.

Exercise 1

Choose the correct option.

1 That's the woman *which / who / where* lives upstairs from me.
2 It's one thing *that / who / where* just really annoys me.
3 That's the shop *which / that / where* I bought my shoes.
4 He's the guy *which / who / where* owns the whole factory.
5 English is the subject *which / who / where* I enjoy most.
6 That's the room *that / who / where* you get your lunch.

DID YOU KNOW?

The relative pronoun replaces the noun / pronoun it refers to in the relative clause. Don't write both!

The Boredoms are a group. The Boredoms are from Japan. They have released about ten albums.

The Boredoms are a group **that** ~~The Boredoms~~ *are from Japan and* **who** ~~they~~ *have released about ten albums.*

I spoke to a woman. The woman was the manager.

The woman **who** *I spoke to* ~~her~~ *was the manager.*

You see that place. I used to work there.

That's the place **where** *I used to work* ~~there~~.

Exercise 2

Rewrite each pair of sentences as one sentence, using a relative clause.

1 Sertab Erener is a Turkish singer. ~~She~~ won the Eurovision Song Contest in 2003.
   <u>Who / That won</u>

2 Storaplan is a very trendy area. ~~There~~ are lots of nice shops and restaurants there.
   <u>Where are</u>

3 Sue Briggs was an English teacher. She persuaded me to go to university.
   <u>who / that</u>

4 A campsite is a place. ~~You~~ stay there when you go camping.
   <u>Where you stay</u>

5 Shostakovich was a Russian composer. He wrote some amazing pieces of music.
   <u>who / That</u>

6 Istanbul is a city. Europe and Asia meet there.
   <u>Where</u>

7 What do you call those machines? They do the washing-up for you.
   <u>That</u>

8 I need to buy one of those things. You wear it round your waist and keep money in it.
   <u>That</u>

MUST / MUSTN'T

must and have to

When *must* means something is essential, you can also use *have to*. *Must* often sounds stronger than *have to*.

What goes up, **has to / must come** *down.*

If you **have to / must have** *soft drinks, buy them in recyclable plastic bottles.*

I **have to / must go** *to the shops. I'll be back in a bit.*

You can't use *have to* when *must* means 'I imagine this is definitely true'.

The packaging is biodegradable, so they ~~have to~~ **must be** *OK.*

You **must be** *tired after your journey.*

It **must be** *a horrible job collecting rubbish, but I suppose someone* **has to / must do** *it.*

mustn't and don't have to

Mustn't and *don't have to* mean different things. *Mustn't* means it's essential not to do something. *Don't have to* means it doesn't matter if we do it or not – it's not necessary.

People ~~don't have to~~ **mustn't leave** *rubbish outside without a sticker on the bag.*

I **mustn't be** *late. My teacher's already unhappy with me.*

I'm going to get up late tomorrow as **I don't have** *to go to work.*

Exercise 1

Choose all the correct options.

1 I *must / have to* rush. I'm late for class.
2 Oh, I *must / mustn't* remember to go to the cash machine
3 We *don't have to / mustn't* forget to get your number before you go.
4 I *don't have / mustn't* to be back at any particular time.
5 He *must / has to* be very pleased that he's finally found a job.
6 I guess I'll do the shopping, if I really *must / have to*, but I'd rather not.
7 A: I've already been waiting for over an hour.
   B: You *must / have to* be really fed up.

Mustn't can sound quite strong, so we often prefer *can't* or *be not allowed to.*

People **aren't allowed to / can't leave** rubbish outside without a sticker on the bag.

I'm afraid **you're not allowed to / you can't** eat food in here.

Exercise 2

Complete the second sentence so that it has a similar meaning to the first sentence, using the word given. Do not change the word given. You must use between three and five words, including the word given.

1 People must pay tax for throwing rubbish away.
   People _____ for throwing rubbish away. **HAVE**

2 You mustn't leave rubbish bags on the street.
   You _____ rubbish bags on the street. **ALLOWED**

3 I must remember to call him.
   I _____ call him. **FORGET**

4 I imagine you're very excited about going away.
   You _____ about going away. **MUST**

5 You aren't allowed to enter the building without showing your ID.
   You _____ the building without ID. **CAN'T**

15 MONEY

TIME PHRASES AND TENSE

Present continuous	*currently* *at the moment*
Present perfect simple **(and present perfect continuous)**	*over the last two years* *in the last few months* *since last month / year*
be going to and **will**	*in a few days* *in two weeks' time* *over the next few weeks*
used to or the past simple	*in the past* *when I was younger* *when I was at school*
Past tenses (not *used to***)**	*last night / year* *the other day / week* *five days / years ago*

Exercise 1

Which time phrases from the box can be used to complete each sentence?

over the last five years	in three months' time
in two years	the other week
last month	when I was young
three months ago	since last year
at the moment	in the last six months

1 Prices have gone up a lot …
2 Unemployment is falling …
3 They opened a new factory here …
4 There's going to be a general election …

Exercise 2

Write sentences using the prompts below.

1 The prime minister / lose popularity / in the last year.
2 I / spend a lot more money / in the past.
3 I / get a loan from the bank / the other month.
4 The recession / get worse / at the moment.
5 They / invest more in schools / over the next five years.
6 He / lose his job / three years ago.

PRESENT TENSES IN FUTURE TIME CLAUSES

We can talk about the future using time clauses that start with words like *when, as soon as, before, once, after* and *until*. The future time clause can come first or second in a sentence. We generally use the present simple in these clauses.

You can pay half back **when you have** *the money, OK?*

You'll receive your new PIN number **after you get** *the card.*

In the main clause, we can use modals such as *will* and *can, be going to* or imperatives.

I'll pay *you* **back** *as soon as I get paid.*

We won't see *any improvement until the economy gets better.*

I can help *you with your homework as soon as I finish this.*

When I leave school, **I'm going to study** *Law at university.*

After you finish that, **make** *me a cup of coffee.*

As soon as (and *once*) show that one thing will happen quickly after another thing.

When shows we are sure that something will happen.

Until shows something stops happening at this time.

Exercise 1

Choose the correct option.

1 I'll email you *when / until* I get home tonight.
2 I'm not going to lend you any more *until / after* you pay me the money you owe me!
3 *After / Until* this course ends, I'm going to visit my cousin in the States.
4 I'm not going to talk to him *until / as soon as* he apologises.
5 I'm staying late tonight. I have to finish this work *before / when* I leave the office.
6 We should book a hotel *before / after* we arrive in Paris. We arrive very late.
7 She's still in hospital. *As soon as / Until* I hear anything, I'll call you.
8 My neighbours are going to look after our cat *when / after* we're away on holiday.
9 I'll do it *as soon as / before* I have time, OK?

Exercise 2

Decide which five sentences are incorrect, then correct them.

1 We'll obviously discuss the deal with everyone before we'll make a final decision.
2 When you're ready, tell me, OK?
3 We will can have something to eat when we get home.
4 After you'll register, you'll be able to access your account online.
5 I'll be OK for money when this cheque clears.
6 I'll come and visit you as soon as I'm feeling better.
7 Inflation continues to rise until the government does something about it!
8 I will believe in UFOs until I see one with my own eyes!

16 EVENTS

ARTICLES

the

We use *the* to show we think it's obvious which thing(s) we mean, and that there's no other example.

*It's **the** ninth largest country in the world.*
(There's only one ninth largest.)

*Islam was introduced by **the** Arabs ...*
(There's no other example of Arab people.)

*... in **the** eighth century.*
(It's obvious which one they mean.)

***the** Soviet Union*
(There was only one Soviet Union.)

***the** only thing*
(*Only* shows there's no other thing.)

a / an

We use *a / an* to show a thing could be one of several examples, and it's not important at this stage exactly which one.

*They share **a** border.*
(They have borders with several countries.)

*It's **an** exporter of natural resources.*
(There are many exporters in the world.)

Texts

Following the rules above, when we first introduce a noun in a text we often use *a / an*. After that we use *the* to show we are talking about the same thing.

*There was **a** war during the 19th century. After **the** war **a** new government was established, but **the** government wasn't very popular.*

Exercise 1

Complete the short text with *the*, *a* or *an*.

I go to [1]_____ school near my house. It was established in the 19th century by a wealthy doctor and is one of [2]_____ oldest educational institutions in [3]_____ city. It was [4]_____ private school until [5]_____ Second World War. After [6]_____ war, [7]_____ state education sytem was created and fees were ended.

[8]_____ school is going to celebrate its 200th anniversary next year. We're going to have several events over [9]_____ year, starting with [10]_____ amazing party on 20th September, which is [11]_____ exact date the school opened. [12]_____ president of our region is going to attend.

Names

We use *the* with many kinds of names to show they are the only example:

The Soviet Union, The River Nile, The Hilton Hotel, The Bolshoi Theatre, etc.

But for other kinds of place names we don't use an article at all:

Kazakhstan, Cuba, Europe, Asia, Oxford Street, Mount Fuji, Lake Como

Generalities

We sometimes use *the* to talk about the whole of a group of people or things.

*Islam was introduced by **the** Arabs.*

However, normally we don't use any article when talking about things in a general way. We are talking about the whole / all examples of the thing.

~~*The*~~ ***Islam*** *was introduced by the Arabs*

~~*The*~~ ***War*** *is stupid and ~~the~~ people are stupid.*

*I don't like ~~the~~ **coffee**.*

Exercise 2

Correct one mistake connected to articles in each sentence.

1 He died during Second World War.
2 I think it's very important to study the history .
3 Our friends have the lovely cottage in the Black Forest.
4 I'm meeting the friend of mine later.
5 One day I'd love to try and climb the Mount Everest.
6 My father is pilot, so he's away from home a lot.
7 The happiness is more important than money.
8 I don't like the eggs. I don't know why. I just don't.

VERB PATTERNS

-ing and infinitive with *to*

When two verbs are used together, the second verb can take the *-ing* form or the infinitive with *to*. The choice of form depends on the first verb. There are no rules for this. You just have to learn the patterns.

Verbs which are usually followed by the *-ing* form include:

avoid	enjoy	miss
can't stand	finish	practise
consider	mind	recommend

Verbs which are usually followed by the infinitive with *to* include:

agree	fail	plan
arrange	hope	promise
decide	offer	refuse

Exercise 1

Choose the correct option.

1 My sister offered *taking / to take* me shopping for my birthday last year.
2 I can still remember the day I decided *becoming / to become* an architect. That was a big day for me.
3 I've just finished *writing / to write* my second novel. I'm going out to celebrate!
4 I've got my Chinese exams next week, so I'm practising *speaking / to speak* as much as I can.
5 I've promised *taking / to take* my girlfriend out somewhere tonight. It's her birthday. Would you recommend *trying / to try* that place near the beach?
6 If you can't find anyone else to do it, I don't mind *working / to work* late tonight.
7 I've arranged *meeting / to meet* a few friends in town later on tonight.
8 I usually avoid *working / to work* weekends if I can help it. My boss sometimes asks me, but I usually just refuse *doing / to do* it. I need my time off!

Exercise 2

Decide which seven sentences are incorrect, then correct them.

1 I've decided not going to university.
2 I thought we agreed not to talk about politics!
3 Do you mind to wait here for a few minutes?
4 I don't really enjoy to shop for clothes.
5 I spent nine months to travel round Africa.
6 A friend of mine recommended coming here.
7 I can't stand going to office parties. I find them very stressful.
8 I'm considering to look for work overseas.
9 When I can afford to take some time off work, I'd really like to go to Peru.
10 Sorry we're so late. We stopped having lunch on the way.
11 Can you please stop to make so much noise?
12 I must remember to buy some stamps later today.

INFORMATION FILES

FILE 1

Unit 2, page 19   **READING**

JOCHEM
It was my son's thirteenth birthday a few weeks ago. I decided to buy him a laptop. I looked at lots of different sites and did my research. In the end, I found a great one in a sale. It was £225 – reduced from £300. I paid online and a few days later, it arrived. I didn't want my son to see it, so I put it in my bedroom. On his birthday, I gave him his present. He was so happy! He opened the box in a rush – and dropped the laptop on the floor! Of course, it was so badly damaged it didn't work anymore!

KRISTIN
My car had a problem so I ordered a new part online so I could repair it. The part was out of stock and the company needed to get it from somewhere else – but they forgot to tell me, so I waited and waited. After three weeks and maybe ten phone calls, it finally arrived. My car is now fine, but the service was terrible, so I don't recommend that website.

FILE 2

Unit 3 page 27   **CONVERSATION PRACTICE**

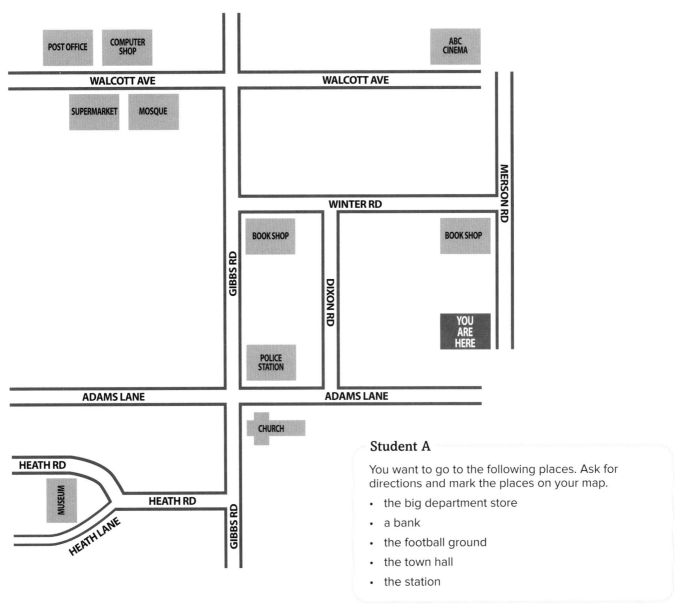

Student A

You want to go to the following places. Ask for directions and mark the places on your map.

- the big department store
- a bank
- the football ground
- the town hall
- the station

Unit 7 page 67 **SPEAKING**

Student A

You are the host. Either draw a plan of your own home or use your imagination and invent one. Think about what you'll say in the conversation, including one or two comments you'll make about some of the rooms or the other people you live with. Also, think of some offers you'll make.

Start the conversation by welcoming your guest like this:

(name of your guest)! Come in. Come in. How was your journey?

Unit 10 page 89 **CONVERSATION PRACTICE**

Student A

Your parents' friends are going to Canada on holiday. There will be two adults and two children – aged fourteen and nine. They have seen an advert for four-bed apartments connected to a hotel. They are interested in going skiing in a place nearby and the adults want to spend some free time on their own. Ring the hotel in Canada and ask for information.

Unit 11 page 99 **CONVERSATION PRACTICE**

Student A

1	The police caught some terrorists with nuclear material. The police don't know where it came from. It's not clear what they planned to do with it.	**Ask:** Did you see the news about those terrorists with the nuclear material?
2	They're going to build a new zoo in a city near you. It's going to cost around $3 billion.	**Ask:** Did you hear about the zoo that they're going to build in … (say the place)?
3	It's going to snow at the beginning of the weekend and then it's going to be cold and sunny.	**Ask:** Did you see the forecast for the weekend?

FILE 6

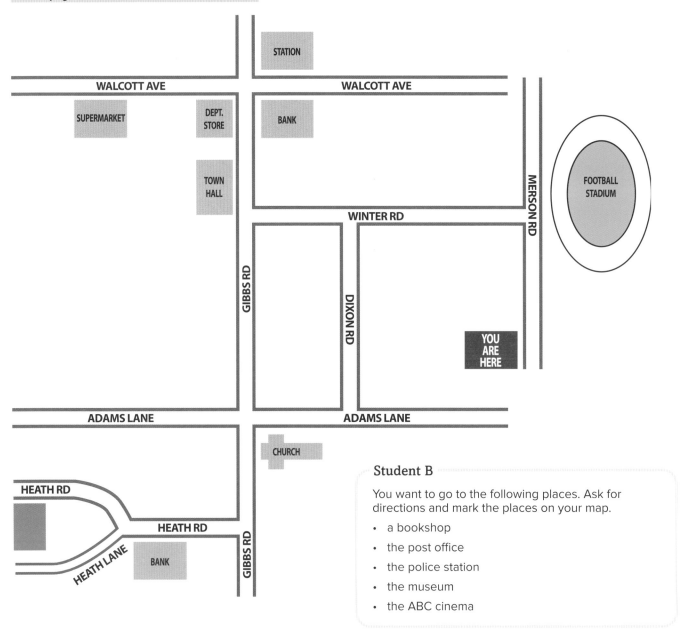

Student B

You want to go to the following places. Ask for directions and mark the places on your map.

- a bookshop
- the post office
- the police station
- the museum
- the ABC cinema

Unit 15 page 135 **CONVERSATION PRACTICE**

Student A

You are from a country called Remonesia, which is somewhere in South East Asia.

- Invent exactly where it is.
- Decide what the quality of life is like there and give one or two reasons for this.
- Decide how the economy is doing and give one or two examples.
- Say you are thinking of moving. Explain why.

Unit 12 page 107 **CONVERSATION PRACTICE**

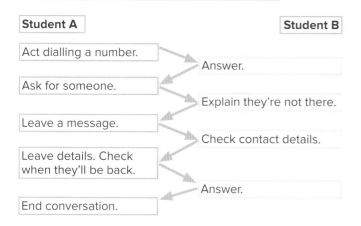

Student A	Student B
Act dialling a number.	Answer.
Ask for someone.	Explain they're not there.
Leave a message.	Check contact details.
Leave details. Check when they'll be back.	Answer.
End conversation.	

Unit 14 page 125 **CONVERSATION PRACTICE**

Student A

Unit 7 page 67   **SPEAKING**

Student B

You are the guest. Think about what you'll say in the conversation. In particular, decide:

how to describe your journey to the house / apartment.

- what you'll give your host and why.
- two or three requests you'll make.

Then have a conversation with your partner. They will start.

Unit 15 page 135   **CONVERSATION PRACTICE**

Student B

You are from a country called Lidland, which is somewhere in northern Europe.

- Invent exactly where it is
- Decide what the quality of life is like there and give one or two reasons for this.
- Decide how the economy is doing and give one or two examples.
- Say you are thinking of moving. Explain why.

Unit 10 page 89   **CONVERSATION PRACTICE**

Student B

You have friends who have found a hostel 20km from Edinburgh in Scotland. They want to stay for four days and go to the arts festival in the city. They also want to go on a day trip round the Scottish countryside. They are students and don't want to spend too much money.

Unit 7 page 64   **READING**

Student B

YOHANNES

Until last year, I lived with my parents in the capital of Eritrea, Asmara, but here everyone under the age of 50 has to do military service, so now I'm living in a big base out in the desert. Luckily, we're not at war with anyone at the moment, so I don't have to fight. Mainly, we work on construction projects: helping to build roads and airports and factories and so on. I'm paid about $30 a month and I try to send most of that to my parents as I don't have to buy much for myself here. Still, I worry about my parents because I was supporting them more before.

Officially, we have to do eighteen months in the army, but some people have been here much longer. Actually, some of my friends decided to leave the country to avoid all this. I understand them, but personally I hope I can help my country develop – and then go home to help my family again!

ELSIE

My husband died three years ago after 50 years of happy marriage and I decided that I didn't want to stay in our old house. It contained too many memories. I think it's one of the best decisions I've ever made. I'm now living in an old people's home on the south coast of England. I know they don't have a very good reputation, but my family looked at lots of places and chose very well.

I have my own room, which is very important, and I don't have to do anything I don't want to. If I want to spend the whole day in bed reading, I can. Having said that, the home often organises nice trips out, and of course I go and visit my family regularly. The staff here are wonderful: they're always polite and they treat us with respect. They look after us really well.

Unit 11 page 99   **CONVERSATION PRACTICE**

Student B

 They have found a cure for the flu. It's a new drug that deals with 90% of all cases. It could save thousands of lives.

Ask:
Did you hear about the new cure for the flu?

 There's going to be a storm this weekend. It's going to rain a lot and be very windy.

Ask:
Did you see the weather forecast for the weekend?

 The right whale is almost extinct. There are only around 500 left in the wild. Scientists don't know if there are enough to survive.

Ask:
Did you see the article about the right whale?

Unit 11 page 101   **GRAMMAR**

1 Guards caught and arrested a pigeon in a jail. The pigeon had carried drugs to prisoners at the jail. Apparently, it had flown over 60 kilometres from one prisoner's home town.

2 Fishermen found a pet dog on a desert island. The dog had disappeared when its owner was travelling on a cruise. The dog had fallen into the sea and had swum to the island. Fishermen who sail near the island found the dog several weeks later. It had survived by eating small animals.

3 A pet rabbit saved his elderly owners. The couple hadn't turned off the gas on their cooker properly and the house was filling with gas. The rabbit detected the smell, ran up the stairs and woke his owners, who were sleeping.

Unit 14 page 125   **CONVERSATION PRACTICE**

Student B

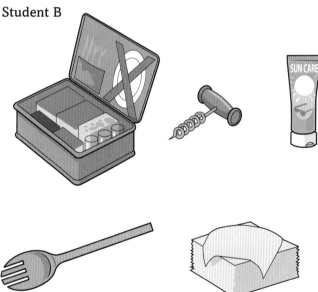

AUDIO SCRIPTS

UNIT 1

▶ TRACK 1

actor, engineer, journalist, lawyer, nurse, photographer, pilot, police officer, politician, sales manager, scientist, soldier

▶ TRACK 2

1

A: So what you do?

B: I'm an engineer.

A: Oh, right. Where do you work?

B: Well, I travel around quite a lot, actually.

A: Oh, OK.

B: Yeah, I'm working in Scotland at the moment – in Glasgow. They're building a new sports stadium there and I'm working on that.

A: Really? So where do you live, then?

B: Well, in London most of the time, but I'm renting an apartment in Glasgow while I'm there. I usually come down to London every two weeks, if I can.

A: And do you enjoy it?

B: Yeah, it's great. I don't really mind the travelling and the money's good. Plus, I don't really have much time to spend it!

A: Well, I guess that's good, then. What are the hours like?

B: Oh, I usually work quite long hours. I mean, I often do a sixty-hour week.

A: Really? That sounds hard.

B: No, it's good and I get on really well with the other people I work with.

2

C: So, what do you do?

D: Oh, I work for a small company back in Korea, but I'm actually a student at the moment.

C: Oh, OK. What are you studying?

D: I'm doing a Master's degree in Marketing.

C: Is that what you do in your company? Marketing?

D: Yes, kind of.

C: So how long have you worked there?

D: About two years now.

C: Only two years and they're sending you to another country to study! That's fantastic!

D: Yeah, well, actually my father runs the company and he wants me to become the marketing manager.

C: Oh, right. I see. So do you get on with the other people you work with?

D: Yeah, we get on OK, but it can be difficult sometimes because I'm the boss's daughter, you know?

C: Yeah, I can imagine.

D: I sometimes feel like I have to work harder to show everyone I can actually do my job.

C: I'm sure.

▶ TRACK 3

1

T = Tula, M = Martin

T: Hey Martin.

M: Oh hi, Tula.

T: Are you busy?

M: Well ... kind of. I'm just answering some emails. Why?

T: Oh, I need a break.

M: Why? What are you doing?

T: I'm trying to write something for marketing, but I'm finding it difficult.

M: Oh, right.

T: Do you want to go for a coffee? Maybe you can give me some ideas.

M: I don't know. I'm meeting a customer at twelve.

T: You have time!

M: Yeah, but I need to finish these emails and I've got an appointment with the dentist at one.

T: So, you can answer your emails this afternoon.

M: Yeah, but I'm giving that presentation on Friday and I need to start preparing.

A: So you need a break now!

M: Oh, alright. Where do you want to go?

T: Just to the place on the corner.

M: Hey, by the way, are you going to that training session tomorrow?

T: No. What's that?

M: Time management. There was an email about it.

T: Really? Maybe I missed it.

M: It said all the sales staff have to attend.

T: Really. What's it about?

M: The usual thing, I imagine – using your time more efficiently, making lists, deciding what your priorities are. Things you probably know already.

T: It's probably a waste of time then.

M: Almost certainly.

T: You ready?

M: Yeah. Let's go.

2

M = Mum, R = Rachel

M: Rachel? ... Rachel? ... Rachel!

R: What?

M: I said it three times.

R: I'm watching something!

M: I'm going. Can you do a couple of things for me?

R: Ohhhh. What?

M: Don't talk to me like that!

R: Just tell me what you want me to do. I'm trying to watch this.

M: The washing machine's on. Can you hang the clothes outside?

R: OK.

M: And can you sort out your room. It's a mess.

R: Ohhh. I'll do it another day.

M: But you told me you don't have classes today.

R: Yeah, but I need to study. I've got a test tomorrow. And I need to finish a project before Thursday. And I'm meeting Jane tonight.

M: Why can't you meet her at the weekend? Or stop watching TV? You need to change your priorities, my girl. You're nineteen, not a child!

R: Mum! I have to relax too! I can't work *all* day!

M: *I* work all day and then do housework.

R: Yeah, but you get paid for your work. And anyway, you're my mum. That's what mums do!

M: Is that right?

R: I'm joking.

M: Well, I'm not. Please tidy your room!

R: OK. OK.

M: I'll be back at seven.

R: Oh! What time are we having dinner? I need to leave at eight.

M: I'll get a pizza on my way home.

▶ TRACK 4

/trə/, /drə/, /ɑːt/, /te/, /tɪ/, /dɪ/, /steɪ/, /stɑː/, /draɪ/, /treɪ/, /ənt/, /end/

▶ TRACK 5

1 You need to make an appointment.
2 Staff only get very basic training.
3 It's hard to keep good staff.
4 I need to pass a test in English.
5 I'm phoning because my train's delayed.
6 She's now the head of her department.
7 it depends on the day.
8 They really need to develop a new policy.

UNIT 2

▶ TRACK 6

K = Keira, C = Claire, D = Dan

K: Did you have a nice weekend?

C: Yeah, it was good.

K: What did you do?

C: Oh, nothing much. I went for a walk with some friends round Sutton Park yesterday.

K: Oh, nice. It was a lovely clear day.

C: Yeah. It was a bit cold, but it was great. I was taking photos with my new camera.

K: That one? Let's have a look. Wow! That's really neat. Where did you get it?

C: In Jessops in town. I'm really pleased with it. It's really good quality and it's got quite a few different functions.

K: Really? Is it complicated to use?

C: No, not really. There are a few things I don't know yet, but it's OK.

K: Yeah. Well, the pictures look good and it's nice and light as well.

C: Hmm, yeah. It's cool, isn't it? Anyway, what about you two? Did you do anything?

D: Yeah, we went shopping.

C: Oh, OK. Did you buy anything nice?

K: Well, I got these earrings.

B: They're lovely! They look quite old.

K: Yeah, they are. I got them in a second-hand shop near here. They've got all kinds of things there – books, CDs, clothes. Dan got that jacket there.

C: Really? I love it. It looks really nice and warm.

D: Yeah, it is. It's pure wool and it's nice and thick. And it only cost fifteen pounds.

C: You're joking! That's fantastic. It really suits you as well. It's a great style and colour!

D: Thanks.

C: Did you get any clothes, Keira?

K: No, there were some really nice things, but I didn't find anything that fitted me. Everything was either too big or too small.

▶ TRACK 7

did you	What did you do?
did she	Where did she go?
did it	Did it take long?
were you	Were you OK?
was it	What was it like?
were they	Were they expensive?

▶ TRACK 8

1 I love your ring. Where did you get it?
2 That's a great bag. Is it new?
3 Hey, cool phone! How long have you had it?
4 I love your shirt. It's a really nice design.
5 I like your boots. They look really comfortable.
6 That's a lovely jacket. It really suits you.

▶ TRACK 9

1 recommended
2 delivered
3 ordered
4 dropped
5 arrived
6 needed
7 loved
8 decided
9 looked
10 returned
11 wanted
12 opened

▶ TRACK 10

1
A: Is that all you have?
B: Yeah, it is.
A: Well, do you want to go first?
B: Are you sure?
A: Yes, of course. I have a lot to get.
B: Great. Thanks.

2
C: Would you like it wrapped?
D: Um … what's the paper like?
C: It's this green paper.
D: Hmm, it's a bit plain. Do you have anything a bit prettier? It's a special present.
C: Well, there's quite a big selection in the stationery department. Do you want to choose something and bring it here and I'll wrap it for you?
D: Really? You don't mind?
C: Of course not.
D: Thanks.

3
E: Yes Sir. How can I help you?
F: I bought this the other day and it's damaged. When I got it home and took it out of the box, I found the button was loose and it's damaged here. Look, you see?
E: Are you sure you didn't drop it or anything?
F: No, of course not!

E: It's just that this kind of damage doesn't happen unless you do something. It's not a manufacturing fault.

F: Honestly, when I got home I took it out of the box and it was already damaged.

E: Have you got a receipt and the box?

F: I didn't bring the box. I've got the receipt, though.

4

G: Is there anyone serving here?

H: Yes, but I don't think you can pay here.

G: That's OK. I just want to find out if they have something in stock.

H: Well, there was a guy here and he said he would be back in a minute, but that was ten minutes ago.

G: Oh right.

H: It's typical! The service is always terrible here.

G: Hmm.

H: Hatton's is better really. Their service is much more reliable and their things are generally better quality.

G: Really? Well, why didn't you go there?

H: Well, I do normally, but I saw in the window they had a sale here.

G: Ah!

H: There he is! About time!

I: Sorry.

H: That's OK.

5

J: Excuse me. Do you have one of these in a smaller size? This one's a bit big.

K: I'm afraid not. That's why they're at a reduced price.

J: Never mind, Timmy. You'll grow into it.

L: But I don't like it.

J: Don't be silly. You look lovely. It really suits you.

L: It's not as nice as the other one we saw.

J: That was much more expensive. This one's fine.

L: It's not fair.

▶ TRACK 11

/sə/, /ʃ/, /ɪːs/, /st/, /ɪst/, /siː/, /ʃt/, /ʃən/, /sɜː/, /vɪs/, /ʃɜː/

▶ TRACK 12

1 I missed the last class.
2 They increased sales.
3 For the last several years …
4 Ask for a receipt.
5 We need to rush to the station.
6 Make sure you wear a smart shirt.
7 They've got a good selection of shoes.
8 They've got an efficient delivery service.

▶ TRACK 13

1 It doesn't really suit me.
2 Do you have anything a bit bigger?
3 It's not as good as my old one.
4 What did you think of it?
5 I'm thinking of buying it.
6 I work late most nights.

UNIT 3

▶ TRACK 14

1

A: Listen, we're obviously lost. Ask this guy here.

B: OK, OK. … Sorry. Do you speak English?

C: Sure.

B: Oh, great. Do you know the way to the museum from here?

C: Yes, but it is far. It's better to get a bus.

B: OK. So how do we get to the stop?

C: Go down this road. Take the second road on the right. Then cross, turn left and then left again and it's directly opposite the town hall.

B: OK, great.

C: No problem.

B: So did he say second right or second left?

A: I'm not actually sure, you know. And what bus did he say we need?

B: No idea! Anyway, it's down here somewhere, I think.

2

B: It's your turn. Ask that old lady.

A: Excuse me. Is this the right bus stop for the museum?

D: Eh?

A: The bus? Brmm … To the museum?

D: Eh?

A: To the museum?

D: Eh?

E: You want the number 67 bus.

A: Oh, thanks.

E: You need to go over the road. This stop, it goes the wrong way. Go over the crossing. It's after the traffic lights there.

A: I see it. Thanks.

E: They come often.

A: Thanks.

3

A: Excuse me, sorry. Do you speak English?

F: Sure I do. How can I help?

A: Do you know the way to the museum? Is it near here?

F: Yes, quite near, but you got off at the wrong stop, really. Go down this road until you come to a church. Then turn left. It's quite a big road. Then go past a monument and a football ground – and just keep going. It's maybe half a mile. It's on the right. You can't miss it.

B: I told you that was it! Why do you never listen to me?

▶ TRACK 15

1 I was going to work the other day …
2 The other day, I was coming home …
3 He was driving along the motorway …
4 She wasn't looking where she was going …
5 It was late and we were trying to get to sleep …

▶ TRACK 16

M = Mark, L = Lisa

M: And now, over to Lisa Verity for the travel news.

L: Thanks Mark. There's not much good news, I'm afraid. For many travellers today, getting anywhere could be difficult. There are terrible problems in a lot of places out there at the moment.

So, starting with the airports. Air traffic controllers in France are on strike this week so expect a bit of trouble there. Plenty of flights are delayed and quite a few cancelled unfortunately. Not many planes can fly over France. Most have to fly a different route to avoid French air space. There's not much hope of a deal any time soon, so any passengers who are flying in the next few days should ring their airline or check their airline's website.

Onto the roads … a truck crashed earlier this morning on the A516 entering Milton Keynes and lost its load of fruit. Lanes in both directions are closed at the moment while police try to clear up the mess – a big mess I would imagine too! Avoid the area, if you can.

Elsewhere on the roads, the M6 motorway between junctions 5 and 6 is completely closed for repair work. There is a diversion, but you can expect some delays there all day. Traffic's moving very slowly, so best to take other routes.

Large sections of the Northern Line in London are closed today because of continuing repair work to renew the tube. A replacement bus service is in operation.

Also on the underground, East Ham station is closed at present because of a flood. This follows some heavy rain in the area overnight.

Better news elsewhere. The rail service between London and Birmingham is now running normally after a cow was removed from the line.

And I'm pleased to say that there aren't any more problems on the A6 now that the traffic lights are working again at the crossroads with the B761. The traffic's moving freely there.

Finally, one event tonight to tell you about. Just to remind anyone travelling to Wembley for the big concert there – there's no parking in or around the ground. Police in the area will remove any cars parked there, so go on foot or take public transport.

That's all from me – back to you, Mark.

▶ TRACK 17

/krɒ/, /ɒk/, /kræ/, /graʊ/, /kjʊə/, /geɪ/, /kjuː/, /ʌk/, /æg/, /ek/, /aɪk/, /ɪg/

▶ TRACK 18

1 They lost my bags when I missed my connection.
2 Don't forget to set the alarm clock.
3 There was a crash at the crossroads.
4 When we got to the gate it was closed.
5 There's a big queue to go through security.
6 The game was cancelled because the ground was flooded.
7 The coach drivers are going on strike.
8 We got stuck behind a big truck.

UNIT 4

▶ TRACK 19

S = Sarah, V = Victor

S: So Victor. Are you hungry?
V: Yeah, a bit.
S: Do you want to get something to eat?
V: I'd love to, yeah. Where are you thinking of going?
S: Well, there's a really nice Thai place just down the road. Have you ever been there?
V: Yeah, I go there a lot. I actually went there yesterday.
S: Oh right. So maybe you don't want to go there again today.
V: I'd rather not, If you don't mind. And I actually don't really feel like anything very spicy today.
S: OK. No problem. I'm happy to go somewhere else.
V: There's a nice seafood restaurant near the big department store. How about that?
S: To be honest, I don't really like seafood. I prefer meat.
V: Well, why don't we go to Selale instead. Have you been there?

S: No. I've never heard of it. Where is it?
V: It's about fifteen minutes' walk from here. It's just round the corner from the bus station.
S: Oh, OK. And what kind of restaurant is it?
V: It's Turkish. It's really good. I've been there a few times.
S: Really? I haven't ever had Turkish food.
V: You're joking. You'll love it. They do lots of grilled meat, but they also have a great selection of other dishes, so there's plenty to choose from.
S: It sounds great.
V: Yeah. The only problem is that it gets really busy, so sometimes you have to wait a while to get a table.
S: Oh right, well can we ring them to check they have a table?
V: I guess so. Let me see if I can find their number on my phone.

▶ TRACK 20

1 Have you ever eaten anything unusual?
2 Have you ever been to an expensive restaurant?
3 Have you ever complained In a restaurant?
4 Have you ever found a hair in your food?
5 Have you tried any of Jamie Oliver's recipes?
6 Have you watched Masterchef?

▶ TRACK 21

C1 = customer 1, C2 = customer 2, W = waiter

1
W: How many people is it?
C1: There are three of us.
W: And have you booked?
C1: No. Is that a problem?
W: No, but do you mind waiting?
C1: How long?
W: Maybe ten or fifteen minutes.
C2: OK. That's fine.
C1: Could I change the baby somewhere?
W: I'm afraid we don't have any special facilities. You can use the toilet. It's not very big, though.
C1: That's OK.
W: It's just at the end there, down the stairs.

2
W: Is this table here OK?
C1: Yeah, this is fine. Thank you.
W: Would you like a high chair for the little girl?
C1: That'd be great. Thanks. He's actually a boy, though!
W: Oh, I'm so sorry! Anyway, here are your menus. I'll get the chair.

3
W: Are you ready to order?
C1: Not quite. Could you just give us two more minutes?
W: Yes, of course.
…
C2: Right. OK. Could I have the grilled squid for starters, please? And for my main course, I think I'll have the chicken.
W: Uh-huh, and what kind of potatoes would you like?
C2: Roast potatoes, please.
W: OK.
C1: I'll go for the aubergines stuffed with rice for my main course, please. And the soup of the day? Does it contain any meat? I'm vegetarian.
W: Yes. I'm afraid it's got lamb in it.
C1: Oh, OK. Well, I'll just have the tomato and avocado salad, then. And could we get some water as well?

W: Of course. Sparkling or still?

C1: Just tap water, please, if possible.

W: Sure.

C2: And could we have a small plate for our son? We'd like to share our dishes with him.

4

C1: Oh, dear – what a mess!

C2: I'll get the waiter. Er, excuse me. I'm really sorry, but could you get us a cloth, please? My son's dropped some water on the floor.

W: Certainly madam. I'll just go and get one.

C2: Thank you.

5

W: Would you like to see the dessert menu?

C1: I'm OK, thanks. I'm really full, but if you want something ...

C2: No, no. I couldn't eat another thing. It was lovely, though. Could I just have a coffee, please?

C1: Me too. Thank you.

6

C1: Could we have the bill, please?

W: Yes, of course.

C1: Great. Thanks.

C2: That's very reasonable, isn't it? Shall we leave a tip?

C1: No, look. Service is included.

C2: Wow. Then that really is good value for money. We should come here again sometime.

▶ TRACK 22

/vjuː/, /ɜːv/, /fɪ/, /bɪ/, /pɪ/, /bʊ/, /pɔː/, /fæ/, /feɪ/, /ve/, /və/, /pɑː/

▶ TRACK 23

1 The café has a very nice view over the park.
2 They serve the fish with boiled vegetables.
3 I didn't have enough money to pay the bill.
4 Have you booked a table for four people or five?
5 There's a typical French café opposite my apartment building.
6 They have half portions for kids.
7 Chips are bad for you because they're high in fat.
8 It's a fixed price so fill your plates.

▶ TRACK 24

1 Could you get us a cloth?
2 Shall we leave a tip?
3 Could you show me the way?
4 Would you like anything to drink?
5 Could I have the vegetarian option?
6 Shall we call a taxi?

UNIT 5

▶ TRACK 25

C = Corinne, M = Maribel

C: So what are you going to do while you're here?

M: I'm just going to take it easy, Corinne. I guess I might go shopping in the morning. You're working tomorrow, aren't you?

C: Yes – and Saturday morning, I'm afraid.

M: Oh dear.

C: Yeah, I know. I'm sorry, but some important clients are coming and I need to go and meet them at the airport and make sure everything's OK.

M: Right. What time are you going to be back?

C: Hopefully about two.

M: That's OK, then. I'm not going to be up before eleven anyway and I've brought my trainers, so I might go running. Is there anywhere to go near here?

C: There's actually an athletics track just down the road.

M: OK. To be honest, though, I'd prefer a park or somewhere like that.

C: Hmm. There's not much near here. I usually just run on the streets when I go.

M: OK. Well, I'll see. Do you have any plans for us at the weekend?

C: Well, a friend is having a party for his birthday on Saturday night, if you'd like to go.

M: Oh great. You know I always like a dance!

C: And the forecast is really good for Sunday, so we're thinking of going for a walk in the mountains near here.

M: Oh right. That sounds nice.

C: Yes, it's great there. There's a lovely river we can go swimming in.

M: Oh right. Do you have any spare swimming gear? I don't have anything with me.

C: Yeah, I'm sure I can lend you something.

M: Thanks. Isn't the water cold, though?

C: A bit, but you soon warm up.

M: Hmmm. I must admit, I'm a bit soft. I like a heated pool, myself.

C: Honestly, it's not so bad and the water's really clear. It's just beautiful with the mountains and everything!

M: OK. So what time are you thinking of leaving?

C: Well, it's two or three hours by car, so if we want to make the most of the day, we need to leave early – maybe around six o'clock.

M: Six in the morning?!

▶ TRACK 26

Last night I watched the big game in England between Manchester City and Chelsea. I was one of a billion people watching in places as far apart as Peru, Saudi Arabia and Vietnam. Now, when football's good, it can be amazing ... but when it's bad, it can be awful – and this game was maybe the most boring game I've ever seen. It was a nil-nil draw and almost nothing happened for the whole 90 minutes. Honestly, it was terrible! Football's the most popular sport in the world, but it's hard to understand why when you watch a game like that. Knowing that the players earn millions a year just makes it worse! So why do we watch when there are plenty of alternatives? The Olympics features around thirty sports; other countries have different national sports such as cricket; and new sports are being created all the time.

Maybe the main reason is because football is the simplest game to play. The basic rules are among the easiest to grasp of any sport. In contrast, does anyone really understand the rules of cricket? In addition, football doesn't require expensive equipment. In fact, you need hardly any gear at all and on top of that you need no real skill to play – who can't kick a ball? So nearly everyone has played at least once in their life – and of course once you've played a sport, you appreciate it more. Finally, football's different every game. Last night's game was boring, but next time Chelsea might win five-four, with a goal in the last minute! You just never know.

▶ TRACK 27

1 It's the simplest game to play.
2 It's not the easiest game to understand.
3 He's the tallest person I know.
4 She's the fittest person I know.
5 He's the cleverest person I know.
6 It's the ugliest building in town.

▶ TRACK 28

P = presenter, C = Clare Ellis, K = Karen Miller,
T = Professor Townsend

P: Perhaps like me, you spent hours drawing and colouring things when you were young, but then just stopped. Personally, I can't remember when or why, but I suppose I felt it was childish and wanted more adult things – make-up, shopping, boys. So you might be interested to learn that one of the biggest growth areas in publishing at the moment is colouring books for adults. These books have been around for a while, but in France they've become best sellers thanks to some clever marketing, as book trader Clare Ellis explains.

C: Several of these books were actually first published in the UK with only moderate success, but when French publishers added 'anti-stress' or 'art therapy' to the titles, there was a dramatic increase in sales. Thirty-three per cent of French people have taken pills like Prozac for depression, so there's clearly a big market for anything that helps reduce stress.

P: Watching any child with pens and paper, you can see how the simple task of carefully filling in a pattern can completely occupy their attention, and it's that focus on the present which Karen Miller – a lawyer and colouring fan – likes.

K: Law is a very stressful occupation and it's difficult to stop thinking about work, but colouring has really made a difference for me. Some designs are very detailed and complicated, so you really need to concentrate, and I quickly forget about everything else. It really helps me relax. I even sleep better.

P: And it's not just colouring that's coming back into fashion. In the States, there is a growing interest in making things – everything from clothes to furniture to cakes. The sociologist, Professor John Townsend, suggests why.

T: I think the maker movement is a reaction against life being so commercial. We were sold the idea of retail therapy – shopping as relaxation – but many people's experience of shopping is far from relaxing: it involves difficult decisions, debt and worrying about what others have. Making your own things is the opposite: you follow a recipe or instructions; it's cheaper; and it involves sharing ideas and helping each other. There's nothing commercial about the outcome either – you're not buying or selling it. It's personal. It's yours. It's you.

P: Hmm, I'm not sure *my* baking or making are 'me', because I'm awful at it – but anyway here in the studio to discuss the rise of making, I have Professor Townsend, Karen Miller and a keen maker, Lisa O'Sullivan. Lisa, if I could ask you first …

▶ TRACK 29

/pleɪ/, /uːl/, /əʊl/, /læ/, /reɪ/, /træ/, /θruː/, /eɪl/, /əl/, /pəl/, /ləʊ/, /treɪ/

TRACK 30

1 I play football every Friday in a local park.
2 There's an Olympic-size swimming pool just round the corner.
3 The cycle race usually attracts lots of spectators.
4 I like to relax with my family at the weekend.
5 I have to drive miles to get to the nearest athletics track.
6 He threw me his keys, but I dropped them down a hole.
7 I bought these trainers in a sale.
8 The rules are simple and easy to follow.

UNIT 6

▶ TRACK 31

L = Laura, M = Maya, A = Anna

L: Maya.
M: Hi Laura. Sorry I'm a bit late.
L: That's OK.
M: How long have you been here?
L: Oh, not long. Ten minutes.
M: Sorry. The traffic was bad.
L: Are you looking for something?
M: Another chair. Oh … there's one.
L: So, who else is coming?
M: My friend Anna from Poland.
L: Oh yeah? How do you know her?
M: I met her on an exchange trip.
L: Really? Why Poland?
M: There was some connection between the schools. Anyway, it was great and I got on really well with Anna. Here. I've got a picture of her on my mobile.
L: OK.
M: Here. She's the girl on the right.
L: Oh wow! She's very pretty.
M: Yeah.
L: So is she just visiting?
M: No, she's studying here.
L: OK. Quite clever too, then.
M: Definitely. She's one of those people who's good at everything: studying, languages, sports … . We play tennis sometimes, but she always beats me.
L: How annoying!
M: Isn't it! No … she's really nice. You'll like her.
L: So, who's the guy? Is that her boyfriend?
M: No! That's my brother!
L: Really? You don't look very similar.
M: I know. He's quite dark – but look at the nose and mouth.
L: Let me see. Yeah, I guess. So what does he do?
M: He's a nurse. He lives in the States.
L: Really? Why did he go there?
M: His wife's from there.
L: Really? He's married? How old is he?
M: 24.
L: OK. That's quite young.
M: I guess.
L: Do you get on well?
M: Yes, we're quite close. Although, obviously, I don't see him very often now. We Skype a lot.
L: Right.
M: I might actually go over there in a few months because they're having a baby.
L: Really? That's great. A boy or a girl?
M: A boy, apparently. My first nephew or niece.
L: OK. So, Auntie Maya. Amazing.
M: I know.
L: Do you have any other brothers or sisters?
M: Just my little sister.
L: Is that the other girl in the picture?
M: No, she's a friend from my Spanish class.
A: Maya!

Audio scripts   197

M: Anna! How are you? We saved you a seat. Anna – I don't think you know my friend Laura. She's a friend from work. Laura, this is Anna.

A: Nice to meet you.

L: Hi – I've heard a lot about you.

A: All good I hope!

▶ TRACK 32

1 Where do you live?
2 Do you know anyone in this class?
3 How long have you known them?
4 Why are you studying English?
5 Have you studied in this school before?
6 Are you enjoying the class?
7 Did you have a nice weekend?
8 What did you do?

▶ TRACK 33

We have a wedding planning business which we've run for almost twenty years now. I was a model when I was younger and I did work for several wedding magazines, which is how I first got interested in the business. I stopped modelling after I got married and had my two babies, but I never wanted only to be a mum and my husband was very supportive when I decided to start my company.

I think he thought it would always be small – something like a hobby – but it grew and grew – and eventually he left his job to work with me as the finance director. We have three kids now and they're all part of the business too. Even my little boy – who's only six – sometimes welcomes the guests. He's so cute in his little suit! The clients love him.

I hope my daughter, Sophie, will take over the business eventually. I think she combines the best of her parents. She and I are both very determined – she doesn't stop until she succeeds at something! And then, she also shares her father's head for figures. They're both very good at negotiating prices, whereas I think maybe my son, Jerome, is a bit too soft. He loves fashion and design, but I don't think he has the business skills. We'll see.

▶ TRACK 34

Sophie: Yeah, the wedding business, it's OK. I guess it's nice to do things together as a family. It means we're pretty close, I guess, and of course, we have nice things from the success, but it is work and Mum can be quite strict sometimes. My mum sometimes says things like 'When you take over the business, blah, blah, blah' or 'When I retire, you need to know blah, blah, blah', but I actually don't want to run the business – none of us do! Well, I guess Ben might, but he's only six. I want to make a difference in the world. I want to become a scientist. Discover things.

Jerome: Did she say I wasn't interested? I suppose I've never really said anything to her when we've talked, because she gets so, kind of, angry about it. It's easier just to agree. She's like my mum. They're very strong characters. Neither of them take no for an answer. Me and Dad, we're more the calm, quiet types. Anyway, I love the business. I like the fashion and design aspect, but also you meet people, you make this amazing special day for them. It's so happy and romantic. And you can make money from it. What's not to like? Of course I'd like to run the company.

▶ TRACK 35

1 friendly and open
2 fit and healthy
3 calm and patient
4 clear and confident
5 strong and determined
6 peace and quiet
7 cooking and cleaning
8 more and more
9 bigger and better
10 try and help
11 go and see
12 scream and shout

▶ TRACK 36

/wɪər/, /gəʊ/, /weɪ/, /wiː/, /we/, /waɪ/, /kwəʊ/, /kwɪ/, /gən/, /eɪg/, /wɜː/, /gæ/

▶ TRACK 37

1 We're going away for the weekend.
2 I found a really funny quote on the web.
3 His wife negotiated a special deal.
4 We organised a quiz night.
5 It was a very vague answer.
6 I need to go to work.
7 I want to go into the wedding business.
8 There's a big age gap, but we get on very well.

▶ TRACK 38

1 We might go running at the track.
2 Is there a pool near here?
3 Who's the guy with the basketball?
4 A friend from university is coming to stay.
5 How do you know each other?
6 I'm going to watch the game with some friends.

UNIT 7

▶ TRACK 39

1

A: Where are you from?

B: Italy.

A: Oh nice! Which part?

B: Treviso.

A: Oh. Where's that?

B: It's a small city in the north-east. It's about 40 kilometres from Venice. So, say that's Venice, OK? Well, Treviso is just here – to the north.

A: Oh, OK. So what's it like?

B: It's great. The centre's very old with some beautiful old buildings, but the city's also quite modern. You know Benetton? The clothes?

A: Yes.

B: Well, Benetton's based in Treviso.

A: Oh wow! OK. So where do you live? In the centre?

B: Not exactly, but everything is quite near. It's small – only eighty thousand people. And it's easy to get round. I live near the river and you can walk along the banks, which is nice. There's a nice park too.

Conversation 2

C: So, where are you from Chuck?

D: Texas.

C: Whereabouts?

D: I doubt you'll know it. It's a little town called Harlingen. It's right in the south – by the Mexican border.

C: Yeah, I know it. In fact, I've been there! I have a friend who lives in Port Isabel.

D: Port Isabel! Wow, that's real close. So what did you think of Harlingen?

C: Yeah, it was lovely. I mean, it's a bit quiet, but for a holiday it was great.

D: When were you there? What time of year?

C: February, but the climate's lovely. It's so warm. We went to the beach quite a lot.

D: Sure.

C: And we took a boat along the coast a couple of times and went fishing.

D: Did you catch anything?

C: Not much, but it was just nice to be on the sea.

D: So what's your friend called?

C: Harry Dancey.

D: You're kidding me! Skip Dancey? I went to high school with him!

C: No! Really? What a small world!

3

E: Where are you from?

F: Oman.

E: Oh, OK. Oman. I'm really sorry, but where is that exactly? My geography isn't very good.

F: It's in the Middle East – on the Indian Ocean. So imagine you've got Saudi Arabia here and then the UAE – the United Arab Emirates – is up here and Oman goes down here to the right.

E: Oh, OK. I think I know where you mean. And where do you live?

F: In the capital, Muscat – in the north of the country.

E: Oh OK. And what's it like? Is it a big city?

F: Yes, quite big – it's about a million people and it spreads along the coast.

E: Oh, sounds nice.

F: It is. It's beautiful because you have the sea and the mountains behind. And it's a very exciting place because lots of people from different countries live there and, you know, there's lots to do there.

▶ TRACK 40

1 We can walk there in ten minutes.

2 Do you have to pay extra for the bills?

3 Friends can stay at my house if they want to.

4 She doesn't have to do any housework at all!

5 I have to help with all the cooking and cleaning.

6 I can't talk to her.

▶ TRACK 41

I=Isabel, O = Oliver, M = Maksim

O: Hi there Maksim. Come in, come in.

M: Oliver, good to meet you finally.

O: This is my wife Isabel.

I: Welcome. Nice to meet you. How was your journey?

M: OK, but very long.

I: I can imagine. Anyway, you're here now. Do you want me to take your coat?

M: Oh, yes. Thank you.

O: You can just leave your bag and things over there for now.

M: OK. Is it OK if I take my shoes off?

I: Sure. Go ahead. You don't have to, though.

M: I've brought some – what do you call them? House shoes? ... I'll find them ... .

I: Oh – sure. Slippers.

M: Oliver, I also bought you this. It's a traditional knife from Uzbekistan – it's called a *pichok*. And Mrs Isabel, this is a special hat – very traditional in my country.

I: Gosh – thank you.

M: And your son?

I: He's sleeping.

O: How did you get this through security?

M: Oh, it's not hand luggage.

O: Doh. Of course. Ow! Wow, it's sharp!

M: Yes – yes.

O: I think I've cut myself.

M: Oh yes. So sorry.

O: No, don't be silly. It's amazing, thanks.

I: Would you like a cup of tea or something to eat, Maksim?

M: No, no, thank you. I'm fine. Maybe just some water.

O: Sure. Come through to the kitchen.

M: Thanks.

I: Are you sure you're not hungry?

M: No really. I ate on the plane, but er ... do you mind if I smoke?

O: Well, actually, I'd rather you didn't inside. Isabel goes outside.

I: To be honest, it's better – it means I smoke less. I'm trying to give up.

M: Of course – no problem. I'll go now, if you don't mind.

I: You can go in the garden, if you like. The door's here.

M: OK, great, great.

▶ TRACK 42

1 A: Do you mind if I open the window?
   B: No, of course not. It is quite hot, isn't it?

2 A: Do you mind if I use your computer?
   B: No, of course not. One minute. I'll just log off.

3 A: Do you mind if I borrow your phone for a minute?
   B: Actually, I'd rather you didn't. I don't have much credit.

4 A Is it OK if I leave class early today?
   B: Yes, of course. Just make sure you do your homework.

5 A: Is it OK if I close the window?
   B: Yes, of course. It is quite cold, isn't it?

6 A: Is it OK if I leave these papers here?
   B: I'd rather you didn't. I'm trying to tidy up.

▶ TRACK 43

O: Oh gosh. Sorry. I forgot to tell you about Boris. Did he scare you?

M: A little.

O: He won't bite you. I promise. He's very friendly.

M: I'm sure, but maybe I'll go out the front next time.

O: Sorry.

I: Let me show you around the house.

M: OK, yes. thanks.

I: So you've seen the garden, and obviously this is the kitchen. Please help yourself to food.

M: Could I use the washing machine while I'm here?

I: Oh, I'll do it for you if you like.

M: Oh really? Are you sure?

I: Absolutely.

M: Thanks

I: So this is the living room. You're welcome to watch TV. Although you'll probably have to watch repeats of *The Big Bang Theory* as that's all my son Theo seems to watch – or play video games.

M: Oh right. Like my little brother. And here?

I: Oh, that's Oliver's study, but we won't go in there. It's a mess! So come up the stairs. The toilet's in here. It's a bit, er, funny. Look – you need to press quick for the water ... Like this.

M: Oh right. OK. Quickly.

I: This is the bathroom. We just have a shower. It was actually installed last month.

M: Very nice. Do I use this?

I: Yes. There's only one bathroom. We share it.

M: Oh, OK. So is it OK if I have a shower in the morning?

I: Of course. I'll get you some towels in a moment. Just go in if it's free. There's a lock on the door. OK, this door is our room and that's Theo's.

M: How old is he?

I: Sixteen.

M: Oh yes? Like my baby brother. He'll remind me of home.

I: I hope not. He's very messy, too.

M: Oh really? No. I think my brother is quite tidy. My mother is very strict with him.

I: Yes, maybe I'm too soft.

M: Oh, no. I didn't mean ... I'm sure you are a very good mother.

I: I try. So this is your room.

M: Oh, it's so lovely.

I: So, you can use these drawers and there's space in the wardrobe to hang some things.

M: OK.

I: I think you'll be warm enough, but I can get you a blanket if you want.

M: Oh, no. I'll be fine. It was minus six degrees in Tashkent this morning.

I: Minus six? Wow. I'm sure you will be OK then.

▶ TRACK 44

/æ/, /ɑː/, /aɪ/, /mæ/, /mɑː/, /maɪ/, /bæ/, /fɑː/, /faɪ/, /kæn/, /kɑːn/, /kaɪn/

▶ TRACK 45

1 You can cycle along the path by the river bank.
2 The climate's warm and the people are kind.
3 My family have a farm where they grow rice.
4 It's a financial centre where many banks are based.
5 It's a large island off the south coast of France.
6 I don't mind travelling, but I prefer to stay at home.
7 I can't find it on a map because it's so tiny.
8 There's a market in the square on Fridays.

UNIT 8

▶ TRACK 46

design, economics, geography, graduate, history, interested, nursery, primary, secondary, university

▶ TRACK 47

1

A: So, how's school, Ollie? Your father told me you're doing well.

B: It's OK, I suppose. Some bits are good.

A: Yeah? What are your favourite subjects?

B: Spanish and art. And history's OK as well.

A: And what year are you in now?

B: Year eleven.

A: So how long have you got left?

B: Well, if it all goes well, I'll have two more years.

A: What are you going to do when you finish? Have you got any plans?

B: Well, if I can save enough money between now and then, I'll try and take a year off. Dad doesn't want me to, though.

A: No?

B: No, he just wants me to stay in the system and go straight to university and study Business or something and graduate and become just like him.

A: Yeah, well. He's probably just worried about you.

B: Yeah, right. Whatever!

2

C: So what course are you doing, Pep?

D: Pure Maths.

C: Wow! OK. That sounds hard.

D: Yeah, it can be, but I'm really enjoying it. To be honest, the most difficult thing for me is doing the whole degree in English, but my tutors are great. Everybody has been very helpful.

C: What year are you in?

D: My third, unfortunately. I've got my finals next April!

C: Oh, OK. Well, good luck!

D: Thanks!

C: What are you going to do after you graduate? Any plans?

D: Well, if I get the grades I want, I'll probably do a Master's somewhere.

C: Oh, OK. What in? The same subject?

D: Maybe. I'm not sure. I'm thinking of maybe doing Astrophysics, actually.

C: Oh, right. Have you applied anywhere yet?

D: No, I haven't, actually – not yet. But I probably will in the next few weeks.

3

E: So, did you go to university, Dhanya?

F: Yes, I did. The Paul Cézanne University in Marseille. It's one of the oldest universities in France.

E: Oh, OK. What did you study?

F: International Law.

E: And did you enjoy it?

F: Yes, up to a point, I suppose, but to be honest, it was quite theoretical. It wasn't very practical and I think I've learned much more since I started working.

E: I know what you mean! I mean, I left school at sixteen and started working straight away. To begin with, I did lots of horrible jobs, but I learnt a lot as well and it made me hungry for success. I was running my own business by the time I was 22. I'm not sure many university graduates can say the same!

F: You can't beat the university of life, eh?!

▶ TRACK 48

I = Interviewer, R = Rebecca

I: So, how did you find school when you came here?

R: A bit mixed. I made friends quickly. I knew a bit of Spanish and people were friendly, but I remember that to begin with, my brother just stood in the corner of the playground watching everyone play. It was sad!

I: But he made friends in the end?

R: Yeah.

I: So you spoke Spanish?

R A bit, but in class I couldn't understand very much. It was horrible.

I: Did you have to do extra Spanish classes?

R: Not really. There was another girl in the class who spoke English so she translated a lot at the beginning. Then Mum and Dad helped me at home with my homework. And, oh my gosh, we have to do so much here!

I: Really?

R: Yeah – I remember really crying about it when I first came because we didn't have to do much in primary in England – a bit of reading or something. Even now my friends in England complain when they have to do 45 minutes in secondary school, but I often have two hours – and sometimes study for tests on top of that.

I: OK. So are classes different?

R: Primary was. For some reason, I did the last year of primary here, although I'd already done it in England. Maybe it was because they have five years of secondary school in England, but there are only four here. Sorry, what was the question?

I: Are classes different?

R: Oh yeah. Basically, in primary in England we had the same teacher all day, but here we changed teachers. I liked some, but some – like Don Miguel – were really boring! Sometimes we just had to copy from the book. We didn't use textbooks much in England and we did more projects and arty things.

I: Right. So which do you prefer?

R: It's difficult to say. Now I'm at instituto ...

I: Instituto?

R: Sorry, secondary school. We finish at two o'clock every day and then we get almost three months off in the summer, whereas in England my friends finish at four and they only get six weeks' summer holiday. I chat to my friends in England still or read their updates on Facebook and they say school is boring too, and they get stressed with exams and stuff, but then they have this thing here, where if your teacher fails you in some subjects, you have to repeat the whole year! I don't like that stress.

▶ TRACK 49

You hear politicians and parents here saying education is bad, but you get the same complaints in Britain, where there are generally more resources. Parents send their kids to private schools or move house to be near good state schools.

From what Rebecca says, her teachers here are generally more traditional in the way they teach, but I don't mind that. Students probably learn to listen and concentrate better. Anyway, no method's perfect. There's good and bad everywhere. Luckily, Rebecca's very responsible and she has some great teachers. She's happy and the school has a good atmosphere, small classes, and there's no violence or bullying – that's the most important thing. And if we stay, university will be much cheaper here. Fees in England are very high, even though nearly all universities are state run.

The only policies I really don't like here are textbooks and holidays. I spend 400 euros on books every year. In Britain, they're free. Schools buy the books and the students borrow them. And the summer holidays here are too long when you both work! When we were in the UK, my wife and I could organise our holidays to be at home with the kids most of the time, but here it's impossible!

▶ TRACK 50

/dʒə/, /tʃe/, /tʃeɪ/, /dʒɒ/, /ʃən/, /tʃɪ/, /ɪʃt/, /ɪdʒ/, /iːtʃ/, /əʊtʃ/, /tʃæ/, /dʒu/

▶ TRACK 51

1 They rejected my application for university.
2 We need to change our traditional approach.
3 You need to challenge students to succeed.
4 Did you check your work after you finished?
5 All children have religious education in primary school.
6 I have to do a project before I can graduate.
7 The website has a jobs section for teachers.
8 You can't mention some subjects in conversation.

▶ TRACK 52

1 I'll do it in a minute.
2 Is it OK if I use it?
3 It won't happen.
4 Sorry, I had to leave early.
5 I couldn't hear anything.
6 I'll let you know.

UNIT 9

▶ TRACK 53

1

A: Hi, how are you?

B: Not very well, actually. I think I have the flu.

A: Oh no! You poor thing! Are you sure it's not just a cold?

B: It might be, I suppose, but it doesn't feel like it. I've had it for a few days now. I just feel really weak and tired all the time and my muscles ache a lot.

A: That sounds horrible. Maybe you should go home and get some rest.

B: Yes, maybe you're right.

A: No-one will thank you if you stay and spread it!

B: That's true. Could you tell Mr Einhoff I'm sick?

A: Yes, of course.

B: Oh, and could you give him my homework?

A: Yeah, of course.

B: Thanks.

A: No problem. Well, you take it easy and get well soon.

B: I'll try! Bye.

A: Bye. See you.

2

D: Atchoo!

C: Bless you!

D: Oh! I am sorry! That's the fifth time in as many minutes!

C: That's OK.

D: I always get like this at this time of year! It's awful, because I hate winter, but then as soon as the sun comes out, I can't stop sneezing! And my eyes get really sore as well. I really want to rub them, but that just makes them worse!

C: Oh, that sounds horrible. Are you taking anything for it?

D: Yes, I went to the chemist's last year and they recommended these pills so I take four of these every day, and they help, but they don't stop it completely.

C: Well, why don't you get some sunglasses to protect your eyes a bit?

D: That's not a bad idea, actually ... but I think I might feel a bit funny walking round in sunglasses all day!

C: Yeah, I know what you mean, but maybe you ought to try it. You never know. It might work for you.

D: Well, maybe if things get really bad.

▶ TRACK 54

1 It's just a question of mind over matter.
2 What's the matter?
3 I don't mind.
4 It doesn't matter.
5 Never mind.
6 To make matters worse …
7 You don't mind?
8 I've got a lot on my mind.
9 That's a matter of opinion.

▶ TRACK 55

1

A: Are you OK?
B: Hic! Yeah, I've just got hiccups. Oh gosh! Hic! It's really annoying.
A: Here. I know a cure. It never fails.
B: Hic.
A: Take some water in your mouth, but don't drink it.
B: Mmm.
A: Now put your fingers in your ears. Bend down and put your head between your knees and swallow the water slowly.
B: Mmmm?
A: Swallow the water!
B: Mmm.
A: OK. You can breathe now. Have you still got them?
B: Um, no. No, I don't think so.
A: You see. It works every time.
B: Maybe, but I wouldn't want to do it in public! People would think I was mad!

2

C: Yes. Can I help you?
D: Yes, I would like something for a bad stomach, please.
C: Does it hurt or have you been sick?
D: Not sick. It's more gas. It's uncomfortable.
C: OK. It sounds like indigestion. It's after you eat, right?
D: Yes.
C: And you're going to the toilet normally? No diarrhoea?
D: Diarrhoea? No.
C: OK, so I think these are what you need. They're indigestion tablets. You mix them with water and drink them after your meals. They're the most effective, I think.
D: OK.
C: What flavour would you like? Orange or blackcurrant?
D: Oh, orange.
C: That'll be 4.25. Don't take more than four tablets a day – and if they don't deal with the problem, consult your doctor.
D: OK. Thanks. I will.

3

E: The burn's not too bad. We'll give you some cream for it, but you'll need some stitches in that cut. It's quite deep. What happened?
F: Well, I cut my head dancing with my son.
E: I'm sorry?
F: I was dancing with my five-year-old son and I stepped on one of his toys and I fell and hit my head on the side of the table.
E: Oh dear. What about the burn, then?
F: Well, my wife came in when she heard me shout and while she was helping me stand up, she knocked a cup of coffee off the table and it went all over my leg.
E: Oh dear. I am sorry. I shouldn't laugh!

F: Don't worry. It was very stupid!
E: Nurse, could you dress the burn after I've done these stitches?
G: Of course.

▶ TRACK 56

/bliː/, /fiː/, /niː/, /breɪ/, /sweɪ/, /beɪ/, /heɪ/, /tʃeɪ/, /peɪ/, /reɪ/, /eɪk/, /feɪ/

▶ TRACK 57

1 My eyes ache and I need to sleep!
2 I can't bend my knee very well.
3 She was bleeding from her head.
4 Can you take a deep breath for me, please?
5 These shoes really hurt my feet.
6 I had a terrible pain in my chest.
7 Raise your head and face me, please.
8 The bed was wet with sweat.

UNIT 10

▶ TRACK 58

R = receptionist, D = David

R: Hillborough Hotel.
D: Oh, hello. I'm ringing on behalf of a friend. He wants some information.
R: Sure. What would you like to know?
D: Um, well, do you have any triple rooms?
R: I'm afraid not. We only have doubles.
D: Oh, right. Is it possible to get a double with an extra bed? They have a small kid.
R: That should be possible.
D: And how much would that be per night?
R: For the room, that's 110 euros per night, with a supplement for a child's bed.
D: Sorry. Does that include the cost of the extra bed or not?
R: It does include it, yes.
D: And breakfast is included too?
R: I'm afraid not. It's 125 with breakfast. What dates are they thinking of coming?
D: Um, Tuesday the twelfth to the seventeenth of August.
R: OK. Let me just check our availability. Hmm, I'm afraid we're fully booked that weekend on the sixteenth and seventeenth.
D: And what if they came the previous weekend?
R: Saturday night no, but from Sunday through to Friday we currently have rooms available.
D: So that's the tenth till the fifteenth – including Friday night?
R: That's correct.
D: OK. I'll need to check with them about that. And just a couple of other things.
R: Sure.
D: They're thinking of hiring a car. Can they get any reduced rates if they book through the hotel?
R: They can, actually. We have a partnership with a local hire firm. The cost starts at 25 euros a day.
D: OK. Great. Do you have parking at the hotel?
R: There is a car park, which is 20 euros a day, and there is some street parking nearby.
D: Right. OK. Well, I think they're travelling around Ireland after Dublin, so maybe they could hire the car later in the week.
R: Of course, whatever suits them.
D: OK. Let me just talk to my friends. Could you tell me your name for when I call back?

R: Yes, it's Jackie, but any of my colleagues can deal with the booking.

D: Oh wait, sorry – one last thing. Will they need to make a payment when they make the booking?

R: Yes, we'll need to take a 10% deposit on a credit card.

D: So if for whatever reason they didn't come, they'd lose that money?

R: I'm afraid so. The complete payment is made on arrival.

D: OK. Thanks.

TRACK 59

R = receptionist, C = Customer

R: OK, so can I take your credit card details for the deposit?

C: Sure.

R: What kind of card is it?

C: Visa.

R: And the name on your card?

C: Mr D E Gwaizda. That's G – W – A – I – Z – D – A.

R: OK. That's an unusual name.

C: Yeah, it's Polish originally.

R: OK. And the card number on the card?

C: 1003 6566 9242 8307.

R: And the security number on the back of the card – the last three digits there?

C: 718.

R: And the expiry date?

C 06 17

R: And can I just take a contact number in case there are any problems?

C: Sure. 0044 796 883 412.

▶ TRACK 60

A, B, C, D, E, F, G, H, I, J, K, L, M, N, O, P, Q, R, S, T, U, V, W, X, Y, Z

▶ TRACK 61

R = receptionist, M = manager, L= Lady Zaza

R: Hello. Reception.

M: Hi. I'm calling on behalf of Lady Zaza, in the presidential suite.

R: Oh, yes. It's a real pleasure to have her in the hotel.

M: Yeah, well, there was no way we could stay in that last place. The service there was a joke!

R: Well, I hope everything's OK with our rooms. We really didn't have much time to prepare them.

M: Yeah, everything's fine, basically, but there are just a couple of things she's asked for.

R: OK.

M: Well, first, can you ask room service to send some fresh flowers to the room? Lady Zaza enjoys arranging them. She'd like a hundred bunches of red flowers and eighty bunches of white.

R: Certainly. I'll send someone up with them in a minute.

M: And tell them to bring more of her favourite chocolates too, please. And please remember to remove the ones with nuts. She'd be very ill if she ate one by mistake. And the hotel wouldn't want that.

R: Absolutely not. I'll make sure they're taken out.

M: She'd also like the light bulbs in her room changed. She said it's too dark.

R: Oh … of course.

M: And can you bring her a kitten?

R: Er, a kitten?!

M: Yeah. Stroking it helps her relax. She wants a white one.

R: I doubt I can find one …

M: What Lady Zaza wants, Lady Zaza gets.

R: Would it be OK if the cat was a different colour?

M: No. It needs to match the colour of the flowers. Oh, and one last thing. Can she get a wake-up call at four a.m., please? She'd like to use the gym.

R: Well, the gym doesn't usually open until six, but I'm sure we can organise something for her.

M: Great. That's it for now. Oh, wait. Just one second. She's saying something.

L: They did it again! You've got to do something!

M: Yeah, OK, OK. Hello?

R: Yes, hello.

M: Lady Zaza can hear the people downstairs. They're talking or watching TV or something and she wants them to be moved.

R: Moved? I'm afraid that's just not possible.

M: Sure it's possible. You've got hundreds of rooms in this place.

R: I know, but I'm afraid we're fully booked. We don't have any other rooms available.

M: So you're telling me you can't move them?

R: I really would move them, if I could, but I'm afraid it's absolutely impossible. I'm terribly sorry.

M: Well, that's just not good enough. I'd like to talk to the manager.

R: She's not here at the moment, I'm afraid, but I'm sure that if she was, she'd tell you exactly the same thing.

M: Is that right?

R: I'm afraid so, yes.

M: OK. Well, I'll tell her … but she's not going to like it.

▶ TRACK 62

1 I never used to like camping.

2 I used to do judo when I was younger.

4 He used to smoke quite heavily when he was younger.

5 I used to have really long hair when I was at college.

6 It never used to be crowded before.

▶ TRACK 63

/rʌʃ/, /hɒl/, /lʊk/, /puːl/, /mʌn/, /pɒ/, /bʊk/, /luːz/, /dʌb/, /hɒs/, /kʊd/, /ruːm/

▶ TRACK 64

1 Could I make a booking for Friday?

2 We don't want to lose our deposit.

3 I never used to like group holidays, but now I do.

4 Could I have a look at your book?

5 How much money did you spend?

6 I spent the whole week by the pool.

7 I'd like to book a double room.

8 I lost my toothbrush somewhere in the hostel.

▶ TRACK 65

1 Where would you go if you could go anywhere in the world?

2 I never used to enjoy camping, but I've grown to really love it.

3 Don't have any more of that coffee if you want to sleep tonight!

4 I don't think you should worry too much about it.

5 I used to get terrible nosebleeds, and then one day they just stopped!

6 I'd never go to work again if I didn't really have to.

UNIT 11

▶ TRACK 66

1

A: Did you read this article about bees?

B: No.

A: They're all dying, for some unknown reason.

B: Really? That's terrible!

A: I know. It's really bad news because we really depend on bees. If bees become extinct, we won't have any fruit or vegetables.

B: I hadn't thought about that. They should do something – fund research or something.

A Absolutely.

2

C: Did you see the forecast for tomorrow?

D: No.

C: It's going to be nice – really hot and sunny.

D: Really? That's great!

C: I know. It's good. It's been so wet and windy recently.

D: We should go out, then – go to the beach or somewhere.

C: Yeah, that's a good idea.

3

E: Did you hear what they want to do in Morovia?

F: No. What?

E: It said on the news that they're going to pull down a lot of the horrible houses they've built along the coast and create a national park instead.

F: Really? That's great.

E: I know. It's good news.

F: They should do more to protect the countryside here, too.

E: Definitely. We need more green spaces.

4

G: Did you see they've discovered a new way to kill the mosquitoes that spread malaria?

H: No.

G: Yeah, it said it could save millions of lives.

H: Really? That's great.

G: I know. It's really good.

H: It makes a change to hear some good news.

G: Absolutely.

▶ TRACK 67

1 Really? That's great!
2 Really? That's interesting.
3 Really? That's nice.
4 Really? That's bad news.
5 Really? That's awful.
6 I know. It's fantastic.
7 Yeah. It's good news.
8 Yeah, I know. It's really bad news.
9 I know. It's terrible.
10 That's a good idea.
11 Absolutely.
12 Definitely.

▶ TRACK 68

P = presenter, S = scientist

P: OK. So the first question from listener Mary Martin is based on a recent news story: Are there crime genes?

S: Well, yes and no. First, remember we share 50% of our genes with bananas, but you wouldn't say humans were half banana! There are studies that have found some violent criminals share a particular gene. But, BUT, this is one of many, many factors. Many people have the gene, but aren't violent. Violence and crime can be learned. Home life, culture, war, even the environment and pollution can be factors.

P: OK. Something rather different now. Yevgeny from Russia asks: How do spiders walk on ceilings?

S: OK, right, yes, well researchers have discovered that spiders' feet are covered in hairs. But then each hair is also covered in hundreds of thousands of tiny hairs, each about an atom wide. Basically, when these tiny hairs move next to the atoms of the ceiling material, it creates a small electric charge so the hairs and ceiling atoms are attracted to each other. It's a bit like how you can rub a balloon on your hair, then stick it to a wall. The spider has so many hairs, the attraction is quite strong – strong enough to hold 100 times the weight of the spider.

P: Right, well, from some very thin hairs to Graphene and Jamie Seguro's question: What is Graphene?

S: Graphene, OK. Well, this is probably the most important discovery of the last 20 years.

P: Really? So what is it and who discovered it?

S: It's the world's thinnest material. It's just one atom thick, and it was discovered by two Russian scientists working at the University of Manchester. The first amazing thing is, it's very easy to find, because it's basically a very, very thin layer of the stuff in a pencil.

P: What, a normal pencil?

S: Yep. That stuff is called graphite. Basically, you take some graphite and put it on some sticky tape – normal sellotape. Then you take some more tape, press it on the graphite. If you peel this tape away, some layers of graphite come off. And if that process is repeated a few times, it eventually leaves a layer one atom thick.

P: So can you see it?

S: Not without a microscope, no, but even though it's so thin Graphene is incredibly difficult to tear: it's the strongest material we know. But then because it's thin you can bend it easily. And it's really, really good at conducting electricity – much better than the wires that are used in our home or the chips in computers.

P: So could those things be replaced by Graphene?

S: Some day, hopefully, because it's so easy to get and so efficient. We could save a lot of money. It's an incredible discovery and it was awarded a Nobel Prize.

▶ TRACK 69

/laʊ/, /lɔ:/, /rɒk/, /pɒ/, /paʊ/, /faʊ/, /stɔ:/, /dɒ/, /kɔ:/, /bɒ/, /mɔ:/, /ɔ:t/

▶ TRACK 70

1 You're not allowed to keep pets.
2 They found the bomb before it went off.
3 They took it to court and won.
4 You ought to feed your dog less.
5 The last version was launched in October.
6 They have a policy to fund more research.
7 The rocket lost power and crashed.
8 The storm caused a lot of damage.

UNIT 12

1

A: Hello.

B: Hi, it's Brendan. Is Neil there?

A: No, he's not got up yet. Is it urgent?

B: No, it's OK. Just tell him we're meeting earlier – at seven, not eight. And tell him he's very lazy! Twelve o'clock and still in bed!

A: Well, he was out late last night. Has he got your number, Brendan?

B: Yeah, he has. So what time will he be up?

A: I imagine in about an hour. He didn't get back home till four.

B: Oh right. Well, I'll see him later. Thanks.

A: That's OK. I'll give him your message. Meet at seven, not eight.

B: Yeah.

A: Bye now.

2

C: Good morning, DBB. How can I help you?

D: Yeah, hi. Could I speak to Jane Simpson, please?

C: Of course. I'll just put you through to her.

D: Thanks.

...

E: Hello.

D: Hi, Jane?

E: No, it's actually Poppy. I'm afraid Jane's out visiting a client. Would you like to leave a message?

D: Yeah, could you tell her Diane called? I've already spoken to my boss and he's fine with the price, so we can go ahead with the work. Can you ask her to phone me when she gets back so we can sort out the details?

E: Of course. Has she got your number?

D: I don't think she has my mobile. It's 07729 651 118.

E: OK. 07729 651 118. And what was your name again? Sorry.

D: Diane Lincoln. L-I-N-C-O-L-N. So when will she be back?

E: Probably later this afternoon. I think she said she was going for lunch.

D: Oh, right. Well, hopefully I can speak to her today. I'm actually away on holiday from tomorrow.

E: Oh, right. Well, I'll let her know anyway.

D: OK. Thanks. Bye.

E: Bye.

▶ TRACK 72

A: No, he's not up yet. Is it urgent?

B: Just tell him we're meeting earlier – at seven, not eight.

▶ TRACK 73

1

A: Hello. Better Banking.

B: Oh, hello there. I need to cancel my cards, please. As soon as possible.

A: OK, no problem, but I'm afraid I have to take you through security first. Can I get your full name, please?

B: Um … oh, yes. Of course. It's Bettina Kraus. That's B-E-double T-I …

...

A: OK. That's fine. I'll just put you through to the right department. One moment, please.

...

C: That's fine. So I've cancelled your cards and ordered new ones, and they'll be with you in the next three or four days. We'll also send you a new PIN.

B: Oh, that's great. Thank you so much for your help.

C: You're welcome. Is there anything else I can do for you today?

B: No. That's all for now. Thanks again. Bye.

2

D: OK. So can you just tell me how it happened?

B: Yes. I was walking from the bus stop to my friend's house and I was talking on the phone so I wasn't really paying attention. Then someone came past me on a bicycle and just grabbed my bag and rode off. The strap on the bag broke because he pulled so hard.

D: And can you give me a description of the person on the bike?

B: Not really. Young. Maybe fifteen or sixteen. Wearing dark clothes. And a hood.

D: Anything else?

B: I'm afraid not. It all happened so quickly, you know.

D: OK. Well, I can give you a reference number so you can contact your insurance company, if you have one.

B: OK. And what about my bag?

D: Well, it's a big city out there and obviously we don't have the people to go and look for the person who did this, but if we do hear or find anything, we'll let you know.

3

E: Hello. Abbey Locks. How can I help you?

B: Yeah. Hello, er, basically, my bag's been stolen and it had my keys in it, so I need to get into my apartment.

E: OK. Do you want us to change the lock or just get you in? Was there anything with your address in the bag?

B: Oh gosh, yes. I had my driving licence in my purse.

E: OK. You'll want new locks then. Are you at the property?

B: No, I'm phoning from my friend's house.

E: Right, well I suggest you go back home. We can send someone within an hour. Can I just get the address, please?

B: Sure. It's Apartment 4, number 72 Montague Terrace, BR2 0SZ.

E: OK. Got it. Someone will be with you soon. Do you have proof of ID and proof of address?

B: No, I don't. No. Everything was in my bag. I mean normally I'd ask my landlady who lives next door, but she's away.

E: Wait, you rent the apartment?

B: Yes – is that a problem?

E: Well, we would normally talk to the owner of the property.

B: But she's abroad!

E: Don't you have a contact number?

B: I did – in my phone … oh what a nightmare!

▶ TRACK 74

F: Hello there. You're speaking to Alan. I understand you're calling about your cash and credit cards. Is that correct?

B: Yes, that's right. I called last week. Someone stole my bag and I phoned to cancel my cards.

F: OK.

B: And the guy I spoke to told me he'd cancelled them and that the new cards would be with me in three or four days … but I still haven't received them.

F: Right. Let me just check. OK. I can see that the cards were actually sent out as promised. Last Tuesday. And in fact, your credit card was used just yesterday.

B: No, that's not possible.

F: £1,845, spent in IKEA in Aberdeen.

B: But I've never even been to Aberdeen. How did that happen?

F: I'm not sure. I'm very sorry. I think I have to speak my manager.

▶ TRACK 75

/jʊə/, /stəʊl/, /həʊm/, /aʊə/, /fəʊ/, /ʃʊə/, /fəʊn/, /kjʊə/, /məʊ/

▶ TRACK 76

1 He had to pay a 200-euro fine.
2 I usually work from home.
3 She'll be back in about an hour.
4 Do you have insurance for your phone?
5 I've lost my mobile somewhere.
6 Take a photo with your phone.
7 I'm lucky my job's quite secure.
8 My car was stolen from outside my home.

▶ TRACK 77

1 We've only just left the house.
2 I suddenly realised I'd left my keys in my flat.
3 I was stopped by the police as I was driving home.
4 The lions are usually fed at about three in the afternoon.
5 I knew we'd met before, but I just couldn't remember where.
6 They said the new battery would be here within three or four days.

UNIT 13

▶ TRACK 78

A: What a boring lecture!

B: I know. It wasn't very good. I was starting to fall asleep near the end!

A: So what are you doing this afternoon? Have you got any plans?

B: Yeah, I'm thinking of going to see a movie and … um … listen, would you like to come with me?

A: Maybe. What's on?

B: Well, there's this film called *In the Heat of the Moment* – directed by Umberto Collocini. It's supposed to be really good.

A: Yeah, I've seen it already, actually. I saw it the other day.

B: Oh yes? What was it like?

A: Not bad, but not as good as everyone is saying. The costumes were great and it's set on an island in Thailand, so it looks amazing.

B: Yeah, that's what I'd heard. So what was wrong with it?

A: Oh, I don't know. I just found it a bit too slow. I got a bit bored with it after a while – and the ending was very predictable.

B: Oh, right.

A: And that Scottish actor's in it as well. You know. What's his name?

B: Bryan McFletcher?

A: Yeah, that's him. I just find him really, really annoying. He can't act! Anyway, what else is on?

B: Um … let me see. Oh, there's *The Cottage*.

A: Yeah? What's that?

B: It's a new horror movie. It's supposed to be really scary.

A: OK. To be honest, I don't really like horror movies. I'd rather see something a bit lighter, if possible.

B: OK. Right. Well, how about this? *It's a Love–Hate Thing*. It's a romantic comedy set in Paris and New York and it stars Ellen McAdams and Ryan Rudd.

A: That sounds more like it! Where's it on?

B: The Galaxy in Cambridge Road.

A: OK. And what time does it start?

B: There's one showing at two thirty and then another one at quarter to five.

A: So shall we try the half past two one? We could go and have a coffee or something first.

B: OK. Great.

▶ TRACK 79

cash machine, city centre, crossroads, flatmate, film industry, football boots, heart disease, security system, success story, sunglasses, tennis court, traffic lights

▶ TRACK 80

1

I'm a big fan of a Turkish singer called Sertab Erener. I first heard her when she won the Eurovision Song Contest and I've liked her ever since then. I think she's got an amazing voice. She actually trained as an opera singer. I've got five or six of her albums and a couple of years ago I went to Istanbul to see her sing live. In fact, I've discovered Turkey through her music and want to spend more time there. I've been learning Turkish since 2012 and I'm now starting to understand her songs better too. My all-time favourite is *Life Doesn't Wait – Hayat Beklemez*. Excuse my bad pronunciation.

2

I've been playing the trumpet for ten years now with El Sistema, which is a programme that helps young people from poor backgrounds learn classical music. I really, really love playing, and without El Sistema I would probably be in a bad situation! When I joined, I was only eight, but I was already in trouble with the police. My favourite composers are Russian – Shostakovich and Stravinsky. We've been rehearsing The Rite of Spring recently for a concert. It's fantastic – the best.

3

My favourite author is the Swedish crime writer Henning Mankell, especially his stories with the detective Wallander. The stories are good thrillers. They're unpredictable, but they're also about social issues and are a bit political which makes them extra interesting. For the last few weeks, they've been showing a series on TV based on the books. It's OK, but the main character is different to the character in my imagination and, of course, there's less suspense because I've already read the books! I don't know if I'll keep watching.

4

I'm at art school, where I'm studying Fine Art. I've known I wanted to be an artist since I was three. I've always been more of a painter, especially people – portraits, but recently I've become much more interested in sculpture. I think my favourite artist at the moment is an English sculptor called Henry Moore. He did these beautiful, strange, abstract sculptures – often based on human figures. I saw an exhibition of his work last year. I don't know why I liked it so much, I just did – especially a sculpture called King and Queen.

▶ TRACK 81

1 How long have you been going there?
2 How long have they been doing that?
3 How long has she been learning?
4 How long have you been playing?
5 How long has he been training?
6 How long have you known him?
7 How long has she been going out with him?
8 How long have you been married?

▶ TRACK 82

/haɪnd/, /həd/, /hɒrə/, /hiːz/, /hæ/, /hɑːf/, /hɪs/, /hɒŋ/, /hɒb/, /hɜːs/, /hɔːl/, /hɪə/

▶ TRACK 83

1 The woman behind me had a horrible laugh.
2 He's got some really annoying habits.
3 I left about halfway through the film.
4 It's quite sad, but it has a happy ending.
5 It's a historical drama set in Hong Kong.
6 Everyone needs to have a hobby.
7 I really hate horror movies.
8 We rehearse every week in a hall near here.

UNIT 14

▶ TRACK 84

A: It's nice.
B: Yes, it is, but it's also very dirty!
C: I know. We'll have to give everything a good clean and sort the place out. Maybe we should go into town and buy some stuff.
A: Yeah, it's a good idea. One minute. I'll get a pen and we can write a list. OK. So ... .
B: Well, we need those things for cleaning. A brush and a ... I don't know the name. The thing that you put rubbish in. What's the name?
C: Do you mean a rubbish bin?
B: No, not that. When you use the brush, what do you call the thing that you use to get rubbish from the floor? The thing that you put the dirt into with the brush?
C: Oh, you mean a dustpan. A dustpan and brush.
B: A dustpan and brush. Yes, that's very useful.
C: And maybe we should get some cleaning stuff as well. Have we got any bleach?
A: What is bleach?
C: Oh, it's a kind of liquid that's really good for cleaning things, you know, like for cleaning the floor and the toilet. It's a kind of chemical. It's quite strong.
A: Oh, we have some. It's in the kitchen – in the cupboard under the sink.
C: Oh, OK. I didn't notice that, but that's good.
B: We need to buy that machine that you use for the clothes. After you wash them. I can't remember the name. Oh, and I know this word as well.
A: You mean an iron?
B: Yes, an iron! And also the thing that you put the clothes on when you use the iron.
C: Yeah, an ironing board. OK. What else?
A: Oh, for the bathroom we need a thing for the shower. You know, the plastic thing that stops the water from leaving the shower – and the metal thing that holds it.
C: A shower curtain and a shower rail. Yeah, I noticed there wasn't anything like that in the bathroom. It's crazy, isn't it? Why doesn't the landlord provide things like that? It's so basic.

B: I know!
A: We should charge the landlord for these things.
B: Oh, one more thing. Before I forget. We need the machine that makes hot water – to make tea and coffee.
C: Oh, yes, of course. A kettle! I can't live without a kettle! I need my tea in the morning!

▶ TRACK 85

I must remember to call her later.
You mustn't forget to set your alarm.
You can, if you must.
We mustn't leave it here.
You must be tired.
He mustn't do anything till the doctor's seen him.
I must speak to them later.

▶ TRACK 86

1 For my birthday this year, my big sister bought me my own website. She's really good with computers and I'm not, but the website has become something fun we work on together. I also loved the way she told me. She sent me an email where she gave me clues about the present for me to guess what it was, but I didn't know. Then she sent me another email with a link to a website. When I clicked on the link, I understood everything and I realised that the site was the present. I was really excited! It's my favourite ever gift because, as I said, it's something we do together.

2 I got a mountain bike for Christmas a few years ago and it's been one of the most useful presents ever. Over the last year, I've lived close enough to work to be able to cycle and so I've saved loads of money on petrol. A birthday present that also saves me money! Excellent. I'm also fitter and have lost weight.

3 One of my ex-boyfriends was the king of bad presents. One year, he gave me an iron for my birthday! An iron! I mean, what kind of message does that send about our relationship and the way that he saw me? The following year, he bought me a dress that HE really liked and told me that he wanted me to start wearing more clothes like that from then on – because they would make me more attractive. I couldn't believe it! A couple of weeks after that, we broke up!

4 A few years ago, I went out with a girl and as we were getting out of the taxi to go to dinner, she suddenly said, 'I got you a present.' I was quite embarrassed because it was our first date and I hadn't thought of getting her anything. Then she handed me a rock from a beach. I was confused. Why had she given me this thing? She said, 'I wanted to give you something you'd never forget and you could tell your children about'. I said thanks to be polite, but I actually thought it was a bit stupid and it was a bad start to the evening!
Now, though, I use that rock to stop papers on my desk blowing away and that girl is my wife!

▶ TRACK 87

/e/, /ə/, /ɔː/, /ɜː/, /be/, /bɜː/, /pre/, /pɔː/, /zənt/, /zɜːrv/, /drɔː/, /tɔː/

▶ TRACK 88

1 I burnt my hand on the cooker.
2 We found some money buried in the garden
3 You mustn't pour chemicals down the sink.
4 There's a torch in the drawer over there.
5 There are strict laws to protect the environment.
6 I didn't get any birthday presents this year.
7 The old church is perfectly preserved.
8 Where do you store all your food?

▶ TRACK 89

1 I've been wanting to see that for ages.
2 It's just one of those things that happen sometimes.
3 I don't have to work tomorrow, so I guess I can, yeah.
4 How long have you been working in the music industry?
5 He's one of those people who can always make you laugh.
6 There's been an accident on the crossroads in the city centre.

UNIT 15

▶ TRACK 90

L = Laima, A = Aidan

L: So how long have you been living here?
A: Almost two years.
L: Wow! You must like it.
A: Yeah, it's nice. I have a good quality of life here – warm climate, near the beach, not too much work.
L: It sounds fantastic.
A: Yeah, it's great, but I'm actually going back to Canada in a few months.
L: Forever?
A: Yeah, I think so.
L: Why? It sounds perfect here.
A: Well, the economy's doing quite badly at the moment. I mean, unemployment has gone up quite a lot over the last few months, so I'm not sure I'm going to have a job in a year's time.
L: Really?
A: Yeah, and also salaries aren't so high here, you know. I could get paid a lot more back home.
L: Sure, but I bet the cost of living's a lot higher in Canada as well. Everything's so cheap here. I mean, eating out is twice the price in my country. You can get a three-course meal for about six dollars here.
A: Yeah, that's true, but it used to be cheaper in the past. Inflation has gone up over the last two years and if it stays high, well, you know, it won't be so cheap.
L: I know, but it's still a big difference, no?
A: Yeah, maybe, but anyway, in the end, I miss my family and friends and maybe money isn't so important, but I'll still have more opportunities back home, I think, so work might be more interesting there.
L: I guess so. It seems a shame, though. It's so nice here. Won't you miss the heat?
A: Yeah, probably, but I don't mind the cold weather so much. You get used to it after a while.
L: Mmm.
A: So what about your country? How are things there? Is it a good place to live?

▶ TRACK 91

The lawyer continued reading. It seemed Dad had actually been a good salesman. He earned quite a good salary, but he just preferred to save it. And he had been good at investing money too. The most expensive technology he had was a radio, but he bought shares in some camera and electronic shops. In 1965, the shares cost eight pence each and he sold them 35 years later for £4.12 each.

Of the 2.7 million pounds he was leaving, he had decided to give two million to a charity that looked after teenagers with problems. The rest was divided between me and my sisters.

For a moment, I felt angry. Why hadn't he said anything? Why had we lived like poor people? Why was he giving the money to other children? But then I thought, it's stupid to think like

that. Really, I had a happy childhood and I'm very happy now. I remembered my parents reading us books they'd borrowed from the library and the hours we played cards together. It was fantastic what my parents had done. The love we had was more important than money, but now maybe the money they saved can bring some love to others.

The only problem I have now is what to do with a quarter of a million pounds – when I honestly don't really need anything!

▶ TRACK 92

1 Two million pounds
2 Seven hundred and eighty-one thousand
3 Six hundred and fifty-three
4 Nineteen sixty-five
5 Four pounds twelve
6 Two point seven
7 A quarter

▶ TRACK 93

1 The minimum wage at that time was five pounds seventy-three an hour.
2 Inflation fell to three point four per cent last month.
3 The government is going to invest seven hundred million in schools.
4 Three-quarters of the population own a car.
5 The new factory will create eight hundred and twenty-five jobs.
6 The house cost three hundred and sixty thousand euros.
7 We borrowed a hundred and ninety-four thousand from the bank.
8 We'll finally pay back the mortgage in twenty fifty-one.

▶ TRACK 94

1
A: Yes, Sir?
B: Can we get the bill, please?
A: Certainly. One moment.
B: Thanks.
C: How much is it?
B: Don't worry. I'll get this. It's my treat.
C: Are you sure? I don't mind paying half.
B: No, really. It's fine. After all, I asked you out.
C: Thanks. It's really kind of you.
B: Oh no!
C: What's up?
B: I've just realised I left my wallet in my other jacket. It's got all my credit cards and cash in it! I'll have to go and get it.
C: Don't be silly. It's too far to go. I'll pay today.
B: Are you sure? I'll pay you back as soon as I can, I promise.
C: No, it's fine. Honestly. Oh! Wow! Right. That's a lot! I hope they accept my credit card!

2
D: That looks great on you.
E: Really?
D: Yeah. Really suits you.
E: Maybe. How much is it?
D: Well, it's vintage sixties.
E: Sorry?
D: It's very old. From the nineteen sixties. It's hard to find things like that in this condition.
E: Oh. Yes. So how much?
D: Let's call it 200.
E: Pounds?
D: Yes, of course pounds.

208

E: Two hundred pounds! But it's not in perfect condition. Look – there's a mark here.

D: OK. So let's say 180.

E: No, sorry. It's too much. Thank you.

D: OK, OK. The best price I can manage is 150. Any lower than that and I'll lose money.

3

F: But if I don't buy it, someone else will.

G: So you've said, but a thousand pounds is a thousand pounds

F: I know, but if I don't have a car, then I'll have to keep getting the bus into town. And that's not cheap either. Fares have just gone up.

G: OK, OK. Look, you did well in your exams and we'd be happy to help, but it is a lot of money. You're working now, so why don't you pay half?

F: I would if I could, Mum, honestly, but I haven't managed to save much yet!

G: Well, maybe we can borrow some money from the bank.

F: Really? Oh, that'd be brilliant!

G: And you can pay us half back when you have the money, OK?

4

H: Your card was cancelled because of some irregular activity that we noticed.

I: Irregular activity? What do you mean?

H: Well, for instance, did you have lunch in Singapore last week?

I: No. I've never been there in my life.

H: Exactly. We suspect that your card was copied sometime last month and that someone then used it overseas.

I: Oh no! How did they manage to do that? And will I get a refund?

H: Everything is covered by your insurance and we're sending out a new card today. You'll receive your new PIN number after you get the card. They're sent separately for security reasons.

▶ TRACK 95

/ɪ/, /ɔɪ/, /ə/, /əʊ/, /raʊ/, /ləʊ/, /rɪdʒ/, /gɪdʒ/, /rəns/, /ʃən/, /dʒɔɪ/, /plɔɪ/

▶ TRACK 96

1 What's the average salary?
2 Can I borrow fifteen euros?
3 I don't know what the local currency is.
4 They won't win the election.
5 It was a joint decision to go.
6 The interest on our mortgage is low.
7 Thanks. I owe you a favour.
8 Youth unemployment is almost 50%.

UNIT 16

▶ TRACK 97

1

A: Did you have a nice weekend?

B: Yes, it was great, actually.

A: Yeah? What did you do?

B: One of my oldest friends got married on Saturday, so I went to the wedding in the afternoon and then the reception later on. It was really good.

A: Oh yeah?

B: Yeah. They hired an old castle on the coast for it. It was an amazing venue. And they had a big buffet there, with really good food, and a DJ and everything.

A: That sounds great. What was the music like?

B: Excellent. I was expecting typical wedding reception music, but this DJ played lots of modern things as well. The dance floor was full all evening.

2

C: Did you do anything last night?

D: Yeah, I did, actually. I went to a friend's house-warming. She's just moved into this new place. It's an amazing flat – in a converted church. It's a really impressive place.

C: Oh, wow! So what was the party like? Was it good?

D: It was great to begin with, yeah. All the other guests were lovely. Everyone was really warm and friendly and very easy to talk to, but then my ex arrived with his new girlfriend.

C: Oh no!

D: Yes, and to make things worse, she was absolutely gorgeous!

C: Oh, you poor thing! That's awful.

D: I know. It ruined the night for me, to be honest. I didn't stay much longer after that.

3

E: So what did you do last night? Anything interesting?

F: Yeah, I had a little dinner party.

E: Oh really? What was the occasion?

F: There wasn't one. I just felt like inviting some friends round and cooking for them.

E: Nice. So how did it go? Was it good?

F: Yeah, it was lovely. It was nice to see people and chat.

E: How many people came?

F: Twelve.

E: Wow! That's a lot of cooking.

F: I know! It took me ages to get everything ready.

E: Did you cook everything yourself?

E: Yeah.

F: You must be a good cook.

E: I don't know about that! I just follow recipes.

F: So what did you do?

E: Well, for starters, I did grilled aubergines covered in yoghurt and served with a slightly spicy sauce and then …

▶ TRACK 98

1 We call April the 21st Kartini Day. It's the day that Raden Ajeng Kartini was born in 1879. She's very important in Indonesia because she fought for women's rights and against sexual discrimination at a time when we were very much second-class citizens. She set up the country's first all-girls school and really helped to change the country for the better. There's still some way to go, sure, but it's important to remember her life and celebrate it every year.

2 My great-grandmother on my mum's side was Ukrainian. We never met, as she died before I was born, but a few years ago my mum and I decided to go on a trip to the village that she came from. We spent a night in the house she'd been born in, which was very moving. The people were very welcoming and I felt a real connection with the place. It was incredible – a day I'll never forget.

3 June the 25th will always be a very special day for me as it's the anniversary of the day that Michael Jackson died. His death in 2009 was a real tragedy and I still feel his loss today. I know he was a controversial figure, but he touched the lives of millions of people all over the world. One of my biggest regrets is that I wasn't able to go to Los Angeles for his memorial service. I wanted to be there, but I just couldn't afford to buy a ticket from Bulgaria.

4 When I was 23 or 24, I spent six months travelling round South East Asia. It was an amazing time in my life and I had lots of great experiences, but perhaps the day I remember best was when I climbed Mount Kinabalu in Malaysia, one of the highest mountains in the region. We started climbing at midnight, with a local guide, and we reached the peak just as the sun was coming up. It was incredibly beautiful.

5 March the 24th is a very special day for me as it's the anniversary of the day that my sight was restored. Thirteen years ago, my eyes were severely damaged in an accident at work and I was told I'd never see again. However, two years ago, I agreed to have this special new operation. It was still in the experimental stage, but amazingly, it worked, and thanks to my surgeon, I can now see my two kids. I'll always be grateful for that!

▶ TRACK 99

/graʊ/, /klɪə/, /skrɪ/, /stæ/, /blɪ/, /fre/, /pre/, /spaɪ/, /trə/, /aʊnd/, /end/, /əsts/

▶ TRACK 100

1 They played some nice background music.
2 The DJ almost cleared the dance floor.
3 Women still face a lot of discrimination in the workplace.
4 A new government was established after the war.
5 On my birthday, I had some friends round for dinner.
6 The organisation of the whole event was very impressive.
7 I cooked my special spicy chicken dish.
8 You should try the traditional breakfasts here.

▶ TRACK 101

1 To be honest, I avoid talking to him if I can help it.
2 I guess it'll take some time before I get used to it.
3 He's a computer programmer based in the States.
4 I'm going to go back as soon as I save enough money.
5 He always promises to help, but then he fails to keep all his promises.
6 I'm currently living at home, but I'm planning to leave after I graduate.

Outcomes Pre-intermediate
Student's Book
Hugh Dellar and Andrew Walkley

Publisher: Gavin McLean

Publishing Consultant: Karen Spiller

Development Editor: Clare Shaw

Editorial Manager: Alison Burt

Head of Strategic Marketing ELT: Charlotte Ellis

Senior Content Project Manager: Nick Ventullo

Senior Production Controller: Eyvett Davis

Cover design: emc design

Text design: Alex Dull

Compositor: emc design

National Geographic Liaison:
    Wesley Della Volla / Leila Hishmeh

Audio: Tom Dick & Debbie Productions Ltd

DVD: Tom Dick & Debbie Productions Ltd

For product information and technology assistance, contact us at **Cengage Learning Customer & Sales Support, cengage.com/contact**

For permission to use material from this text or product, submit all requests online at **cengage.com/permissions** Further permissions questions can be emailed to **permissionrequest@cengage.com**

Student Book ISBN: 978-1-305-09010-1
Student Book w/o Access Code ISBN: 978-1-305-65188-3

National Geographic Learning
Cheriton House, North Way, Andover, Hampshire, SP10 5BE
United Kingdom

National Geographic Learning, a Cengage Learning Company, has a mission to bring the world to the classroom and the classroom to life. With our English language programs, students learn about their world by experiencing it. Through our partnerships with National Geographic and TED Talks, they develop the language and skills they need to be successful global citizens and leaders.

Locate your local office at **international.cengage.com/region**

Visit National Geographic Learning online at **NGL.Cengage.com/ELT**
Visit our corporate website at **www.cengage.com**

CREDITS

Although every effort has been made to contact copyright holders before publication, this has not always been possible. If contacted, the publisher will undertake to rectify any errors or omissions at the earliest opportunity.

Printed in Greece by Bakis
Print Number: 08   Print Year: 2020

Photos

6–7 © Yamandu Hilbert/National Geographic Creative; 8 (tl) © Jason Edwards/National Geographic Creative; 8 (tm) © Thierry Grun/Getty Images; 8 (tr) © Sean Gallup/Getty Images; 8 (ml) © David McNew/Getty Images; 8 (mm) © H. Mark Weidman Photography/Alamy; 8 (mr) © Uriel Sinai/Getty Images; 8 (bl) © Marc Piasecki/Getty Images; 8 (bm) © Photofusion/Getty Images; 8 (br) © Peter Macdiarmid/Getty Images; 10 © Krista Rossow/National Geographic Creative; 13 (t) © IPGGutenbergUKLtd/Getty Images; 13 (m) © BSIP/Getty Images; 13 (b) © Jonas Gratzer/Getty Images; 14–15 © Dick Loek/Getty Images; 16 © Anna Bryukhanova/iStockphoto; 18–19 © Andrew Yates/AFP/Getty Images; 20 © PE Forsberg/Alamy; 22 © Niklas Halle'n/Barcroft Media/Getty Images Media; 24–25 © Sivaram V/Reuters; 27 © John Burcham/National Geographic Creative; 30 © Pearl Bucknall/Alamy; 32–33 © A/G Keery/Splash/Splash News/Corbis; 34 © Morteza Nikoubazl/Reuters/Corbis; 36 (l) © Leon Neal/Getty Images; 36 (ml) © Karen Kasmauski/Corbis; 36 (mr) © Axel Fassio/Getty Images; 36 (r) © Plattform/Johnér Images/Corbis; 37 (l) © Cultura RM/Charles Gullung/Getty Images; 37 (ml) © Jun Tukuhashi/Getty Images; 37 (mr) © Ron Levine/Getty Images; 37 (r) © Spencer Platt/Getty Images; 39 (tl) © Paul Cowan/Shutterstock.com; 39 (tr) © RosaBetancourt 0 people images/Alamy; 39 (bl) © Flash Parker/Getty Images; 39 (br) © Radharc Images/Alamy; 40 © Cesar Torres/Demotix/Corbis; 42–43 © Andrew Mills/Star Ledger/Corbis; 44 © Gordon Wiltsie/National Geographic Creative; 47 (tl) © Rodrigo Oropeza/Xinhua Press/Corbis; 47 (tm) © Chris Smith/Popperfoto/Getty Images; 47 (tr) © Eduardo Mariano Rivero/Alamy; 47 (bl) © John P Kelly/Getty Images; 47 (bm) © Leo Mason sports photos/Alamy; 47 (br) © Ryan Pierse/Getty Images; 50–51 © Michael Nichols/National Geographic Creative; 52 © Ezra Bailey/Getty Images; 53 © Mike Goldwater/Alamy; 54 © Robert Madden/National Geographic Creative; 57 © Saiful Azri Mohamad; 58 © Rich Reid/Getty Images; 60–61 © David Evans/National Geographic Creative; 62 © Philip Lange/Shutterstock.com; 64 © VIEW Pictures Ltd/Alamy; 65 © Mario De Biasi/Mondadori Portfolio/Getty Images; 67 © Dean Northcott/Age Fotostock; 68–69 © Blend Images – GM Visuals/Getty Images; 71 © Karen Kasmauski/National Geographic Creative; 72–73 © Mike Theiss/National Geographic Creative; 74 © Ira Block/National Geographic Creative; 76 © Ralph Lee Hopkins/National Geographic Creative; 78–79 © Peter Ginter/Getty Images; 80 © Marser/Getty Images; 83 © Cary Wolinsky/National Geographic Creative; 84 (t) © Greg Elms/Getty Images; 84 (b) © Aleksandra Yakovleva/Getty Images; 86–87 © Matt Moyer/National Geographic Creative; 89 © Stephen St. John/National Geographic Creative; 90 (t) © AJ Wilhelm/National Geographic Creative; 90 (bottom: tl) © mdmmikle/Shutterstock.com; 90 (bottom: tm) © Daria Minaeva/Shutterstock.com; 90 (bottom: r) © hidesy/Shutterstock.com; 90 (bottom: bl) © wongstock/Shutterstock.com; 90 (bottom: bm) © Trinette Reed/Blend Images/Corbis; 93 © G. KNAPP/ClassicStock/Corbis; 94 © Matej Kastelic/Shutterstock.com; 96–97 © Mike Theiss/National Geographic Creative; 98–99 © Paul Zahl/National Geographic Creative; 100 (tl) © Fotokon/Shutterstock.com; 100 (tm) © Maggy Meyer/Shutterstock.com; 100 (tr) © Dan-Alexandru Buta/Shutterstock.com; 100 (bl) © aaltair/Shutterstock.com; 100 (bm) © Jodie Nash/Shutterstock.com; 100 (br) © Erni/Shutterstock.com; 102 © Science & Society Picture Library/Getty Images; 104–105 © Michael Melford/National Geographic Creative; 106 © Philippe Lissac/Photononstop/Corbis; 109 © George Grall/National Geographic Creative; 110 © PeopleImages.com/Getty Images; 111 © Ammentorp Photography/Shutterstock.com; 112 © Michael Austen/Alamy; 114–115 © Joel Sartore/National Geographic Creative; 116–117 © David Bleeker/Alamy; 119 © Robin Hammond/National Geographic Creative; 120 (tl) © Mark Ralston/AFP/Getty Images; 120 (tm) © Photos 12/Alamy; 120 (tr) © Birger Vogelius/All Over Press; 120 (ml) © Pictorial Press Ltd/Alamy; 120 (mr) © Tino Soriano/National Geographic Creative; 120 (bl) © Zatelepina Aleksandra/Shutterstock.com; 120 (bm) © ABM/Corbis; 120 (br) © ATStockFoto/Alamy; 122–123 © Ron Bull/Toronto Star/Getty Images; 125 © Jess Kraft/Shutterstock.com; 128 © Alan Powdrill/Getty Images; 130 © Skowronek/Shutterstock.com; 132–133 © Karen Bleier/AFP/Getty Images; 134 © Aaron Huey/National Geographic Creative; 136 © William Albert Allard/National Geographic Creative; 139 © Jupiterimages/Getty Images; 140–141 © Omar Torres/AFP/Getty Images; 142–143 © Aaron Huey/National Geographic Creative; 145 (t) © Shamil Zhumatov/Reuters/Corbis; 145 (b) © Gerd Ludwig/National Geographic Creative; 146–147 © paulwongkwan/Getty Images; 148 (l) © Greg Balfour Evans/Alamy; 148 (ml) © Hemis/Alamy; 148 (mr) © Mary Calvert/Reuters/Corbis; 148 (r) © Bruce Yuanyue Bi/Getty Images; 150 © foto infot/Shutterstock.com; 151 © Kzenon/Shutterstock.com; 153 © Thanagon_thekob/Shutterstock.com; 154 (l) © Ammentorp Photography/Shutterstock.com; 154 (r) © racorn/Shutterstock.com; 156–157 © Michael Hero/Shutterstock.com; 159 © Viacheslav Lopatin/Shutterstock.com; 161 © Monkey Business Images/Shutterstock.com; 162 © supertramp88/Shutterstock.com; 163 © Delmonte, Steve/Cartoonstock; 164–165 © Chris Howey/Shutterstock.com; 190 (l) © michaeljung/Shutterstock.com; 190 (r) © Lopolo/Shutterstock.com.

Cover: © Johnathan Ly.

Illustrations: 26 Gary Venn (Lemonade Illustration); 28–29, 125 Phil Hackett; 48 Richard Merritt; 63 Daniel Gray; 80, 124, 189, 191 KJA Artists; 160 Mark Draisey.

Acknowledgements

The publisher and authors would like to thank the following teachers who provided the feedback and user insights on the first edition of Outcomes that have helped us develop this new edition:

Rosetta d'Agostino, New English Teaching, Milan, Italy; Victor Manuel Alarcón, EOI Badalona, Badalona, Spain; Isidro Almendarez, Universidad Complutense, Madrid, Spain; Isabel Andrés, EOI Valdemoro, Madrid, Spain; Brian Brennan, International House Company Training, Barcelona, Spain; Nara Carlini, Università Cattolica, Milan, Italy; Karen Corne, UK; Jordi Dalmau, EOI Reus, Reus, Spain; Matthew Ellman, British Council, Malaysia; Clara Espelt, EOI Maresme, Barcelona, Spain; Abigail Fulbrook, Chiba, Japan; Dylan Gates, Granada, Spain; Blanca Gozalo, EOI Fuenlabrada, Madrid, Spain; James Grant, Japan; Joanna Faith Habershon, St Giles Schools of Languages London Central, UK; Jeanine Hack; English Language Coach.com, London, UK; Claire Hart, Germany; David Hicks, Languages4Life, Barcelona, Spain; Hilary Irving, Central School of English, London, UK; Jessica Jacobs, Università Commerciale Luigi Bocconi, Milan, Italy; Lucia Luciani, Centro di Formaziones Casati, Milan, Italy; Izabela Michalak, ELC, Łódź, Poland; Josep Millanes Moya, FIAC Escola d'Idiomes, Terrassa, Catalonia; Rodrigo Alonso Páramo, EOI Viladecans, Barcelona, Spain; Jonathan Parish, Uxbridge College, London, UK; Mercè Falcó Pegueroles, EOI Tortosa, Tortosa, Spain; Hugh Podmore, St Giles Schools of Languages London Central, UK; James Rock, Università Cattolica, Milan, Italy; Virginia Ron, EOI Rivas, Madrid, Spain; Coletto Russo, British Institutes, Milan, Italy; Ana Salvador, EOI Fuenlabrada, Madrid, Spain; Adam Scott, St Giles College, Brighton, UK; Olga Smolenskaya, Russia; Carla Stroulger, American Language Academy, Madrid, Spain; Simon Thomas, St Giles, UK; Simon Thorley, British Council, Madrid, Spain; Helen Tooke, Università Commerciale Luigi Bocconi, Milan, Italy; Chloe Turner, St Giles Schools of Languages London Central, UK; Sheila Vine, University of Paderborn, Germany; Richard Willmsen, British Study Centres, London, UK; Various teachers at English Studio Academic management, UK.

Authors' acknowledgements

Thanks to Karen Spiller and Clare Shaw, and to Dennis Hogan, John McHugh and Gavin McLean for their continued support and enthusiasm.

Thanks also to all the students we've taught over the years for providing more inspiration and insight than they ever realised.

And to the colleagues we've taught alongside for their friendship, thoughts and assistance.